P9-EKE-315

The Temptation of ELIZABETH TUDOR

The Temptation of ELIZABETH TUDOR

Elizabeth I, Thomas Seymour,
and the Making of a Virgin Queen

ELIZABETH NORTON

PEGASUS BOOKS
NEW YORK LONDON

THE TEMPTATION OF ELIZABETH TUDOR

Pegasus Books LLC
80 Broad Street, 5th Floor
New York, NY 10004

First Pegasus Books cloth edition January 2016

Interior design by Maria Fernandez

Library of Congress Cataloging-in-Publication Data is available.

ISBN: 978-1-60598-948-8

10 9 8 7 6 5 4 3 2 1

Printed in the United States of America
Distributed by W. W. Norton & Company

To David, Dominic, and Barnaby

CONTENTS

Prologue

6 FEBRUARY 1559

The great gallery at Whitehall, though capacious, was crowded that afternoon as the Council and a deputation of thirty members of the House of Commons filed in, following their Speaker.[1] The woman who was the focus of their attention seemed slight beneath her canopy of estate, facing the clamorous throng.[2] Gorgeously dressed, in clothes from a wardrobe that included fine satins and velvets, and cloth of gold and silk, Elizabeth had been proclaimed queen only three months before. Now she sat, pale-faced, upon the throne that had once been her father's. Her long yellow-red hair was pinned up, away from her face. She wanted the world to see her as they had done her father—stern-faced, but also serene and majestic.[3] Yet she was still young—only twenty-five. She was also unmarried, which, in a queen, was an aberration.

Elizabeth called her first Parliament on 25 January 1559, not long after her coronation. The Commons and Lords considered the nature of the religious settlement that would replace the Catholicism reintroduced in Queen Mary's regime and other pressing matters besides; but thoughts also turned to the question of who should take the crown matrimonial and become king. It was unthinkable that the queen should not soon marry. Already offers were being made, both at home and abroad. Voices in the Commons proved the boldest in raising the issue, and on 4 February 1559 they petitioned for an audience with the queen.[4] It was granted two days later.

Now, as a hush fell over the room, Sir Thomas Gargrave, Speaker of the Commons, stepped forward.[5] He was nearly forty years older than his monarch, a blunt Yorkshireman with thin lips and a serious face that tapered almost to a point at his chin.[6] With considerable Parliamentary experience behind him, it must have seemed a simple matter to come before this inexperienced young woman.[7] But her dark, intelligent eyes scrutinized him keenly from the dais. As he began to read his prepared speech, his monarch's gaze "made him fear the unworthiness of every word which he was about to present to her ears." He stumbled over his lines. He stuttered out a request to the queen to marry, "as well for her own comfort and contentment, as for assurance to the realm by her royal issue."

There was silence as the queen considered his words. Then, with a "princely countenance of voice" and a sudden, quick gesture of her hand, as though she was surprised, she answered. She gave them "great thanks," she said, "for the love and care which they did express, as well towards her person as the whole state of the realm." She liked the petition and took it in good part, as she assured the Commons, who must have breathed a communal sigh of relief. "If it had been otherwise," she continued, "if you had taken upon you to confine, or rather to bind, my choice; to draw my love to your liking; to frame my affection according to your fantasies; I must have disliked it very much." It was for them to obey her, not her to obey them.

Elizabeth then turned her attention to the matter of their suit. Ever since she had reached her "years of understanding," being (as she said) "first able to take consideration of myself," she had made a decision. Matrimony was not for her. She had, she said, "made choice of a single life, which hath best, I assure you, contented me, and, I trust, hath been most acceptable to God." She meant, she assured them, to "preserve in a virgin's state."

Elizabeth's words must have seemed fanciful to those assembled. Nobody believed that a queen could hope to reign alone.[8] It was, those who were present must have reasoned, inconceivable that she would not marry and provide England with an heir. Indeed, the queen was already showing her interest in men, for was not her handsome Master of Horse, Robert Dudley, often by her side at court?

As she made her answer, Elizabeth assured the Commons that "as for me, it shall be sufficient that a marble stone shall declare that a queen, having lived and reigned so many years, died a virgin." She claimed that, since her youth, she had "always continued in this determination," but there were those standing by, including her chief gentlewoman of the bedchamber, Kate Ashley, who might have disagreed.[9]

Once, her virginity had not been so jealously guarded. Ten years ago to the day, as a fifteen-year-old, she had been closely questioned on her attempts to take a husband of her own choosing, who was already known to have visited her bed. When she was a teenager, there was one man who had caught her fancy enough to tempt her to abandon herself to him.

The Virgin Queen was born out of the ashes of his fall.[10]

Part One

THE SEEDS OF SCANDAL

Sir Thomas Seymour, second in command of Henry VIII's invasion force in France, surveyed his troops. He was not a man of half measures. He entered into everything with gusto and determination, but not always skill or foresight. Everyone liked him, even the rapidly aging king who, by this year of 1543, was a gross caricature of his former self, yet—in his decrepitude—still longed to conquer France.

That July, Seymour began burning and taking French castles as a prelude to the main invasion, which was scheduled for the following year. As cannons smoked and men charged into French territory, the thirty-five-year-old commander had finally been given the chance to begin satisfying his overweening ambition.

Pale-faced, but certainly not unpleasing, Thomas Seymour resembled his younger sister Jane, the sibling to whom he was closest in age. The road to France, and to military glory, had started with her only a few years before. It had begun with a birth.

Chapter One

AFFECTION SHALL LEAD ME TO COURT . . .

It was bracingly cold in London on the morning of 11 October 1537. The weather the previous year had been so piercing that the Thames had frozen, forcing water traffic onto the already crowded streets of England's capital.[1] This year would not prove so frigid, but at this time of day, as the sun slowly began to rise, the assembled crowds still had their hands tucked away against the frost, and there was a murmur in the air.[2] They were waiting for news—but as yet, there was none to report.

The friars, priests, and clerks gathered there pulled on their ceremonial copes, which appeared vivid against the monochrome-looking buildings. The mayor and aldermen of the city, along with members of all the crafts guilds in their liveries, joined them, forming into a line. It was a companionable scene, since such gatherings were frequent enough for the participants to know each other well; but that day they walked with downcast eyes. Slowly, they processed through the narrow, tunnel-like streets of the city, passing ancient buildings of timber or stone, their feet pressing on the rutted, cobbled streets. Prayers were on the lips of the priests. Crowds watching from the streets or from jettied windows above adopted the invocation. It was a prayer for the queen, Jane Seymour, who had already been in labor for a day and two nights. All England's hopes rested on her good hour.

An anxious King Henry VIII, at Hampton Court, recalled the last royal birth, four years ago. He had ascended the throne as a seventeen-year-old, nearly thirty years before. He had been young, handsome, and vigorous, yet his first marriage had produced a daughter, Mary, but no son. Instead, in around 1527, he had turned his attentions to the exotic, dark Anne Boleyn, but the road to the altar proved a long one. Anne was over thirty and past her childbearing prime when she became queen in January 1533; yet she was already pregnant. Henry, who had broken with the pope to marry his love, expected a son, any doubts about it assuaged by the fortune tellers engaged to reassure him. He had wasted his money. The letters carefully prepared in advance to announce the birth of a "prince" were clumsily amended for a "princess." Anne's daughter, Princess Elizabeth, caused consternation at her birth on 7 September 1533. But she was, for a time, heiress to Henry's throne.*

Elizabeth was born to gilded splendor. When she was a baby, four rockers were engaged whose sole purpose was to gently push her cradle and soothe her off to sleep. When she changed residences,

* In 1533, Princess Mary had been delegitimized and removed from the succession by Act of Parliament.

which was frequently, she was carried in a velvet litter at the head of a snaking procession of servants. This all changed with the swing of a headsman's sword in May 1536 and the execution of her mother on trumped-up charges of adultery. Although not yet three years old, Elizabeth noticed her drop in status, precociously asking her governess, Lady Bryan, "how happs it yesterday Lady Princess and today but Lady Elizabeth?" Within a few months, she had outgrown all her clothes, but there were no replacements forthcoming from a king who was preoccupied with a new bride. Elizabeth had not visited court for eighteen months by the time her stepmother Jane, the new queen, went into labor.

By the standards of the time, Jane Seymour was, at twenty-eight, rather old for her first confinement, having failed to attract a husband in her youth. It was her air of quiet virtue, so different from the outspoken Anne Boleyn, that drew the king to her. He had been entranced by her refusal to accept a gift of money from him early in 1536, because she had "no greater riches in the world than her honour, which she would not injure for a thousand deaths."[3] Within days, Jane's brother, Edward Seymour, and his wife had been installed as chaperones in fine court apartments. Conveniently, they had access to Henry's own private rooms via a secret stair.

Edward Seymour intended to rise with his younger sister at court.[4] They were the children of Sir John Seymour, of Wolf Hall in Wiltshire, and his wife, Margery Wentworth, a "benign, courteous and meek" woman with solid family connections.[5] Both Edward and his brother Henry, the eldest surviving sons, were born at the turn of the sixteenth century. They had a comfortable childhood in their father's 1,200 acres, which offered hunting in the parks and strolls through the fine walled garden or fruitful orchards.[6] Fifty servants attended to the family's needs. There was a private chapel for the Seymours, and they could also worship down in the village of Great Bedwyn, which lay close to Wolf Hall.

Infant mortality, which was then so virulent, left a hole at the heart of the Seymour family and divided the Seymour children into two groups. By the time that Edward's youngest siblings abandoned babyhood, he had left home and was using family connections to take the first tentative steps toward a court career, while Henry, not sharing his brother's ambitions, later chose the conventional life of a country squire.[7] The third surviving son, Thomas, who was born around 1508, was followed by Jane and two other sisters.

The Seymour children were literate, learning their letters with the parish priest, but none of them showed Edward's intellectual promise. With no inheritance prospects and few routes to advancement, Thomas struggled to follow his brother to court.[8] Indeed, it was only the intervention of his cousin Sir Francis Bryan, the infamous "vicar of Hell," that rescued him from country obscurity, taking him into his service around 1530.[9] At about the same time, Bryan also secured a place at court for Jane.*

Jane's marriage to the king increased Thomas's standing too, bringing appointments to the Privy Chamber and other minor offices soon afterwards. He hoped for more if Jane could only bear Henry a son. It was in the early hours of 12 October 1537, at the point of total exhaustion, that the queen did as desired—and London erupted in celebration. At nine o'clock in the morning, a new procession formed up at St. Paul's, among the booksellers and market stalls that crowded the churchyard. As the church bells rang and *Te Deums* were sung in church, Jane issued the official birth announcements from her fine gilt bed.[10] All seemed well and, at forty-six, Henry VIII finally had his longed-for male heir.**

---

* Bryan's "vicar of Hell" nickname related to his irreverent, libertine nature, and it was given him by Henry VIII after asking Bryan "what sort of sin it was to ruin the mother and then the child." Bryan replied drily that "it was a sin like that of eating a hen first and its chicken afterwards" (Sander, p. 24). Thomas Cromwell also used the nickname in a letter dated 14 May 1536 (in Merriman, Vol. II, pp. 12–13). Bryan, a longstanding member of the court, had been appointed, before 1522, to act as chief cupbearer to the king (*Rutland Papers*, p. 101).

** Henry had also had a son, Henry Fitzroy (born 1519), Duke of Richmond and Somerset, but he was illegitimate—the result of the king's relationship with Elizabeth Blount. Fitzroy died in 1536.

Edward Seymour must have heard the cannons, fired from the Tower of London, and the carousing crowds, drunk on hogsheads of wine distributed by the proud new father. London was kept up until past ten o'clock that night with the celebrations, while preparations were put in hand for the newborn Edward's christening on 15 October. By convention, neither the king nor queen attended their son's baptism. Instead, Jane, wrapped in velvet and furs against the cold, was carried to an antechamber close to the chapel at Hampton Court in order to receive her guests and—if all proved well—revel in her role as royal mother. She gave the fine, healthy baby boy her blessing before he was carried into the torchlit great chapel.

Sir Francis Bryan, benefitting from his royal cousin's success in the birth, took charge of the font, carrying towels and wearing an apron to protect his clothes. He spotted his kinsman, Edward Seymour, who had received an honorable but burdensome appointment, carrying the four-year-old Princess Elizabeth. Thomas Seymour, too, was there, holding one corner of the canopy above the baby. This was Elizabeth's first meeting with either Seymour brother, although only the elder brother—her bearer—can have made any impression on her.

Just nine days after the christening, the jubilation was followed by a bitter blow for the king. After succumbing to septicemia following the birth, Queen Jane died. Only six days earlier, as Jane feverishly hovered between life and death, Henry had shown his appreciation of her two brothers with an earldom (of Hertford) for Edward and a knighthood for Thomas. Edward proudly received his patent from the king's own hand and was so overcome with gratitude that, after thanking God in a short speech, he promised humbly to "do His Grace such service that might be to his pleasure."[11] Privately, the new Earl of Hertford mused that "affection shall lead me to court, but I'll take care that interest keeps me."[12] The unexpected death of Queen Jane threw Henry into mourning for the wife who had finally given him his son and heir; but it did not dampen the Seymour brothers' sense of triumph or hinder their ambitions.

Both now motherless, Elizabeth and the infant Edward found themselves thrown together. From her birth, Elizabeth had been attended by a suite of servants. Her great-aunt, Lady Bryan, who had originally cared for Princess Mary, served as her "lady mistress," filling a mother's role in her day-to-day life. Lady Bryan, who by 1537 was approaching sixty, understood the needs of the royal children better than anyone else. In spite of her gray hairs, she was energetic and sprightly and would live to a ripe old age. She took charge of Prince Edward from birth, plainly adoring the sweet little boy who, by the time he was seventeen months old, could tap his tiny feet to music, enjoying himself so much that "he could not be still."[13] With chubby fingers, he took the instruments from the minstrels employed to amuse him and tried to pick out his own tunes. Elizabeth was with him during such times, watching her little brother lovingly.

Lady Bryan could not be expected to raise the royal children indefinitely, and within a few years she retired to Essex. Elizabeth's new lady mistress came from within the household. As a "wise lady of dignity," she was as solidly respectable as her predecessor.[14] Blanche, Lady Troy, had been raised in the Welsh Marches and, along with her niece Blanche Parry, had joined the princess at her birth. As a widow, she could focus her energies on her charges, so that the nursery she presided over was as warm and affectionate as in Lady Bryan's day.[15] But times were changing, drawing the two children away from their nursery songs and early letters. In 1543 Elizabeth was called to court for a wedding.

Late in 1542, Catherine Parr, Lady Latimer, a pretty auburn-haired woman of thirty, arrived in London with her second husband. The couple were northerners by descent, although Catherine had been born and raised close to the court. Left a penniless widow when she was barely out of her teens, Catherine had hurriedly wedded the older John Neville, Lord Latimer. As his bride, she took up residence at Snape Castle in Yorkshire and occupied herself in raising her stepchildren. It was a quiet, domestic life, but not one that suited her very considerable intellectual talents. She was also caught up in the events of the Pilgrimage of Grace late in 1536, when the conservative north rebelled against the king's religious policies, including the dissolution of the monasteries. Catherine had no sympathy for Roman Catholic tradition, but her husband did. After agreeing to act as the rebels' captain, Latimer was strongly suspected of treason, while Catherine's own life was endangered when the insurgents occupied her home. It was only with difficulty that Latimer cleared his name and slowly regained royal favor. In September 1542 he fell sick at York and returned to London.[16] By the following March he was dead—and Catherine was widowed for the second time.

Although she dutifully arranged her husband's funeral and took on responsibility for her stepdaughter, Margaret Neville, Catherine was no retiring widow. Even before Lord Latimer had passed away, she had attracted two suitors. The favored gentleman, whom Catherine wished to marry "before any man I know," was Sir Thomas Seymour.[17] But the other was King Henry, whose own fifth marriage, to Catherine Howard, had ended nearly a year before with an axe blow to the imprudent queen's neck.

When, in early 1543, Catherine Parr began to attend the household of her old friend Princess Mary, the king caused gossip by visiting his eldest daughter with surprising regularity. On 16 February 1543, while Lord Latimer was still lingering on his sickbed, Henry made his intentions very clear when he insisted on paying a tailor's bill for clothes for both Catherine and Mary. The gowns for Catherine, made of gorgeous fabrics and cut in Italian, French, Dutch, and Venetian styles, were lavish and must have been meant by Henry as a wedding trousseau—in anticipation of the object of his affections soon becoming free to wed. Catherine, however, intended to resist.

By 1543, Sir Thomas Seymour was a highly eligible bachelor of thirty-five who regularly attended the court. As uncle to Edward,

Prince of Wales, he punched above his weight in the marriage market. Even the great noble the Duke of Norfolk sought him for his daughter, the widowed Duchess of Richmond.[18] The duke had first raised the match personally with the king at Westminster in 1538, amid the hustle and bustle of a royal move to Hampton Court. Henry had agreed, laughing, that if Norfolk was "so minded to bestow his daughter upon the said Sir Thomas Seymour, he should be sure to couple her with one of such lust and youth, as should be able to please her well at all points."[19] Thomas was well-built and handsome, with a thick auburn beard. Although the scheme continued, on and off, until the 1540s, the duchess's "fantasy would not serve her to marry with him."[20] Instead, Seymour flirted with Catherine Parr—but stepped away when the king declared an interest.

Catherine resisted the king's advances for as long as she could. Privately, she was horrified at the thought of marriage to a man who was now—at fifty-one—old (for the time), grossly overweight, and disabled by an open ulcer suppurating in his leg, a lingering injury from falling under his horse during a joust in 1536. It was said that she complained he wronged her in marrying such a young woman.[21] Catherine was a vivacious woman. She had already endured two arranged marriages and she wanted someone young and vigorous. But the king, who was still "lusty" in thoughts if increasingly less able in the actual deed, wanted her in his bed.[22] The modestly born and, seemingly, infertile gentlewoman was otherwise a surprising royal choice.

The widow was not, though, easily won. Reverting to his romantic youth, Henry attempted to woo her with poetry, urging this fair "nymph" in his own poetic hand to "set doubts aside" and couple herself with him.[23] His wife would be required to swear to be "buxom in bed."[24] Catherine prayed to be released from the king's ardor, yet, as she later lamented, "God withstood my will therein most vehemently for a time."[25] She took the Almighty's silence as evidence of divine purpose, making "possible which seemed to me most impossible; that was, made me renounce utterly mine own will, and to follow his will most willingly."[26] She believed that she did God's work when she finally accepted him in July 1543. In preparation for this living martyrdom, she noted down Bible verses by which she intended to live, hoping to be a force for good and "refuse not the prayer of one that is in trouble, and turn not [a]way thy face from the needy."[27] In Henry's younger daughter, Elizabeth, whom she first met that month, she found a child badly in need of a mother's love.

On 12 July 1543, the nine-year-old Princess Elizabeth woke at Hampton Court and made her way to the queen's tiny private chapel. She squeezed herself in among the company, which included her half-sister Mary, as well as her cousin Margaret Douglas and Catherine Willoughby, the Duchess of Suffolk—the young wife of her uncle (and the king's old friend) Charles Brandon.[28] Much of the Privy Council had also crowded in, including Edward Seymour, Earl of Hertford, and his wife. They had come for a wedding. As King Henry took Catherine's hand in his, Bishop Stephen Gardiner recited the words of the marriage ceremony—the sixth time Henry had heard it and the third for Catherine. Quietly, the widow gave herself to Henry "as long as they both shall live," promising to obey and serve him, while for his part he vowed to "love and honour her as a spouse and husband ought to love and honour his wife."

Although childless, the new queen was an experienced step-parent; already her two Neville stepchildren were devoted to their "dear sovereign mistress."[29] But Catherine was denied the opportunity to become an immediate influence over Elizabeth, as her "obedient daughter" was sent back to the nursery within days of the wedding. It was to be a year before the pair met again, by which time Elizabeth's world had changed.[30] On 7 July 1544, the king decreed that it was time for his son, Edward, by now six years old, to learn how to become a man. Edward Seymour and the conservative Lord Chancellor Henry Wriothesley were sent to strip the boy's female attendants of their posts.[31] It was an event that seared itself in the memory of Edward, who recorded years later that "he was brought up among the women until he was six years of age."[32] Henceforth, the prince was to be cared for and instructed by men, and there was no place in this establishment for his ten-year-old sister. Instead, Elizabeth now came to spend more time at court and in the company of her father's new queen.

Edward Seymour's commission to take charge of his royal nephew's household was far from the only time that he had been of use to King Henry. Dour and unsmiling, he was a born politician. In 1544 he was appointed part of a five-man council tasked with assisting Queen Catherine, who was acting as regent while Henry tried to recapture his youth on campaign in France.[33] The somber and black-clad Earl of Hertford had little respect for the queen, who delighted in pretty things, treasuring a set of six gold buttons decorated with Catherine wheels.[34] If he could have seen under her skirts, he would have noted that even her underwear was gilded, including a gold girdle enameled with blue and white—just one of her fine items. She could check her appearance in a mirror garnished with blue sapphires, rock rubies, and twenty-six pearls of assorted sizes, or screen her face from scrutiny with a fan of black ostrich feathers, set in gold and bejeweled. Such a love of jewelry did not mean, however, that she was an intellectual lightweight. She was the first Englishwoman to publish under her own name. Her *Prayers, or, Meditations*, which appeared in 1545, was an immediate best-seller.

Sir Thomas Seymour, aware of the danger of his former connection with Catherine, mostly kept away from the queen's household—although he watched from afar.[35] In the summer of 1542, Henry had sent him on an embassy to the Habsburg monarch (and future Holy Roman Emperor) Ferdinand, King of the Romans, in Vienna.[36] In an age when very few Englishmen ventured beyond the shores of Dover, this was an exciting venture, and Thomas wrote enthusiastic reports of his time abroad, recording military preparations as he joined Ferdinand's camp in his war against the Turks.[37] He showed a particular interest in the Habsburg king's navy, taking the time to draw a picture of a boat in one letter to Henry to illustrate the strange, flat-bottomed craft that he saw being carried on wagons by the army.[38]

Such zeal was not enough, though, to mask Thomas's lack of talent in diplomacy. He was often uncertain of just what he was supposed to report to the king.[39] He also failed to secure the German mercenaries that Henry had specifically requested he hire.[40] In May 1543, some weeks before the king's marriage to Catherine, he found himself sent to the Netherlands—an appointment that he owed more to his status as Henry's love rival than to his ability.[41] He returned a few days before Henry's wedding, once the bride was safely promised to the sovereign.

Undistinguished in diplomacy, Thomas next tried the military—and a successful French campaign ensued in July 1543.[42] In recognition of his newfound military expertise, he was appointed Master of the Ordnance for life, a role that placed him in charge of equipping future military expeditions.

His experiences in recent years had also given him a taste for the adventure of the sea—a contrast to a childhood growing up in landlocked Wiltshire. In 1537, Thomas had sailed under the command of Vice Admiral John Dudley, when the pair had had instructions to guard the English Channel against the French.[43] All that summer they patrolled the coast, although they saw little action.[44] Undaunted, Thomas could not leave the ocean behind him—and this was an exhilarating time to be involved with an English navy that was rapidly growing in strength and which was Henry's pride and joy.[45]

In October 1544 Thomas presented a detailed "advice" for King Henry regarding naval tactics in his new war with France.[46] It was a comprehensive report, and it achieved the desired result: Seymour was appointed an admiral of the king's navy that month and ordered to convey provisions to supply Boulogne, the captured prize of the campaign.[47] He gathered up his possessions in a wooden trunk and hurried up the gangplank to his ship, the *Peter Pomegranate*.[48] At five hundred tons and carrying four hundred men, it was a floating fortress, armed to the teeth with guns on wheeled carriages, ready for action against England's old enemy across the Channel.[49]

Despite having previously sailed only under John Dudley, Thomas Seymour was placed in command of a fleet of fourteen ships. He looked the part of the dashing mariner, with his handsome face and excellent bearing; but the voyage, on ships laden with supplies, seemed cursed from the start. As the vessels lay close to Harwich, sheltered in the mouth of the River Orwell, "such a mist" arose that the sailors could not see their fellows only a few feet away.[50] It was icy cold, but Thomas, still full of enthusiasm for his first naval command, set out to sea as soon as the weather calmed on 5 November. That night, a gale roared around his ships, puffing up their sails and pushing them out into the English Channel. It was nearly too much for the novice admiral, who wrote to the King's Council the following morning from his cabin: "God be thanked we got to Dover."

As he dipped his pen in the inkwell, and as the ship rolled in the harbor, an easterly wind rose. Thomas gave orders to make at once for the French coast, for he had already heard rumors of seventeen French ships at Dieppe; after dropping off his supplies at Boulogne, he wanted to test his guns on them and win glory. He hoped to earn such a reputation that the Frenchmen should "fear our wind, that should bring us thither."

Sailing the wintry seas, as the wind and salt whipped around his face and hardened his skin and hair, proved a rather less certain route to military glory than Thomas had anticipated. That night, as he approached the French coast, the "wind veered to the north-east," forcing the ships westward, although (as Thomas later lamented to the Council) "we had meant no such thing."[51] As a tempest squalled around them, the ships were buffeted on the waves, out of control. It was dark, it was terrifying, and it was deadly. Mariners clung to wooden rails to avoid being cast into the sea. The heavy iron guns "flew about, and shook the ships."[52] Seymour abandoned all plans to reach France; eventually, his own vessel finally found safety in the harbor of the Isle of Wight. He was lucky. Three of the great ships that followed him overshot the chalk cliff coast. They were forced to fight their way on to a bay to the east of the island, where one of them broke up in the struggle, drowning nearly 260 of those on board.

The storm lasted all through the night and the next day, and some of the ships were still in open water. The vessel containing Thomas's older brother Henry, who had surprisingly decided to join him for the adventure, was dashed to pieces on the rocks. Miraculously, all lives on his ship were saved. Surveying the disaster of his expedition in the cold light of day, Thomas Seymour accounted himself fortunate to be alive. He was indignant when word arrived from the king complaining of his negligence. The admiral was genuinely hurt that his ability to command a fleet was called into question, and he sat down with five of his captains, still dazed from the drama, to write in his defense of their actions.

Thomas Seymour was nothing if not confident, and the king duly forgave him.[53] He remained a vice admiral, staying with the fleet for much of the following year and making occasional assays out into open water.[54] But he was not trusted with real authority. Henry liked him but had little confidence in his abilities—unlike the older brother, Edward Seymour, who, by the second half of the 1540s, was rising to a position nearing preeminence in the king's estimation. And as King Henry grew increasingly decrepit, Edward Seymour kept a close eye on the throne and the person of his nephew Prince Edward, who was likely—should matters come to it—to be in need of a regent.

Chapter Two

. . . INTEREST KEEPS ME THERE

By the end of 1546, Henry VIII had loomed over his realm for nearly forty years. But now his health was failing. That September, he and Queen Catherine took their court hunting at Guildford, before indulging in more sporting pursuits the following month at Windsor. These exertions took their toll on the monarch. On 5 December he was well enough to meet the Ambassador of the Holy Roman Empire, François Van der Delft, at Oatlands Palace in Surrey. Only nine days later, such access to the king was barred. A sudden fever had beset Henry, burning for thirty hours and leaving him "greatly fallen away."[1] He declared himself "quite restored" soon afterward, but he did not really believe it.

On Christmas Eve Henry abandoned any pretense, abruptly sending his wife and Princess Mary away to Greenwich to celebrate the season without him. There was no cheer that Christmas at Westminster as the king retreated into his private rooms. The plate and glassware, kept carefully for banquets and other great occasions, were left dusty in the ancient palace. The many musical instruments, all stored carefully for a king who loved music, were ignored.[2] Henry kept at least ten clocks in the palace, which produced a cacophony as each marked the hour or half hour; they included the copper-and-gilt clock still engraved with the initials of Henry VIII and Anne Boleyn. Now, the chiming of the clocks uncomfortably marked the passing of time.

Henry himself expected his end to be imminent. After his secluded Christmas, he called his brother-in-law Edward Seymour (Earl of Hertford), John Dudley (Viscount Lisle), and four other members of his Council to him, asking them to bring his will. As they read the document, which had been prepared in 1544, the king expressed his surprise at its contents: they were not what he wanted at all.

Although weak, Henry remained largely in control of affairs. Accordingly, on 30 December a new will—drafted in accordance with his instructions—was presented to him. Although doubts would later be cast on the authenticity of this document (including by Princess Mary), the king appeared to be active in its drafting.[3] He ordered the removal of Bishop Gardiner from among the names of the executors before he consented to sign it. Three of his physicians acted as witnesses.

Unsurprisingly, Henry's chief concern was the succession. He named Edward and then, optimistically, any further children that he should himself beget as his heirs.[4] After them came the princesses of the earlier marriages, Mary and Elizabeth, in that order, while a Regency Council of sixteen equal-ranking executors was appointed to govern during Edward's minority. There was considerable discussion about whether Henry should appoint someone Lord Protector to lead the Council, but Henry's conservative Lord

Chancellor, Thomas Wriothesley, won the argument against in a bad-tempered exchange.[5] The Earl of Hertford cannot have been pleased to be named only fourth on this list of the Regency Council; but he did rather better than his younger brother Thomas, who was to be merely the eighth of ten assistants to the executors. But Thomas was ignorant of the will's contents. He was, instead, still busy at the Tower of London with his ordnance, supervising the dispatch of military equipment northward in accordance with the Council's instructions on 2 January.[6] Once the will was signed, it was locked in a coffer for safekeeping—and the key resided with Hertford.[7]

Henry was gravely ill at New Year. When the French ambassador attempted to see him, he was refused. The Council members, who had been meeting at nearby Ely Place, were sufficiently concerned to move their meetings to Westminster by 9 January, beginning a long vigil over their master.[8] The kingdom still required its day-to-day government, and so, for example, on 16 January the Council sat to discuss matters such as the delivery of tents and ensuring that there were sufficient scythes to mow hay in the Scottish borders.[9] While these concerns occupied the Archbishop of Canterbury, Wriothesley, Dudley and other leading councilors, Hertford noticeably absented himself: his own plans were rather more ambitious.

As Hertford began to flex his influence, the queen remained adrift from proceedings. Yet, although miles downriver at Greenwich, she was far from inactive and looked for a means to return to her husband and to power. Catherine had worked hard to become Prince Edward's "dearest mother." Despite spending Christmas away from this important boy, she had sought to keep herself in his remembrance by sending a portrait of both herself and the king as his New Year's gift.* The pair regularly corresponded in Latin, too, and it pleased the queen to receive the boy's thanks, which arrived around 11 January—more than two weeks since she had last seen

* In the Tudor era, gifts were exchanged at New Year rather than at Christmas.

her husband.[10] She replied at once.[11] Her Latin was good, but the corrections in her draft betrayed her emotional state. Squeezing her own words into the space left at the foot of Edward's letter, she begged the boy to "keep this depicted image for always before your eyes," before crossing through the words. Instead, she expressed the pious hope that the picture should bring to his mind "the deeds of your most distinguished father, he of whom it will be pleasing in a great degree to keep the depicted image before your eyes." It sufficed that she was included in the portrait; when the soon-to-be king looked upon his father's face, he would also see hers. Even a child king would have some authority.

Gathering the last vestiges of his strength, Henry rallied unexpectedly in mid-January. He was well enough to meet with both the French and Imperial ambassadors on the sixteenth of the month.[12] Van der Delft kept his own meeting brief, since he could see the king was ill. Nonetheless, he found a monarch in good spirits. He was on the mend, Henry assured him, although "he had suffered and passed through a good deal" since their last meeting at Christmas. The French ambassador spent rather longer with the king, taxing the health of the ailing monarch. It all proved too much for Henry, who retreated to his sickbed, abandoning his ornate, silver-gilt walking stick in the little study off his bedchamber.[13] He would have no further need of it. From 16 January 1547, the only people who saw the king were members of the Privy Council; and access was strictly controlled by his secretary, William Paget.

Sir William Paget was a self-made man who saw himself as a king-maker.[14] He had a quick wit, carefully weighing each word before he spoke, something that gave him an air of calmness even in a crisis.[15] This wily son of a constable and a "mean creature" had already brought about the ruin of the elderly Thomas Howard, 3rd Duke of Norfolk, and his son Henry, the Earl of Surrey, in the politicking of that winter.[16] The religiously conservative pair had been committed to the Tower on 12 December 1546, although it was the younger man who was the focus of his sovereign's rage. In truth, Surrey was his own worst enemy, since his words and actions could be easily twisted. At this moment of acute sensitivity over the succession, he was found with a banner of the royal arms of England—something that could be construed as reflecting his own, treasonable ambitions.

More damagingly, as far as Paget and his friend the Earl of Hertford were concerned, Surrey had asserted that "his father was the most qualified person, both on account of his services and his lineage, to be entrusted with the governance of the prince and of this realm."[17] He repeated this at his trial on 13 January 1547, when he also verbally attacked Paget for bringing about his ruin. It was down to Hertford, who presided, to give the verdict. Unsurprisingly, Surrey was sentenced to die. As far as Hertford was concerned, there was no person more qualified than himself to be entrusted with the governance of the prince and the realm.[18] Paget also thought so.

In the long waiting days of January 1547, the pair was seen standing quietly together in the gallery at Westminster, talking among the potted plants that were tended carefully by the royal gardeners.[19] Together, "before the breath was out of the body of the king," they made a bargain to rule together during the prince's coming minority.[20] Paget promised to support Hertford's bid to become Lord Protector while, in turn, his fellow councilor agreed to follow the secretary's advice "more than any other man's." Paget—the "catchpole," or bailiff, as he was disparagingly called by his blue-blooded contemporaries—could never have looked so high for himself. However, for the last twelve days of Henry's life he held the key to the king and was prepared to hand it to Hertford.[21]

Unsurprisingly, after a long and eventful reign, Henry VIII had accumulated a diverse range of councilors by the time of his death. They differed in their politics and religion. The reforming Archbishop Thomas Cranmer shared the Council table with the conservative stalwart Stephen Gardiner, Bishop of Winchester. Thomas

Wriothesley also disapproved of the religious changes during the reign, yet, as Henry's Lord Chancellor, he was close to his master and influential.[22] Hertford had little time for him; importantly, neither did Paget.

Henry VIII genuinely liked his secretary. Paget sat with the king in conversation all through the night as Henry's end approached.[23] At first, the pair was alone, which placed Paget in the unique position of being the only man to know Henry VIII's thoughts at this time. But then, rather than working for his own self-interest, Paget ensured that Hertford was also admitted into the midnight discussions.[24]

The three spent several hours alone together before, finally, the rest of the Council was admitted. They all later reported that the monarch had been active until the end, even going so far as to make the arrangements for his own death to be notified abroad.* It was probably while he was earlier alone with the king that Paget took the opportunity to search Henry's study, which was connected to the bedchamber by a small door and used as a store for items required for the ailing monarch's care. When finished, he left some papers relating to Jane Seymour lying on the desk.[25] Other, more significant documents concerning the Seymour queen were probably taken away.

The bedchamber in which the Council joined Henry was small but richly furnished. A depiction of these final days, painted two decades later by an unknown artist, is a work of a vivid imagination.** It shows the pope lying vanquished at the foot of Henry's bed while Prince Edward sits magnificently enthroned beside his father. Henry, wearing the fine nightclothes and cap in which he died, sits propped up against the pillows, giving his final commands

---

* Although whether Henry actually gave the commands or not can never be known, since the only record lies in the words of Paget and the Council (*CSP Foreign*, No. 7).

** Entitled "King Edward VI and the Pope," the painting survives in the National Portrait Gallery, London (NPG 4165).

to the assembled Council. One figure stands central to the picture. Sallow-faced, with a serene but stern countenance, it is the Earl of Hertford. Only a prominent vein to the side of Hertford's forehead suggests the strain of these last hours of Henry's reign.[26]

On 23 January 1547, Queen Catherine made her final attempt to reach her husband. Over the preceding weeks she had become increasingly frantic for news, sending sixteen anxious messages to her courtier brother-in-law, Sir William Herbert.[27] There was little positive that he could tell her. On 11 January she had sent six of her servants to Westminster to prepare her lodgings there; but still she received no summons.[28] Even after she ordered her luggage to be carried to Westminster, she heard nothing.[29] Finally, and still uninvited, she took to her barge on 23 January, sailing down the Thames.[30] But on her arrival she found access to Henry firmly barred. She was hurried away from prying eyes. No doubt protesting, all the queen could do was to send a servant to fetch her bargemen, who had dispersed to the amusements of nearby Southwark.[31] They took her slowly back to Greenwich and to the agony of waiting. No one was to be admitted to the king without the consent of Paget and Hertford.

On the same day that Catherine was rebuffed, Thomas Seymour experienced a rather different fate—he was admitted to the fold. Hertford was eight years older than his brother. But he was affectionate toward him, envisaging a useful alliance, albeit one in which he, naturally, would be the senior partner. On 23 January Hertford informed King Henry that Thomas was to be admitted to the Privy Council. He had probably waited so long to raise the matter out of fear of the king's reaction, and indeed now Henry cried out "no, no"—but in his weakness was overruled.[32] The other councilors went along with this act of *lèse-majesté* for love, or fear, of the coming new power in England; yet Hertford's partiality for his youngest brother was noted and was a cause of concern. John Dudley, Viscount Lisle, who had been close to Hertford since their shared boyhood with Cardinal Wolsey, saw *himself* as Hertford's natural second in command. Now he decided to make himself "familiar with them both and loved of them both and trusted of them both" and so use that as a means to promote discord and sever the possibility of any alliance between the brothers.[33]

Thomas was oblivious to the circumstances of his appointment when he strode into the Council chamber at Westminster later that day. Unsurprisingly, given the alarming state of the king's health, the entire Council was in attendance to witness his advancement. For Thomas, it was a proud moment. He listened as Paget announced that "the King's Majesty, having in remembrance the good service of Sir Thomas Seymour, and minding to have him trained in the knowledge of His Majesty's Council, had appointed him to be sworn of the same."[34] Rather more down to earth was Thomas's first experience of government in the Council: discussions of judge's payments in Norfolk, and the matter of agreeing a reward for one "Patrick Craggy, Scot," who had assisted the English forces in Scotland. The Council sat only one further time during Henry VIII's lifetime, to arrange the wages for the garrison at Boulogne.[35] Rather than being humbled by his new appointment, Thomas Seymour saw his advancement to the Council as his by right. He was, after all, the prince's uncle and surely destined for greatness in the reign that followed. Moving upward with Thomas at the palace were his closest servants, including John Harington, a young gentleman from Stepney, who was just approaching his thirtieth birthday. Harington was a new addition to Thomas's service. After a decade trying to make his place as a musician in the Chapel Royal, he was glad of this promotion. He was a dreamer and a romantic—a poet and composer—but utterly devoted to his master.[36] In January 1547, he was newly married too; in this respect, he might have had a better reason than many for lurking around the royal apartments, since his bride, Etheldreda Malt, was believed to have been fathered by the dying king.[37]

Harington was determined to prove his loyalty to Thomas Seymour. Leaving the palace one day, he made the short journey to the house of Henry Grey, Marquess of Dorset, which was also in Westminster.[38] Dorset, who was himself a cousin of the king and had married his niece Frances Brandon—daughter of Henry VIII's sister Mary Tudor—was an uncomplicated fellow, priding himself on his faithfulness to his royal wife, to his friends, and to his reformed faith.[39] He admitted Harington, inviting him into his frosty gardens, where they could speak in private. Would he, Harington asked his host, "make friendship" with Thomas Seymour? Dorset did not know Thomas well, but appeared "inclinable and glad to be friend and familiar" with him, words that Harington rushed to convey to his master. The servant would later claim that he had acted on his own authority in making the meeting, but it got Thomas thinking. His future as the boy-king's uncle held a palpable promise of power. He began to form plans for Dorset and, more particularly, for the marquess's eldest daughter—Jane Grey.

Henry VIII slipped quietly away at two o'clock on the morning of 28 January 1547. But no sign was given to the outside world.[40] Within twenty-four hours, Ambassador Van der Delft was receiving whispered words that the king had died ("may God receive His Grace"), yet "not the slightest signs of such things were to be seen at Court." The middle-aged diplomat, who had reported on the old king's rages and his melancholy, itched to tell his master, the Emperor Charles V. But the roads out of London were closed and guarded, and all ships confined to port. Instead, he waited.

The Earl of Hertford had no such difficulty in traveling. As soon as Henry's death was confirmed, he set out northward for the county town of Hertfordshire, where his young nephew, the new king, was staying. He had already laid the political groundwork for the regency, but he needed to act quickly. Parliament had been sitting daily during Henry's final illness, with Hertford occasionally in attendance in the House of Lords. He had not liked what he had heard. There was some suggestion that Edward be placed in the government and possession of the state.[41] Nonetheless, he was confident as he rode out on 28 January, accompanied by Sir

Anthony Browne. Only a select few were even aware that England had a new king, and he would soon have the king's person in his possession.

He approached Hertford Castle by way of icy roads that January day. A convenient distance from London and "a competent lodging," the castle had been used by Henry as a nursery.[42] All three of his children had stayed in the apartments, which were arranged around a large courtyard, and the old king had spent considerable sums on the building to ensure that it was comfortable for his precious only son. It had strong walls, although the domestic buildings into which Hertford was now shown were timber, slotted within the mighty fortress as if as an afterthought.

The earl passed through the gates, close to strong round towers, before entering the courtyard and on into the galleries to await his nephew. He greeted the boy as Prince of Wales, ordering the child's household to prepare to move to London the following day. Hertford had slept very little the previous nights. He was still awake at one o'clock that morning when a letter arrived from Paget. He drafted his reply in the small hours, handed it to a messenger, and ordered: "haste, post haste, haste with all diligence, for thy life, for thy life."[43] It was past four o'clock when Hertford finally snatched a few hours of rest.

Although separated by some miles, Paget and Hertford had agreed to coordinate their actions in the hours following the king's death. Their main concern was Henry VIII's will, which, although it placed them at the center of power, did not name anyone to stand in overall control. Its existence was widely known, and so it could not be concealed; but both men were concerned to agree, as Hertford put it, "how much thereof was necessary to be published."[44] Hertford was anxious that "for divers respects" much of the content should be concealed. The document could, he believed, be carried to Parliament, "to show that this is the will," but closer scrutiny should not be permitted. It was sufficient that only the names of the executors should be provided, those in whom "the king did specially trust." As a token of his own faith in his ally, Hertford sent Paget the key to the chest that contained the will. By letter, the pair agreed that they would wait until Wednesday 2 February to notify Parliament—and the world—that England had a new king.

Edward was entirely oblivious to the fact of his accession. The nine-year-old had been surprised by his uncle's unannounced visit, but he went willingly with him the next morning, riding beside him. In spite of his haste to return to London, Hertford showed kindness to the pale boy who so resembled his own late sister. He resolved to bring him first to the person he loved best. Edward and Princess Elizabeth were well known to share "a concurrency and sympathy of their natures and affection."[45] To the new king, Elizabeth was his "sweet sister." Both had been saddened when they had left their stepmother in the autumn of 1546 to spend the Christmas season separately, north of London.

For Elizabeth, this had meant the pleasant royal hunting lodge at Enfield.[46] With the feast celebrated on trestle tables lined up in the great hall, she could think back to the Christmas four years before, when she had visited with both her siblings.[47] By Christmas 1546, she had turned thirteen and was considered to be on the cusp of womanhood. Around this time she also sat for her first individual portrait, standing solemnly while the artist captured her sparse, still childlike frame and pale, serious face. She carried herself well, though, her poise and the way in which "every motion of her seemed to bear majesty" evident in the portrait.[48] True, no one ever said that the girl was a beauty, with her long, narrow face. But, in common with her mother, she had striking eyes. They were her best feature, sparkling "lively and sweet." Other people compared her to her redoubtable father: she certainly had his fair coloring.[49]

The large oriel window, built by Henry VIII for his great chamber at Enfield, offered Elizabeth a panoramic view as her unexpected visitors approached,[50] the horses' hooves clattering over the wooden bridge at the entrance to the house. Once they were all together in the great hall, Hertford came straight to the point, informing the siblings that their father was dead and that Edward was now king. The two children fell into each other's arms and simply wept.[51]

Henry VIII had overshadowed their lives and would remain constantly in the remembrance of his younger children. For Elizabeth, Henry had been a distant, but fond, father who once enjoined his "own good daughter" to "remember me most heartily when you your prayers do pray for grace to be attained assuredly to your loving father."[52] For her, in particular, this was bitter news; she knew that when Hertford and Edward rode away the following morning, she would be left behind.

As the children grieved, Hertford, still functioning on minimal sleep, was soaring high. While it remained light enough to see, he pulled Sir Anthony Browne aside, inviting him to walk with him in the gardens.[53] Henry VIII's trusted and influential Master of Horse was conservative in religion and no friend to Hertford, but he saw the logic in the new king's uncle taking control. Although named as one of the old king's executors, he had his own concerns about Henry VIII's plans for a Regency Council, considering instead a protectorship to be "the surest kind of government." From the security of his own position, it seemed "a pleasure to stand upon the shore, and to see ships tossed upon the sea."[54] Browne believed in three parts to any business—"preparation, debate and perfection"—and could see that Hertford had already done his preparation. After some debate, he gave his "frank consent" to a protectorate. Hertford's ambitions were closer to realization.

That evening, the pair was deep in conversation when a letter arrived from the Council, deferring to Hertford as master. His response, which he wrote at eleven o'clock that night, was imperious. The tension released, he slept late into the next morning, finally helping the king mount his horse at eleven o'clock. They arrived before three o'clock at the Tower of London, where the boy was to be lodged to await his coronation.

As yet, Henry's fate was still only known to the few. The regular rituals were even maintained. Ambassador Van der Delft, knowing more than he ought, stood quietly by as trumpeters announced the arrival of the royal dinner, and as servants hurried past with their gilt dishes of rapidly cooling food.[55] Behind them, the door to the

Privy Chamber swung resolutely shut. The Imperial ambassador could have been forgiven a wry smile at the charade.

But as the ambassador watched, on 31 January, things were changing. There was no further need to conceal Henry's death, since Hertford held both the king and the levers of government. The Privy Councillors—with Thomas Seymour now counted among them—met in the Tower that day. Almost unanimously, they elected Hertford as England's Lord Protector.[56] And the new king was proclaimed.

Van der Delft was finally able to send his letter.

Chapter Three

ADORATION UNTIL DEATH

On 29 January 1547, the day after King Henry's death, Queen Catherine was waiting anxiously at Greenwich.[1] She was unsurprised when the arrival of a visitor from Westminster was announced, agreeing to meet with him privately. It was some months since Thomas Seymour had last seen the thirty-four-year-old queen—and he liked what he saw. Her beautiful hair was still auburn, peeking out from beneath a jeweled cap.[2] Untroubled by childbearing, she was tall and still girlishly slender, with unblemished pale skin helped by the regular milk baths that she favored. She was more regal and assured, but otherwise very much the woman that had caught his eye four years before.

Alone, in the privacy of the queen's apartments, they spoke of love, for Thomas made overtures toward Catherine even as he told her of the death of her husband.[3] He returned to Westminster later that day, but over the next few weeks the couple managed a few snatched visits. Soon they were kissing passionately, but in secret.[4] Thomas Seymour left the question of marriage dangling, however. After all, might he—the king's uncle—be able to make a better match than a dowager queen?

It took Catherine some time to accept that her status now was only as dowager queen. She had expected to be appointed regent, as she had previously been when Henry was campaigning in France. On hearing that the Council had other plans, she assembled a formidable legal team, headed by the eminent barrister Roger Cholmeley, who had acquired decades of experience in the Court of King's Bench.[5] She remembered, she informed them, that the old king had ordered his servants to swear an oath in her support. Did they think it was invalid now he had died? The answer the lawyers gave to her vice chamberlain was a positive one: the oaths remained binding. But Catherine lacked a party to support her. She might, for a time, have begun to sign her letters as "Kateryn the Quene Regente KP" but—if so—this was quickly dropped.[6] She had to resolve to live with the pretensions of the new king's "dear and well beloved uncle," Hertford, whose office of Protector was soon confirmed by commission.[7] Thomas Seymour received nothing more than a confirmation of his seat on the Council. Even this was far from assured, since Thomas could be dismissed by his brother on a whim.

Nonetheless, although Hertford would not share his preeminence, he did resolve to be generous in other ways. Sitting with the Council at the Tower on 6 February, William Paget rose to his feet. Henry VIII's last hours, he declared, had been troubled, since he was grievously concerned that "the nobility of this realm was greatly decayed." New blood was needed, and Paget—conveniently—had a list, apparently composed by the old king himself. Ignoring the fact that Henry had declined to name Hertford first among the executors, the earl was apparently foremost in his thoughts, to be granted the hitherto royal Dukedom of Somerset. There was something for the others too. John Dudley was to become Earl of Warwick, and Catherine's brother William Parr, the Earl of Essex, would rise to become Marquess of Northampton. Even Lord Chancellor Wriothesley, whom the new Duke of Somerset despised and who had opposed Somerset becoming Protector, received an earldom (of Southampton). Thomas, too, was not forgotten, although he had to make do with the title of Baron Seymour of Sudeley (in Gloucestershire)—the lowest rank of the nobility. The sizable grant of lands made to him at the same time was small consolation for the modest elevation, even though it made him a substantial landowner.[8] Unlike many of his fellow councilors, he failed to make himself available to sign the final version of his brother's commission.

Thomas's disaffection was plain to see. His brother leaned on the new Earl of Warwick to resign his post of Lord Admiral and pass it to him. Warwick had been an active Lord Admiral and likely resented transferring it to his former subordinate, in whose abilities he had little confidence.[9] Nonetheless, the appointment gratified the younger Seymour. It was an office that he coveted, giving him command over nearly sixty ships and authority over the men who packed the decks.[10]

It was still not enough, however. His brother—as Duke of Somerset and Lord Protector of England—was now accompanied everywhere by two gilt maces borne before him. Somerset was willing to share authority with no one, in spite of his promise to Paget as the old king lay dying.[11] As he vied with the other leading men of the Council he was viewed as "heady," "peevish," and "proud disdaining" in his manners.[12] But the duke grasped power with an iron fist, dissolving Parliament that February but refusing to allow the members to return home, "in order to prevent them coming back with changed opinions."[13] He meant to rule the young king, making a prominent show of knighting the boy on Sunday 9 February.[14] At the same time, he waved around several large pieces of paper, all bearing the great seal of Henry VIII. They were, he claimed, letters patent appointing him as Protector even in the lifetime of the old king; but he refused to allow anyone to scrutinize them.

Despite his disappointments, to begin with Thomas was yet unaware of just how limited his own power was intended to be. At his first Council meeting he suggested openly—and ill-advisedly—that Princess Mary and Wriothesley, both opposed to religious reform, should immediately be sent to the Tower.[15] Given the fact that Wriothesley was seated among them, while Mary—the cousin of the Holy Roman Emperor—was heir to the throne, this was naïve in the extreme.* As Somerset so often did in the face of his brother's outbursts, he maintained a stony silence, with Warwick instead employing "strong language" to disabuse Seymour of his delusions, remonstrating with him that "he had come to occupy such a high position through the favor of his brother and the Council, who had admitted him among their number against the late king's wish." This was news to Thomas, but the furious earl was not finished with him, declaring: "be content, therefore, with the honour done to you for your brother's sake, and with your office of Lord High Admiral which I gave up to you for the same motive, for neither the king nor I will be governed by you; nor would we be governed by your brother, were it not that his virtue and loyalty toward the king and the kingdom make him the man fittest to administer the affairs of the country during the king's minority."[16]

Humbled, Thomas apologized to his brother for his presumption, averting any quarrel—for the moment. Yet the rebuke smarted.

John Dudley, Earl of Warwick, was a wily and highly intelligent politician. He was not content with merely knocking Thomas Seymour off his perch for his presumption. As the son of an executed traitor, he had clawed his way almost to the summit of society

---

* Seymour had also already managed to alienate Thomas Cranmer, Archbishop of Canterbury, when he complained about his hospitality to the king (*Narratives*, pp. 260–263).

with his wits alone.* He saw weakness in Somerset's regard for his brother and was determined to use it as a way of sowing discord. Shortly after their exchange in the Council room, Dudley came to Thomas and pointed out that, since his brother was Lord Protector, he himself might aspire to the role of governor of the king, Edward's guardian, and he offered "all his help and furtherance."[17] The possibility that he could become governor had not occurred to Thomas before and he gave his hearty thanks, asking if his old naval superior would raise it himself in Council. Dudley refused. After all, he argued, how could such a reasonable request be denied?[18] Thomas could see logic in this, since he was entirely oblivious to his own political shortcomings. He was accordingly full of confidence when he raised it in front of the Council the next day—and shocked when his brother, listening in furious silence, suddenly rose to his feet and dissolved the meeting.[19]

Later that day, Dudley came to Somerset and whispered: "Thus, Your Grace may see this man's ambition."[20] He reminded him that he had previously warned the Protector that his younger brother "would envy your state and calling to his room."[21] The duplicitous John Dudley—who was trusted by both siblings—counseled Somerset to be wary of his brother.[22]

Thomas Seymour, his ambitions roused, now had no intention of abandoning his claim to the governorship. It must, after all, have seemed terribly unfair. Apart from the accident of birth order, *he* could have been Protector and governor—he and Somerset even looked similar. He began to take steps to enlist others to his cause, beginning with a carefully composed letter to the Marquess of Dorset, outlining plans that he had conceived for his daughter Jane Grey. Sealing it, he passed it to John Harington, with whom

* He was the son of Edmund Dudley who, along with Sir Richard Empson, had attracted opprobrium under Henry VII for their assiduous implementation of royal measures to squeeze money out of England's nobility. Henry VIII, on his accession in 1509, courted popularity by having both men arrested and charged with treason. They were executed in 1510.

he had consulted as he wrote. The persuasive young servant was the perfect emissary. He hotfooted it over to Dorset's residence for the second time that winter.[23]

On taking Harington aside, the marquess's face grew "cold" and unfriendly as he scanned the letter, which proposed that he pass his eldest daughter into Seymour's care. The eminent marquess can only have supposed that Seymour meant to marry his nine-year-old heiress, and it was left to Harington to hastily reassure him otherwise. Had Dorset not heard Seymour say of his daughter "that she was as handsome a lady as any in England, and that she might be wife to any prince in Christendom"? Why, Harington had heard Thomas declare this, he assured the peer. Confidentially, he informed his host that Seymour had gone further, saying: "if the King's Majesty, when he came to age, would marry within the realm, it was as likely he would be there, as in any other place, and that he would wish it."

Dorset believed that his pretty red-haired daughter was worthy of a crown, so the suggestion was a tantalizing one. Confidentially, Harington whispered that "being kept in My Lord's house, who was uncle to the king, it were never the worse for her; and that My Lord would be right glad, if the King's Majesty could like any in his house." Dorset must have heard of Seymour's claims to become the king's guardian—was it true that the king would soon be lodged in his uncle's own house? Harington shook his head, saying "he durst not tell what it was," although Jane "were as like in his master's house to have a greater and better turn, than he would think." To Dorset, who was kept even further from power than Seymour, such a prospect seemed highly likely. He gave the order for his daughter to pack her things. She was going to join Thomas Seymour's household.

Jane Grey's marriage was not the only one that Thomas Seymour was pondering in the early months of 1547. Surprisingly, he was still a bachelor at almost forty and a desirable one at that. His own marriage could lead him to greatness—and his thoughts turned to Princess Mary, the thirty-year-old heir to the throne. The daughter of Catherine of Aragon was slight, with reddish hair and pale skin. Henry VIII, who had declared her illegitimate, never troubled himself to arrange a marriage for her. There had been offers, most notably Don Luis of Portugal, who renewed his addresses before the old king was even buried.[24] Yet Mary's cousin, the Emperor Charles V, who kept a fatherly eye on the princess, was under few illusions that she would be permitted to marry during her brother's minority.[25] She was still the best match in England, as England's most eligible bachelor realized.

Although he was frantically busy, Somerset agreed to meet with his younger brother in private one day at Westminster. He was shocked when Thomas got straight to the point, boldly asking for consent to his marriage to Princess Mary, as though it were almost a foregone conclusion.[26] The certainty with which he spoke would have thrown a less self-assured man; but the duke kept his composure, merely declaring reproachfully that "neither of them was born to be king, nor to marry king's daughters; and though God had given them grace that their sister should have married a king, whence so much honour and benefit had redounded to them, they must thank God and be satisfied." Somerset must have found Thomas's proposition laughable; for good measure he added that "besides which he knew the Lady Mary would never consent."

Somerset had good reason to know that Mary had little love for the new regime. The pair clashed over religion, with the Catholic princess dismissing the Protector's reformed beliefs as "new fangledness and fantasy."[27] While Mary heard two, three, or even four masses a day, Somerset was in the process of stripping the churches of their ornaments to push ahead with his planned program of Protestant reform. He had also offended the heir to the throne when he failed to pay her a courtesy visit after her father's death.[28] She recognized that "in the end everything will depend upon the good pleasure and unfettered discretion of the Protector," but she had no desire to marry his brother. Thomas declared to Somerset that "he had merely asked for his brother's countenance, and he would look after the rest." The Protector, his anger rising at his younger brother, chided him even more sharply and indicated that the matter was finished. As Somerset stomped away, even Thomas must have recognized the hopelessness of his cause. When told of his suit, Mary merely laughed.

Princess Mary kept herself away from the festivities surrounding King Edward's coronation on 20 February, at which the Protector insisted on being at the center of things. In the coronation procession he rode alongside the Earl of Warwick, both vying for the place closest to the king.[29] To cap an awkward day, during which the Imperial ambassador's invitation was mislaid, the boy-king was so nervous that he forgot both his French and Latin. His ignorance was gleefully reported to his counterparts across the Channel. Little Edward, who had previously survived black magic and other attempts on his life during his apprenticeship as Prince of Wales, showed the world the child that he still was, rather than the great king he so wanted to be.* By contrast, Thomas Seymour acquitted himself well, taking part in the jousts and tournaments that followed the coronation and hosting his fellows for dinner one night in his London house.[30] His thoughts, though, were still on matrimony—albeit now in a different quarter.

Princess Elizabeth, left alone at Enfield following Edward's departure, had slowly begun to pack up her household. With the loss of her "own matchless and most kind father," she was now an orphan. At thirteen years old, she was too young to live without family supervision, even within her own household.[31] Her "beloved mother," Catherine Parr, was the obvious candidate to be her guardian, and Catherine welcomed her at Greenwich when she arrived there, which was by late February 1547. During his frequent

* Records at The National Archives (TNA E36/120 f.70) describe the discovery of a wax effigy of Prince Edward, struck through with a knife in 1538. Prophecies and other such attempts on his life are also recorded.

and passionate visits to the queen, Thomas Seymour was able to catch a glance at the princess—black-clad and pale with mourning. He approved. Confident and handsome, he was certain that he could win Elizabeth.

Once again, he sought an audience with his brother and his other friends on the Council, asking that they should consent to this match. Predictably, they refused. Yet Thomas resolved to ignore this "good advice given to the contrary."[32] He desired a royal bride and Elizabeth fit the bill perfectly. On 25 February 1547, less than a month after the death of Elizabeth's father, Seymour sat down to make her an offer in writing. He wrote of his respect for her, which was so great that "I dare not tell you of the fire which consumes me, and the impatience with which I yearn to show you my devotion."[33] He claimed to be burning with love for her. If she would only show him kindness, she would have "made the happiness of a man who will adore you till death." He was offering the girl marriage, if she would only consent.

Elizabeth was "very much surprised" to receive Thomas's letter. She had previously had little direct contact with him and, although she found him dashing (as most women did), she had never contemplated him as a husband. Thomas flattered her. She thanked him in her response, declaring that "the letter you have written to me is the most obliging, and at the same time the most eloquent in the world."[34] He had taken her breath away, and she did not consider herself "competent to reply to so many courteous expressions," but she knew that she needed to unburden herself to him. She was too young, she insisted, to even think of matrimony. She also reproved him gently, contending that "I never would have believed that anyone would have spoken to me of nuptials, at a time when I ought to think of nothing but sorrow for the death of my father." Her words were not, however, an outright refusal. She required time to enjoy "some years my virgin state" and to mature into womanhood; and she intended to mourn her father ("to him I owe so much") for at least two years. But after that, she would be open to offers. Elizabeth discussed the letter only with her governess, Kate

Ashley—but the decision to reject Seymour's offer was made by her alone. Catherine Parr was entirely oblivious of Thomas's suit.

Attempting to woo the king's sister with the express disapproval of the Council was a desperate act. Seymour cannot have been surprised at Elizabeth's decision "to decline the happiness of becoming your wife," although it disappointed him. She did, at least, assure him of her eternal friendship and the pleasure she would feel "in being your servant, and good friend." While friendship with a princess was potentially useful, it would not increase Seymour's actual status one jot.

Picking himself up from this second rejection quickly, Thomas made a decision. On 3 March 1547, finding a private moment amid the comings and goings of the queen's household, Thomas Seymour and Catherine Parr were married. The queen forgot her station when she promised "to honour, love, and such in all lawful thing obey" her alluring lover, as he later reminded her in a letter.[35] It was only thirty-four days since the death of the old king.* Unsurprisingly, and necessarily, the ceremony was conducted in the strictest secrecy. The couple went to bed together immediately—so soon that they placed the royal succession in jeopardy. For, as it was later alleged, "if she had conceived straight after it should have been a great doubt whether the child born should have been accounted the late king's or his."[36] Although a bachelor, Thomas Seymour was no sexual novice.** He so debauched an earlier conquest that she became known as "a lewd woman that had lived an unclean life."[37] In her fourth marriage, the queen now finally had her young and vigorous husband; but she was not thereby prepared to jeopardize her position or reputation. She swore Thomas to secrecy.

---

* See Vertot, pp. 101–103, for Seymour's declaration of love, and Leti for the date of the marriage. The marriage date is controversial, although the surviving evidence supports an early date. (James, in *Catherine Parr*, p. 269, suggested that the marriage occurred at Baynard's Castle in late May 1547, though this is mere supposition.)

** There is at least one earlier recorded mistress.

The Protector's brother slipped quietly back to Westminster following his wedding and attended a Council meeting the next day. The agenda was dominated by fear of conflict with France. Somerset granted a commission to Lord Russell, the Earl of Warwick, Thomas Seymour, and William Paget to enter negotiations for a defensive league with the French ambassadors,[38] with whom they went to dine on 5 March 1547.[39] They failed to do this discreetly for, as they walked together, the Imperial ambassador's spies noted that Paget was carrying a great packet of papers with which to negotiate a treaty. Although very much a junior partner in the discussions, Seymour could congratulate himself, as he made merry at dinner, that—even before his marriage to the queen was known—this was a sign that he was far from being out in the cold.

It was a starkly different situation to that of others who had displeased the Protector. Stephen Gardiner, who had already been excluded from the Council, had such little credit left that—as he noted—he could not even succeed in banning a play in Southwark scheduled to be performed at the same time as a solemn requiem mass for Henry VIII in the cathedral there.[40] As Somerset established himself, the distribution of power among others was constantly shifting. The day after Thomas's ambassadorial dinner, the Protector struck against Wriothesley, requiring him to resign his office and placing him under house arrest.[41] He went quietly.

Somerset hid his insatiable desire for power and his absolute conviction in his own righteousness beneath a cloak of benignity; but some believed him capable even of murder.[42] In large part, his "sabling" as Protector had been due to his fine personage, the eloquence of his speech, and his learning, all of which were noted, even by his detractors, as the means by which he forged goodwill.[43] By March 1547, he considered himself to be secure. Even Warwick, whose "liberality and splendour" made him more popular than the "dry, sour, opinionated" Somerset, appeared to submit to second place willingly enough, in spite of predictions at court that he would never countenance his colleague's dominance.[44] The Earl of Warwick, with his "high courage," was very good at dissembling.

With the coronation out of the way, Somerset set himself the task of organizing the king's household, as well as considering future provision for the dowager queen.[45] Catherine, along with her stepdaughters Mary and Elizabeth, was still in London in early March. They paid at least one visit to the court at Westminster that month.[46] But Catherine was already considering a move out of London to her fine manor house at Chelsea. She busied herself with her council of receivers, surveyors, attorneys, and solicitors, and took steps to put her financial affairs in order.[47] In the eyes of everyone, Catherine continued to appear the grieving widow—although she did permit her troupe of Italian viol players to amuse her mourning household.[48]

Princess Mary, who continued to grieve openly, was gone from London by the end of March, traveling out into Essex and then to East Anglia and her estates there.[49] Remaining behind, and appearing always in the queen's company, Elizabeth was less oblivious to Catherine's marriage secret than her stepmother realized.[50] Toward the end of the month, the queen and her stepdaughter moved briefly to St. James's Palace, while they prepared for the move to Chelsea.[51] It was warmer now and Elizabeth's lady mistress, Kate Ashley, took her exercise in the park beside the palace. One day she came upon Thomas Seymour, who was probably attempting to visit his wife. She approached, telling him boldly that she had heard it said that he should have married Elizabeth.[52] No, said Thomas, she was mistaken since he did not intend to lose his head for a wife. "It could not be," he continued, but he assured Mistress Ashley that he would prove to have the queen. The forthright Kate merely laughed, saying it was past proof as she had heard he had already married Catherine. To this, Seymour said nothing; but his silence was telling.

Catherine and Elizabeth set out for Chelsea in April 1547, accompanied by their households. The queen, who distributed alms liberally to the poor that she met on the road, had mixed feelings.[53] On the one hand, she was relieved to be leaving behind the strictures of life in the capital; on the other hand, it meant a separation from her new husband. Before parting, the couple promised to write to each other every two weeks.[54] It was an interval that the queen found too long, and she playfully claimed to Thomas that "weeks be shorter at Chelsea than in other places" as she sat down to write to him long before two weeks had expired. Signing herself "by hers that is yours to serve and obey during her life," Catherine settled down to wait impatiently for a reply.

Soon, Thomas was haunting the fields around Chelsea, seeking the privacy of a meeting with his wife. In the early hours of a morning, as the spring sky was just beginning to lighten over Chelsea, a cloaked figure would make her way through the damp grass, intent on being unseen. Reaching the gate at the edge of the field, she would listen for footsteps, and on hearing them open the gate, before slipping back with her visitor to the smart brick manor house. There they could spend a few precious, unnoticed hours alone together. In this way, the woman who to all the world was a grieving dowager queen and the man who was looked upon as the realm's most eligible bachelor could make the most of their still-secret marriage. By seven o'clock in the morning, Thomas had hurried away.

At the same time as Catherine could not prevent herself from writing overfrequently, so Thomas reminded her of a promise she had made, "to change the two years [of public mourning and widowhood] into two months."[55] He had seduced her, he had married her and he had bedded her. The time had come, as far as Thomas Seymour was concerned, for Catherine's ostentatious mourning to end. He wanted to reap the rewards of having a royal bride.

Chapter Four

WHAT WE CANNOT REMEDY

Catherine and Thomas struggled with just how they should present their secret match to his brother. Catherine's relationship with the Duke of Somerset was colored by her belief that he had outmaneuvered her in the dying days of Henry VIII. She had once been close to his wife, Anne Stanhope, and had hoped for more support from her.[1] In the weeks following Henry VIII's death, as the two women's positions shifted, Catherine found Anne neglectful of her affairs, making it "her custom to promise many comings to her friends, and to perform none." Catherine was still stewing about slights that she had received when she arrived at Chelsea, writing to complain to Thomas that his brother had made many promises, but they were as yet "unperformed." She thought Anne "hath taught him that lesson." Thomas was more hopeful that his sister-in-law could be their friend. He spoke to her personally one day at court in March, asking that she would see Catherine. The Duchess of Somerset imperiously declared that she would be at her house in Sheen for the next few days, but that "at her return on Tuesday" she would see the queen.[2]

Neither Catherine nor Thomas was convinced that they could obtain the Duchess of Somerset's favor. Thomas wrote to Catherine asking her: "if ye see yourself in good credit with her, to desire Her Grace to be my good lady. And if I see myself in more favour than you, I shall make the like request for you."[3] But Anne Stanhope, as the Protector's wife, saw herself as the queen of the court, and she was not prepared to cede her place to a woman that Henry VIII had merely married in what a chronicler described as his "doting days, when he had brought himself so low by his lust and cruelty that no lady that stood on her honour would venture on him."[4] The Duchess of Somerset questioned the morals of "Latimer's widow" even before she knew of the queen's secret marriage; either way, she was determined not to "give place to her."

Catherine and Thomas continued with their snatched meetings at Chelsea as summer blossomed around them. Such trysts were highly charged, given the constant danger of detection. On one occasion, while he was lurking in the fields with a letter for his wife, Thomas was spotted by a servant of Catherine's brother, the Marquess of Northampton.[5] Seymour thought no more of it, failing to recognize the man, but he was himself instantly recognizable. The servant rushed to inform Nicholas Throckmorton, Catherine's cousin.

The couple was lucky that it was only Throckmorton, who loved his kinswoman, and the matter went no further. Nonetheless, on realizing how close they had come to being discovered, Thomas threw his letter in the fire. Catherine had already cautioned him to ensure that their correspondence, so full of passion and plotting, did not fall into hostile hands. Yet she had already broken her own commandment and kept his letters. He also could not bring himself to keep away, writing again and hoping that his words would be received with "goodwill." In May he sent her a red deer and a buck that he had killed as gifts. The queen generously rewarded the servants who carried the gifts.[6] She ordered that her plate be brought up from London for a banquet but, without Thomas there, the celebrations must have been muted.[7]

There is no doubt that Thomas, in spite of his earlier attempts to find a more prestigious bride, was deeply attracted to Catherine. He probably even loved her. He certainly swore that when he wrote letters to her they were "from the body of him whose heart ye have."[8] On another occasion, on one of Catherine's letters to him he wrote in reply: "from your highness humble servant, assured and faithful friend, and loving husband during his life."[9] Her intellect daunted him, but he also admired it, excusing his own literary deficiencies by saying that since he never reread his words after they were written, "wherefore if any fault be, I pray you hold me excused."[10]

The problem of how to meet and correspond was a very real one, but Catherine and Thomas were soon forced to put all thoughts of gaining acceptance for their marriage aside. First and foremost, Thomas was Lord Admiral, and he relished the adventure of the role and the outlet it gave to his restless spirit. In April word reached London that a particularly notorious corsair, one Thompson of Calais, had sailed with a fleet of Scottish and French pirates and taken the Scilly Isles by force.[11] The islands, ancient and rocky and far from the coast of Cornwall, were strategically important, since they effectively commanded the entrance to the English Channel. Their windswept isolation conferred protection on them and made them dangerous in the wrong hands. Thompson, with his seven or eight ships safely nestled among the rocks of his island fortress, had free rein to plunder merchant ships as they traveled between England and Spain. This was a dangerous and lawless situation, and one that could not be allowed to continue. Seymour was issued with instructions to grant the pirates a pardon, if they would only surrender to him.

Thomas Seymour set sail for Cornwall, taking residence in the Captain's House at St. Michael's Mount. He sent some of his ships on ahead of him to challenge the privateers, waiting impatiently for news on this ancient outcrop off the Cornish coast. Against a chorus of shrieking gulls and the sounds of the sea rushing over the slate and granite of the shore, he sat down on 20 April 1547 to write to his brother, informing him that "as soon as wind will serve" he would sail to the Scilly Isles, "where I am sure to land safe" since the fine galleass *Greyhound* and the rest of her fellows were already there.[12] Galleasses—adaptations of the trusty galleys—were the pinnacle of naval technology. They had in fact already pacified the pirates, making Seymour's visit a matter of surveying his victorious fleet.

He intended to take order of his ships there before returning to Portsmouth and then hurrying, overland, to London and the court. It was the type of campaign he liked best: short and exciting, with opportunity for glory. There was also the chance of a profit. It was probably at Scilly that Seymour struck a deal with Thompson and the other pirates, whereby they could have free rein in their illegal endeavors in return for a share of the booty—which was quickly to make the Lord Admiral rich.

Thomas Seymour reveled in his role as admiral that spring, becoming familiar with the ports in which he docked, though many of them were "frontier towns" exuding "beggary, misery, and desolation" as they decayed through lack of investment.[13] The local people depended on the sea in all manner of ways. The poor there were employed in knitting nets and making and mending ships and tackle, as well as in fishing. Among those thronging the ports were the pirates. The Lord Admiral, who was popular with all, was soon on friendly terms with some of them.[14] He returned to London in May, a conquering hero. Unlike his earlier attempts at naval command, Thomas's admiralty had gotten off to an excellent start. In addition to the Scilly success, in March his fleet, sailing without him, had captured three fine Scottish ships.[15] Even the news that the Scots had—in revenge—captured some English vessels could not dampen Thomas's jubilation.[16]

There was, though, a price to pay. While enjoying life on the high seas, Thomas Seymour was also being slowly maneuvered away from any pretense of power. With the removal of Wriothesley, the Protector had manufactured a Council of men who "all worship him."[17] Somerset sometimes went to farcical lengths to maintain his preeminence. When, early in May 1547, Ambassador Van der Delft's wife gave birth to a son, the diplomat asked Princess Mary to stand as godmother and both Somerset and the young king to act as godfathers.[18] It was, of course, out of the question that the boy-king should attend in person, while Mary—who was still grieving for her father—sent Lady Russell to act as her stand-in. Somerset also needed a proxy, so the Earl of Warwick arrived to play the part of the Protector. Yet in spite of this, standing beside Warwick at the font was none other than Somerset himself—who had insisted on representing the king. It was a ridiculous scene, but the Protector was single-mindedly determined "to take the first place on every occasion." Thomas Seymour, who lacked his brother's abilities and relentless single-mindedness, surely had no real hope of such power.

Thomas and Catherine still desired, though, to be part of the new regime, if Somerset would only distribute some of his power. By May 1547, they had decided to try to obtain the Protector's support for their marriage—without admitting that it had, in fact, already occurred. The conceit was that Thomas would ask his brother to speak to Catherine in favor of an (intended) marriage. It was an uncertain course and Thomas was "in some fear how to frame" Somerset to speak for him, as he admitted to Catherine's brother-in-law Sir William Herbert.[19] Herbert, who was unaware of the reality of the marriage, was surprised. Catherine came to stay at Baynard's Castle for a few days in early May, where Herbert informed her of Thomas's interest.[20] Catherine startled him even further, seeming unperturbed by the idea of such a suit. Indeed, she merely became indignant at the possibility that Somerset would deny the request. As she ranted at the upstart duke's presumption, she declared that his refusal of his brother's suit would "make his folly more manifest to the world." She was a queen and not prepared to beg. She wrote to Thomas that it was sufficient to ask his brother's aid only once, and "after, to cease." Her own plan was somewhat different. She wanted Thomas to obtain a letter from her stepson King Edward in their favor as well as the support of the Council, "which thing obtained shall be no small shame to your brother and loving sister, in case they do not the like." In other words, Catherine wanted to go above Somerset's head; but her husband counseled her to wait.

The couple continued to meet in secret, but their encounters, though passionate, remained all too brief. Thomas longed for his wife's company, something that also drew him toward her sister, the pretty, charming, and cosmopolitan Anne Herbert, whom Thomas already referred to as his "sister" in letters to his wife. She was clever and urbane, corresponding with scholars and reading Cicero for pleasure.[21] She had also spent a life of service at court. At thirty-one, she was still not past her prime, a woman in whose company, Seymour assured his wife, "in default of yours, I shall shorten the weeks in these parts: which heretofore were three days longer, in every of them, than they were under the plummet in Chelsea."* Time ticked by slowly for Thomas when he was away from Catherine.

Anne and her husband invited Thomas to dine with them on 16 May 1547, following Catherine's stay in their house. As he sat privately with William Herbert, a bluff self-made man, whose father's illegitimacy had proved no bar to his son's rise to the Royal Council, the talk turned to Catherine.[22] Herbert was a "mad fighting fellow," a hothead whose glittering military career had begun with a midnight flit to France after being accused of murder. Age had

* "plummet"—the workings of a clock.

mellowed him, but it did not calm his restless spirit: he spoke as he saw. His wife, too, was determined to be outspoken at the meeting. She arrived later, bringing a message from her sister, addressed to Thomas.

Seymour had to be careful, since he was unaware of just how much Anne knew. When she chided him for visiting the queen at Chelsea, he immediately denied it, saying that he had merely passed Catherine's garden on his way to the Bishop of London's house. He and Anne stood silently for a moment before, smiling, Catherine's sister told him other details of the courtship that could only have come from the queen. As he blushed, aware that he had been caught out with a lie, "like a false wench" Seymour admitted everything.[23] It was a burden off his shoulders: there were now four people in on the secret, and the Herberts rejoiced at the match. They also offered practical aid, since Anne volunteered to pass Thomas's letters—as though they were from her—on to her sister.[24] Seymour was thrilled. He stayed up past midnight, when he returned home to write a lengthy letter to his wife. Seeing Anne, who resembled Catherine, had only increased his desire for the queen. He asked Catherine to send him her portrait in miniature, so that it "shall give me occasion to think on the friendly cheer that I shall receive when my suit [to make the marriage public] shall be at an end."

Thomas soon discovered that the queen had also confided her love for him to her friend, the romantic Duchess of Suffolk, who joked with one of Catherine's servants that she wished Thomas could marry the queen and become his master—hinting heavily about what she knew of the relationship.[25] Word was spreading. But Thomas Seymour had still not informed his brother.

The couple decided to press on with their attempts to speak to Somerset. And so, in late May, while the court was still staying at St. James's Palace, Thomas made his third approach to his brother regarding matrimony. This time, he was humble, requesting only that Somerset ask Catherine to bear him goodwill and her favor toward marriage.[26] Once again, however, Seymour had badly misjudged his brother who—although he agreed to speak to Catherine—offered no support.

Three months earlier, on 7 February 1547, Catherine had been gratified that the young King Edward, despite the whirlwind of his new responsibilities, had found the time to write to her, acknowledging her "remarkable and daily love for me."[27] But she had heard nothing since, and her attempts to meet with him were always postponed. Somerset had no wish to readmit the queen into his nephew's orbit and affections.[28] She nevertheless wrote regularly, "beseeching" some response and reiterating her "everlasting love" for King Henry and her goodwill toward Edward. In May, she commissioned portraits of both herself and her stepson as proof of the continuing bond between them.[29] She could not, for propriety's sake, be ignored, so Somerset finally gave the king permission to write to his stepmother on 30 May: it was the first letter that Catherine had received from him in nearly four months. In it, the boy sent his apologies, explaining that he had not written before as he had hoped daily to see her.[30] Catherine resolved to make that a reality.

In the warm sunshine of early June 1547, Catherine arrived at St. James's Palace, dismounting from her horse with her attendants after passing through the red brick gateway. The palace was a favorite of Edward VI, its fine high walls interspersed with chimneys, resembling his birthplace of Hampton Court. It was convenient for her too—not that far from Chelsea, making it an easy enough day trip. She strode into the palace across the cobbled ground, intent on demanding access to her stepson.

First, however, she had to run the gauntlet of an interview with the Protector and his wife. In anticipation that Somerset would, at Thomas's bidding, represent his suit, Catherine had planned her speeches, intending (as she assured Thomas) "to frame mine answer to him when he should attempt the matter, as that he might well and manifestly perceive my fantasy to be more towards you for marriage than any other."[31] She intended to assure Somerset that she had "a full determination never to marry, and break it when I have done, if I live two years."

Yet Catherine's carefully prepared words remained unspoken. Instead, as she entered the chamber, the ducal couple began to berate her. They dismissed any notion of a marriage between her and Thomas Seymour as "that hell"—something that they would earnestly pray would not happen. They were fearful of permitting Thomas to take such a bride. Their words made the queen "warm" with fury, her anger so hot that, had she been only a little closer to the Protector, she feared that she "should have bitten him." Nevertheless, with a promise of a meeting with the king—probably the next day, but perhaps on Saturday at three o'clock at the latest—she backed down and returned home to Chelsea.[32]

She was not done with her "new brother," and meant to "utter all my choler" when she saw him again with the king. That evening, she wrote to Thomas asking him to calm her down and tell her what to say. He found her anger erotic, writing of his pleasure that she "hath been warmed" for him and that this would mean that she no longer spoke of keeping apart for two years. Nonetheless, in spite of the passion that Catherine's fury raised in her, her goals went largely unmet. She found the doors to the royal apartments firmly closed against her and she was not permitted to see her stepson.[33]

For appearances' sake, the Protector and his wife sent gifts to Catherine at Chelsea, including a pasty of venison, while one of the king's servants sent her a book.[34] Yet they had failed to give her what she really wanted. A different course was required. She had always been close to Princess Mary, who was only four years her junior, and now Thomas and Catherine resolved privately to approach her for her support. Catherine had not seen her stepdaughter for some weeks when Thomas wrote to her at Wanstead, Essex, where the princess was staying, warily keeping her distance from London.

Mary, who had been a pretty, promising child, had grown into a sad figure, moving purposelessly from house to house that spring and summer. She was depressed and lonely and had already resorted to coyly begging the Imperial ambassador to visit.[35] Yet it was not Van der Delft who arrived one day in early June, for he was caught up with affairs in London. Instead, a servant dressed in the Lord Admiral's livery rode quickly into the stable yard and made his way to the princess. Although Catherine had already thrown off her coarse black mourning clothes for dark silk and stylish French hoods, Thomas's servant encountered a princess and her household cast still in deepest black, as gloom hung all around them.[36]

He passed no less than six private messages of his master's support to the princess, before also handing her a letter in which Thomas asked for Mary's help in persuading Catherine to marry him.[37] The princess was horrified by what she read. It was "strange news" to her, for how could Catherine even consider forgetting the duty to her late husband, who, as Mary commented, "is yet very ripe in mine own remembrance." No, she would not do as Seymour asked, not even for her "nearest kinsman and dearest friend alive" since, surely, he should consider "whose wife Her Grace was of late." Mary's response was final and cutting. She would not be "a meddler in this matter" for anything, and she trusted her stepmother to show better judgment. Besides, as she wrote to Thomas, she was embarrassed by this insight into his love life since "I, being a maid, am nothing cunning." She wanted nothing more than to be left alone by this troublesome man with whom her name kept being connected.

Mary's rebuff left only one recourse: the young king himself. A child king was still a king, and the mystique and aura of monarchy—even when embodied in a pale, freckled nine-year-old—possessed authority. Somerset knew this, and so kept a tight rein on Edward and on those who were brought into his presence. Even Thomas—the boy's uncle as much as Somerset was—found admittance difficult. He had, though, already used his considerable charms to win the trust of John Fowler, one of the gentlemen of the king's Privy Chamber and a man who had daily access to the king. Fowler was the grandson of both a chancellor of the exchequer and a lord mayor; but his family had sunk socially, and Thomas Seymour's attentions now flattered him.[38]

One day that June, Seymour called Fowler to the chamber he kept at court, chatting amiably with his guest and putting him at his ease before commanding his servant to leave the room.[39] Finding himself alone with Thomas, Fowler was surprised by the sudden change in tone. Seymour asked him: "Now, Mr. Fowler, how doth the King's Majesty?" Being one of the king's closest attendants, Fowler assured him that the king was well. Thomas then asked whether the boy lacked anything, to which his guest demurred.

Seymour now got to the point, enquiring whether "His Grace would not in his absence ask for him, or ask any question of him?" The king's servant could nod his agreement to this—the king would sometimes speak of Thomas, but nothing else. Fowler asked his host: "What question should the king ask of you?" "Nay nothing," replied Thomas, "unless sometimes he would ask why I married not." The marital status of the king's uncle was hardly likely to be uppermost in the nine-year-old's mind, as confirmed when Fowler assured Thomas that "I never heard him ask me such a question."

The answer was disappointing for Seymour, and he paused. After some uncomfortable, silent seconds, he looked again at his guest, before asking: "Mr. Fowler, I pray you if you have any communication with the King's Majesty soon or tomorrow, ask his highness whether he would be content I should marry or not. And if he say yes I pray you ask His Grace who he would should be my wife." The urgency of the request was clear to Fowler. He desperately wanted the Lord Admiral's patronage and agreed to the request.

That night, Fowler sidled up to the king on finding him alone in his chambers. Almost reciting Thomas's words verbatim, he said boldly: "I marvel that My Lord Admiral marrieth not." Edward ignored him. Undaunted, Fowler tried again, asking directly: "Could Your Grace be contented he should marry?" The king had never given it any thought, but it seemed reasonable to him; he merely answered "very well." Fowler tried to draw more interest from the boy, asking whom he thought his uncle should marry.

Raised as he was among men, Edward had little knowledge of the women of his kingdom, but Anne of Cleves—his father's fourth wife and former stepmother, whose annuity he was still paying—sprang to mind. After a pause during which he considered further, Edward changed his mind: "Nay, nay, what you what I would he married my sister Mary to turn her opinions."

The interview was over, and Edward wandered away, oblivious to the blow with which he had just struck Thomas. Fowler found Thomas in the palace gallery the next day. But Seymour laughed when told of what the king had said, before sending the servant straight back to the king to ask whether "he could be content that I should marry the queen." Pretending that Catherine still needed to be wooed, he also asked the boy to write to her on his behalf.

Given Fowler's earlier lack of success in the matter, Seymour did not entirely trust him. He therefore managed to slip into the royal apartments himself the following day.[40] In private, he entirely persuaded the king that the match was his idea. Edward wrote at once to Catherine to promote his uncle. It was a brilliant piece of maneuvering, making the marriage tantamount to a royal command. Thomas himself brought Catherine's meek reply to the king, in which she made a "gentle acceptation" of the suit—before confirming that she had done as bid and married.[41] Edward was thrilled. He replied on 25 June, thanking Catherine for this proof of her love and obedience.[42] He was sure she would be pleased with her new husband, since Thomas, "being mine uncle, is of so good a nature that he will not be troublesome any means unto you." Furthermore, the king resolved to protect them, promising that "I will so provide for you both that hereafter, if any grief befall, I shall be a sufficient succour in your godly and praiseworthy enterprises." With the king's approval, the couple could now publicize their marriage—it was widely put about as having occurred around 16 June 1547.[43]

The Duke of Somerset was furious at what he took to be proof of his brother's "evil and dissembling nature." He made his feelings known even to the king, who recorded that he was "much offended."[44] In public, Somerset put on a brave face, despite rumors that it was all part of a scheme of Seymour family marriages: there was another advantageous union arranged for Somerset's daughter with the son of the Earl of Derby.[45] Thomas still attended Council meetings, but the atmosphere was frosty. Reviewing some written instructions for the French negotiations, produced that June, the rivalry was discernible in their signatures.[46] The brothers had the two largest signatures, and both signed with similar flourishes, dwarfing the other councilors' marks. But, as always, it was Somerset who dominated, signing above all others. Thomas's florid attempt was constrained within the only space left—the far right of the page.[47]

The Protector was not the only person to be shocked at Catherine's apparent lack of self-control. Princess Mary, who usually had so little in common with Somerset, shared his anger. One evening at dinner with Van der Delft, she spoke candidly of the marriage, asking her guest what he thought of it.[48] The ambassador considered that "it appeared to me to be quite fitting, since the queen and he were of similar rank, she having been content to forget the honour she had enjoyed from the late king." Mary was distressed, laying the blame for the marriage firmly with her stepmother.[49]

The princess was also deeply worried about Catherine's suitability as a guardian. She now saw the queen as a woman filled with lust. She wrote at once to Elizabeth, to remind her that their "interests being common, the just grief we feel in seeing the ashes, or rather the scarcely cold body of the king, our father, so shamefully dishonoured by the queen, our stepmother, ought to be common to us also."[50] Elizabeth should come and live with her, she declared, since she herself could now no longer return visits to the fallen queen.

The letter placed Elizabeth in a difficult position, and she took her time over her response. She had (she claimed) suffered "affliction" when she heard of the marriage, finding comfort only in God. Nonetheless, she thought that "the best course we can take is that of dissimulation, that the mortification may fall upon those who commit the fault" rather than those who merely consoled themselves "by making the best of what we cannot remedy." In truth, Elizabeth had no wish to leave her stepmother for the dour environment of Mary's establishment, writing that "the queen having shown me so great affection, and done me so many kind offices, that I must use much tact in manoeuvring with her, for fear of appearing ungrateful." Despite her talk of "dissimulation," it was to her half-sister that she dissembled. She was staying at Chelsea.

Princess Mary's anger was stoked by Somerset's wife. The forthright, capable, but controversial Anne Stanhope was believed by many to rule her husband with "ambitious will and mischievous persuasions."[51] There was some truth in the characterization, and even Paget rued Somerset's "bad wife."[52] Her husband feared to cross her. On one occasion, when he showed leniency in a political matter, she was said to have complained ominously "that she had never so much displeasure of her husband since she was first Sir Edward Seymour's wife."[53] In spite of the frostiness of Mary's relationship with the Protector, his wife was the princess's greatest friend—her "Good Gossip" or "Good Nan," in whom she could confide.[54] The two of them and the queen had once been so close that Catherine and Mary had shared the same sheet of paper to draft a friendly note to Anne, while Catherine wished her "so well to fare as I would myself."[55] Catherine and Anne also shared their deep commitment to the reformed faith, having both held a dangerous connection to the Protestant martyr, Anne Askew, during the latter years of Henry's reign.[56] But now the relationship between the two Seymour sisters-in-law exploded into outright hostility. If Mary was forced to take sides, she would line up with the Duchess of Somerset.

The duchess had initially gotten on reasonably well with Thomas, but she was deeply jealous of Catherine.[57] The marriage gave her the opportunity to publicly attack her rival, since she was not the only person at court to raise eyebrows at the new Lady Seymour of Sudeley's claims to regal status.[58] The queen's own friend, the Duchess of Suffolk, who had once (playfully) promoted the marriage, cruelly mocked the couple in private, naming a black stallion in her stables "Seymour" and a mare "Parr."* Catherine's haste to the altar made her seem wanton—and she was castigated for it. Given her apparent barrenness, as well as her matronly years, contemporaries were certain that there could be no other motive for Catherine other than sexual desire.** After all, marriages were supposed to be consummated purely for the begetting of children—and most people had strong doubts that the queen could achieve that.[59] In short, Catherine had debased herself.

Despite the murmuring and gossip, Catherine was, though, still the queen. She continued to appear at court proudly in her finery, wearing crimson satin and gold buttons, garnished with small pearls.[60] It may have been an attempt to reduce her pride that led Somerset to confiscate many of her jewels, which she had left in the Tower for safekeeping. Or, it could have been mere covetousness, since both Somerset and his duchess were busily helping themselves to the royal stores. Lady Somerset would soon be seen with her brother, Sir Michael Stanhope, smuggling fine fabrics out of the royal silk house, trussed in a sheet.[61] Somerset was availing himself of Catherine's lands, too, granting leases and inciting her servants to disobey her.[62] That summer, in the face of such hostility, she attempted to secure the return of her jewels, only to find them declared Crown property. Catherine was not short of jewelry, including beautiful rings set with rubies and other gems, kept in a box of crimson velvet

---

* As mentioned by James (p. 276). This seems to have been something of a theme for the Duchess of Suffolk. She also had a dog named "Gardiner" after her enemy the conservative Bishop Stephen Gardiner (Evans, p. 187).

** In the 1540s, marriage had only been recognized as a sacrament by the church for a century. This helped to move ideas away from an ideal life of celibacy; yet there was still something furtive about marriage for the sake of love or sexual attraction (see Haynes 1999, p. 1; Vives, p. 155). Wives, in particular, were enjoined not to "contaminate the chaste and holy marriage bed by sordid and lustful acts" (Vives, p. 227).

garnished with silver and gilt.[63] Yet, unsurprisingly, the Protector's actions filled her with fury. Among the items taken from her were her wedding ring from Henry VIII, as well as a gold cross and some pearl pendants that she had received from her mother.[64]

The Duchess of Somerset remained determined to humble her rival. She refused to hold the queen's train when she came to court, declaring that "it was unsuitable for her to submit to perform that service for the wife of her husband's younger brother." On more than one occasion, as both women walked uncomfortably side by side, the duchess physically shoved Catherine out of the way in order to pass through a doorway first. This was outrageous behavior, and the queen refused to stand for it, declaring to anyone that would listen that "if she does again what she did yesterday I will pull her back myself."[65] To add insult to injury, Somerset informed his brother that he supported his wife's actions.

Thomas retaliated by dredging up his brother's uncomfortable past. Calling in his lawyers, he sought their opinion on reinstating the children of Somerset's first wife as his heirs in precedence to his offspring by Anne.[66] This reopened terrible wounds. Somerset's first wife, Catherine Filiol, was rumored to have been caught *in flagrante delicto* with a certain gentleman—believed to have been none other than the Seymour brothers' own father.[67] Catherine Filiol had been repudiated and ordered to "live virtuously and abide in some house of religion of women," and there must have been whispers over the paternity of her sons.[68] Perhaps no one knew the true parentage of the two boys, although their "father" Somerset paid them an allowance when he became Protector.[69] He had ensured, though, that it was his third son—and Anne's first—who would one day succeed to his lands and titles.

Thomas's meddling only served to cause further strife between the brothers, while Queen Catherine soon began to retreat to her household at Chelsea and the peace of the suburbs. She could at least now bring her new husband there openly, as master of everyone in the house. And this included Princess Elizabeth, who was approaching her fourteenth birthday.

Part Two
THE SCANDAL DEEPENS

June 1547. Princess Elizabeth lay in her bed, alone in her locked chamber. She heard a key turn in the door.[1] The sound of it roused her, and she was still blinking as fingers reached in and forcefully pulled back the curtains from around her bed. To her surprise, it was a male hand, one she knew well. Her new stepfather was already sliding his personal key to her bedchamber back into his belt.

Only thin coverlets lay over the princess, for the summer heat at Chelsea made her room stuffy. Dressed only in her loose-fitting nightdress,[2] she sought to shield herself from Seymour's gaze, pulling the sleep-tousled sheets further over her young body. This shyness only made her visitor smile. Leaning into the bed, he called "Good morrow," before seeming to pounce, as though he would climb in with her.

Stunned and blushing, Elizabeth shrank deeper into the bed, pulling the covers up to her chin and well above the low neckline of her nightdress. She moved as far away as possible "so that he could not come at her"; but she made no attempt to rise. Thomas Seymour stepped back eventually. Surely it was only a playful game. But Seymour noted that the girl did not actually protest.

Chapter Five

THE YOUNG DAMSELS

In the summer of 1547, the teenage Princess Elizabeth, still swathed in mourning black, spent much of her time at Chelsea sitting at her desk. There, she read silently from her books, favoring the classical writers such as Cicero, Plato, and Aristotle, who were so popular in the universities. At other times she wrote, furiously copying out a piece of translation or amending some composition. At a second desk, which faced hers, sat her tutor, the young, solemn-faced William Grindal, who also took the opportunity for his own studies. He was kindly, diligent, and approachable, and the princess was fond of him.

Grindal made the journey to Chelsea with Elizabeth and Catherine in April 1547. He was just one member of a sizable household of servants, many of whom, within a few weeks of Elizabeth's birth, had been sworn to serve her. They wore her livery, thus marking them out as Elizabeth's people. In later life, she would choose stylish black satin for her servants. During her brother's reign, she provided her gentlemen with fine velvet coats, each identical in color and style. Those inferior in rank were similarly, but more cheaply, attired.[1] Elizabeth's household now entered the confusing hustle and bustle of Catherine's new establishment, unpacking chests marked with Elizabeth's arms, which were stored haphazardly among the queen's own possessions.

Elizabeth's servants provided stability in a troubled early life. Appointments were long-term: of the thirty-two people employed to serve her when she was three years old, many still remained with her in 1546 when a second census of her household was taken.* Her establishment was always growing too, so that by her late teens her wage bill was enormous.[2]

The center of Elizabeth's world, as a young girl, had been her "lady mistress," Lady Troy, while five gentlewomen provided female company and support—Kate Champernowne, Elizabeth Garrett, Mary Hill, Elizabeth Candish, and Mary Norris.[3] Below them in rank were two female chamberers, who would remain in her service for at least a decade, as well as gentlemen ushers and grooms of her chamber. Her chaplain, Sir Ralph Taylor, was a similarly longstanding appointment, as was William Russell, one of the grooms of the chamber, who served her all through her childhood. Russell was prosperous enough to maintain his own personal servant, "Charles," who was so skilled in stitching that he made the princess's corsets, artfully lining the garments with fine silk.[4]

* Her half-sister Mary's household showed similar continuity over the years, although it was initially larger because of Mary's status as heir to the throne for most of her childhood (BL Harley MS 6807 f. 2–9). Also, see McIntosh (2010), p. 68.

Agnes Hilton, who arrived each day to take care of the princess's laundry, was a familiar face too: she scrubbed Elizabeth's clothing and linens from the time of the girl's infancy.[5]

By the time of Henry VIII's death, Blanche Parry, earlier employed to rock the princess's cradle, had been promoted to become one of the gentlewomen.[6] Gentle Blanche had left behind her childhood in the glorious countryside of the Welsh Marches to serve the princess. Her arrival heralded a lifetime of devoted service, and she was to prove the girl's longest-serving attendant. She was the niece of the aged Lady Troy and owed her position to this illustrious relative, who was also her godmother.[7] Blanche, whose surname was more correctly "ap Harry" following the Welsh naming tradition, was with Elizabeth for almost every day of her young life. She quietly adored the princess, entertaining hopes that she would, in due course, succeed her aunt as Elizabeth's lady mistress.[8] With the appointment of Katherine Champernowne as governess in 1536, however, a smooth transition of authority became far from certain.

Henry VIII, who had been impressed by Katherine Champernowne's learning and the "distinguished teaching" she could provide, had made the appointment himself. She hailed from the West Country. With her round, puffed face, "Kate"—as Elizabeth called her—was homely looking, and affectionate. Born at the turn of the century, Kate was a spinster without family of her own. Instead, she lavished affection on Elizabeth, whom she treated as a daughter. It was only after 1545, when the middle-aged Kate surprised everyone by marrying, that the princess even had to share her affections with another.

Kate socialized mainly within Elizabeth's household, so unsurprisingly her choice of husband came from within its ranks: a pleasant-faced, fork-bearded fellow who had used a very distant familial relationship with the princess to obtain a place in her service. John Astley had suffered tragedy as a child, when his mother, Anne Astley, died giving birth to twins during a visit to the Boleyn family seat of Blickling Hall, in Norfolk. Anne's sister Elizabeth,

Lady Boleyn, commemorated the triple tragedy in a pathos-filled monument in the parish church. Such calamities were all too common, but the shock of the loss, so far from home, must have been particularly difficult for John and his surviving siblings back home in Kent. He was always quietly reflective, later musing on "the frail and transitory state of man in this life."

When Anne Boleyn—Lady Boleyn's niece by marriage—became queen, there was a place for John Astley in her household.[9] He shared his royal kinswoman's reformist religious beliefs, becoming by 1547 an ardent Protestant. In these views he complemented his bride, Kate. The couple, in spite of some disagreements, were close,* but Kate nevertheless retained great independence following her marriage, even going so far as to adopt her own pronunciation of his family name. While her forty-year-old husband was always resolutely "Astley," Kate, with her Devon accent, preferred "Ashley."** Her refashioning stuck.

Kate's role had initially been to teach Princess Elizabeth her letters and provide her with the rudiments of a good education. The motherless girl was a pleasure to instruct, thriving under what the scholar Roger Ascham described as her governess's "excellent counsel."[10] But there were limits to what even the educated gentlewoman could teach. Kate gave up her place willingly to a new tutor in 1544, when Elizabeth was ready to expand her studies. The new appointee, Grindal, had been suggested to King Henry by John Cheke, who had already been appointed tutor to Prince Edward.[11] Grindal, who most likely hailed from the north of England, was young and badly in need of a job to relieve his poverty, for, although

* Both were also proud of their royal connections; John ended his life as the contented resident of a house in Maidstone, Kent, known as "the Palace."

** In correspondence and even in his own will, Sir John always appears as "Astley." Kate on the other hand is called "Ashley" in most documents, suggesting that the pair pronounced the surname differently. Although Katherine is often referred to as "Kat," Elizabeth usually called her "Kate": the reference to her as "Kat" by the princess in her interrogation in 1549 is most likely an abbreviation.

a gentleman, he had no independent means.[12] He came to Cambridge to study under the renowned Roger Ascham, who loved him dearly, calling him his "most familiar friend." Grindal was particularly celebrated for his knowledge of Ancient Greek, although the paucity of his wages at Cambridge had given him "neither heart for study nor a sufficiency to live on."[13]

The position of royal tutor was, by contrast, a lucrative one, and much sought after, with rewards on top of the salary that could be paid by a grateful princess.[14] The tutor was expected to supply the princess with books and a rigorous curriculum, but in return the holder of the post received privileged entrée into royal society.[15] As a teenager, the princess spent more time with her tutors than almost anyone else, and real affection could grow. Even as an adult, Elizabeth remembered her old schoolmasters fondly, greeting one (as he claimed) "as if I were returning to my homeland after exile."[16] All in all, the opportunity was an excellent one for Grindal.

With a heavy heart, Ascham agreed to send his protégé southward when he was called. He offered a character reference for his friend, recalling that Grindal was "a man of mark, and promise" and that Cheke "shall find him diligent and respectful, zealous in learning and love of you, silent, faithful, temperate, and honest, and in every way devoted and well fitted for your service." The quiet, studious young gentleman slotted perfectly into Elizabeth's household. He immediately introduced his royal pupil to a rigorous curriculum of Plato, treating her like a university student several years older than she was.[17] He was pleasantly surprised that Elizabeth had already been well schooled by Kate Ashley, and he reported to Ascham favorably on her methods.[18] Grindal convened lessons for the princess every day of the week, and as Elizabeth settled down to life at Chelsea the daily routine continued unchanged.[19] Grindal also befriended Kate's husband—the men met up to discuss the works of Cicero and other weighty tomes.[20] John Astley was intelligent and had enjoyed some learning; but Grindal—and Ascham, who started corresponding with Astley—opened up a new world for him, enjoining him to read so that his "ears so resound with the noble precepts of the book."

By 1547, Elizabeth's household was largely harmonious, although wounds from just a few years before were still sore and whispered. In late 1546, Lady Troy was approaching seventy at her retirement, having served for thirteen years as the princess's lady mistress.[21] She returned to Wales. Elizabeth went on diligently paying her pension of half her previous salary up until the elderly woman's death in 1557.[22] It was not much money, but the aged widow had been left comfortable by her husband and she enjoyed a long retirement.[23] She had hoped that her niece would succeed her as head of the princess's household, but the quiet Blanche Parry faced a formidable rival in Kate. The former governess needed a new role after Grindal's appointment. She was more ambitious than Blanche and acutely aware of status;[24] she was also possessive of her royal charge and loved her dearly. When, on one later occasion, Blanche presented Elizabeth with a fine square of velvet edged with silver lace as a New Year's gift, her rival outdid her with a dozen handkerchiefs edged with gold and silver.[25] With Kate lobbying for the appointment as lady mistress, the choice had been left to Henry VIII.[26] It was thus Kate Ashley who arrived at Chelsea in the role.

While Elizabeth spent her Chelsea days with her head bowed over her books or writings, the queen was using her general estrangement from court to work on her own intellectual projects. Catherine was formidably intelligent and a published author. Her early works had been orthodox and unobjectionable, but even as Henry VIII lived she had quietly worked on a more radical composition. As she waited for time to pass between Thomas Seymour's visits to Chelsea, she had pulled out her old manuscript, reading through a work that delved deep into her innermost psyche. She wrote of the loathing that she felt about herself in the face of the perfection of God, "bewailing the ignorance of her blind life." Released from the terrifying shadow of Henry VIII's

wrath, Catherine was able to be more open about her thoughts and beliefs.* She discussed the manuscript in her household. Her visiting brother, the Marquess of Northampton, made an "earnest request" that she print her work, while her friend the Duchess of Suffolk declared publication her "instant desire"—as its subsequent title page recorded. During her now-rare visits to court, the queen also sought the advice of William Cecil, a country squire and a rising star in the Protector's household. He considered it "no shame" for Catherine to "detect her sin." She was persuaded and so prepared the work for publication all through the summer and autumn of 1547. It was a brave decision to expose herself in this way as a "miserable, wretched sinner," particularly following the hasty marriage to Thomas that was still looked on by some as a scandal.[27]

Elizabeth approved of Catherine's *Lamentations of a Sinner*, deciding to revise her own earlier work from 1545 in a show of solidarity for her stepmother. As an eleven-year-old, she had prepared a translation of Marguerite of Navarre's *Mirror of the Sinful Soul*. The child had struggled with the content to produce a tiny, beautiful book as Catherine's New Year's present for 1545, finishing only on the very last day of 1544.[28] She had been too young to understand all of the content, which focused on the dependence of the human soul on God. In the studious environment of Catherine's household, Elizabeth again took up her work, giving it a fresh and more mature eye.

At the same time, the princess also copied out a number of biblical verses that had some meaning to her, including: "there is not a more wicked head than the head of a serpent and there is no wrath above the wrath of a woman." She was thinking about marriage, considering that "he that hath gotten a virtuous woman hath gotten a goodly possession; she is unto him an help and pillar whereupon

---

* In 1546 Queen Catherine had narrowly escaped arrest for heresy after her husband began to tire of her outspoken religious beliefs and her opponents sought to take advantage.

he resteth." Yet, "it were better to dwell with a lion and a dragon than to keep house with a wicked wife," while a man should "depart not upon a discreet and good woman that is fallen to thee for thy portion in the fear of the lord for the gift of her honesty is above gold." As she approached fourteen, Elizabeth knew that she was reaching an age at which she could marry. Thomas Seymour's proposal remained in her thoughts, particularly with the teasing and urging of Kate Ashley, who had a soft spot for the new head of the household. Elizabeth ended her biblical copying with words from the Thirteenth Psalm: "the fool saith in his heart that there is no God."[29]

Many at court considered Thomas Seymour to be just such an ungodly fool. In spite of his estrangement from his brother, he continued to haunt the corridors of power, either riding over from Chelsea or from Catherine's other manor of Hanworth, or stepping out from his London townhouse. The Seymour brothers' falling out was not public knowledge that summer; but it lay heavy on Thomas's mind.

One day, not long after Thomas's marriage became widely known, John Fowler came across him in the gallery at St. James's Palace.[30] He watched Seymour pass into the king's inner chambers, before following him in. Once again, finding themselves almost alone, Seymour ordered his servant to leave so that he could speak to Fowler privately. Furtively, he asked the king's servant, according to Fowler's later report, "whether My Lord his brother had been there or not since his last being there." Fowler said no. Seymour made no acknowledgment of this, instead continuing that his brother had "fallen out with him concerning the Admiralty and how His Grace took their part afore his." Fowler had little sympathy on this score, telling Thomas to "bear with My Lord's Grace, considering he is the Protector of the Realm, and your older brother." "For God's love," Fowler added plaintively, "let there be no unkindness between you two." But there already was. Thomas replied: "Mr. Fowler, nay, nay, My Lord would have my head under his girdle." He then paused, before asking Fowler to tell the king what he had said, for fear that Somerset should otherwise slander him.

Although Thomas did not give Fowler the details of his dispute over the Admiralty, it most likely related to the invasion of Scotland. Somerset had inherited war with England's old enemy thanks to Henry VIII's desire to marry his son to Mary, the young queen of Scots.* By late August, the court had moved to Hampton Court and martial preparations were fully under way, although Thomas's role in them was far from certain.[31] That month, Somerset refused to include him on a list of councilors to remain in London and rule while he was away leading the campaign.[32] At the same time, he also informed anyone who cared to know that "his brother was to go to the west of England to see after anything that might be necessary there." These rather vague instructions to quit the capital must have rankled with Thomas, but his brother certainly did not want him close to his vacant seat of power during the six weeks or so that he intended to be away; and neither did he want Thomas with him as he moved northward at the head of the king's army.

When Thomas first heard that he had been appointed Lord Admiral, he had professed himself pleased, declaring to his friend Sir William Sharington that "he was glad of that office as of any office within the Realm and that no man should take that office from him but he should take his life also."[33] Sharington—a tricky, dishonest fellow looking for a profit—seriously doubted this, pointing out that there were many better offices that Seymour

---

* Mary was the daughter of James V of Scotland and granddaughter of Henry VIII's elder sister Margaret Tudor. She had inherited the Scottish throne in 1542 on the death of her father when she was less than a week old. The Treaties of Greenwich (1543), agreeing on a marriage between the infant Mary and Edward, were repudiated by the Scottish Parliament later that year, and instead Scotland maintained its traditional alliance with France. English attempts to coerce the Scots into accepting the marriage treaty began with punitive expeditions under Edward Seymour in 1545: they became known as the "rough wooing."

might have had. Yet Thomas insisted that he would never give up his patent as admiral, since with it he had "the rule of a good sort of ships and men. And I tell you it is a good thing to have the rule of men."

If he hoped that he would really be given effective command of England's navy he was, however, severely disappointed. The appointment was a largely symbolic one. Instead, he was forced to sit while the Council debated the wisdom of sending to Germany for naval munitions, in order to ensure that the Scots were unable to purchase them.[34] He was denied command of the navy in the waters around Scotland. The Earl of Warwick's brother, Andrew Dudley, had already been appointed admiral to the north within weeks of Thomas Seymour's receiving his appointment, although Dudley was then replaced in readiness for the invasion by the more experienced Lord Clinton.[35] Clinton's instructions, dated 1 August 1547, were full of excitement and promise, as he was sent northward against "our ancient enemies the Scots" to take revenge against them and rid the seas of the French galleys haunting the waters.[36] This was the kind of adventure Thomas Seymour relished; but he was not invited to take part.

Thomas had another reason to be discontented. He was furious when he discovered that Somerset had no intention of leaving him as governor of the king when he was in Scotland. He ranted to all that would listen about Somerset's appointee in his stead, "so drunken a fellow as Sir Richard Page."[37] This appointment rankled particularly, because Page was the stepfather of the Duchess of Somerset, whose family the Protector very clearly favored over the Seymours. Instead of heading westward, as was intended, Thomas remained resolutely in London, kicking his heels about the court as Somerset surged northward, winning a victory against the Scots at the Battle of Pinkie, east of Edinburgh, on 10 September 1547. Gallingly for the Protector's younger brother, the navy, under Lord Clinton, played a notable role, supporting the army from the Firth of Forth. There was, at least, one silver lining for Thomas. With the Protector gone and Page apparently less than fit for office, he was able to gain access easily to the king in his apartments at Hampton Court.

Sitting with his royal nephew one day, Thomas told Edward that Somerset would never be able to dominate in Scotland "without loss of a great number of men or of himself; and therefore that he spent a great sum of money in vain."[38] This hit a nerve with the king, since Somerset was widely believed to be embezzling Henry VIII's treasury and jewels.[39] The Protector was also rumored to be wreaking "havocs" among the king's lands and inheritance, with sales made "under pretence of mere necessity," and with many of the king's best lands transferred to his own possession. These charges were largely unfair, since the royal treasury had been much depleted by the time of Edward's accession, while Somerset's character was "not by any means such as to make him lavish, but rather leads him to parsimony in everything."[40] However, it was an easy charge for Thomas Seymour to make, particularly since the Protector deliberately kept the boy-king short of pocket money.

Thomas chided his nephew that he was "too bashful" in his own affairs, and that he should speak up in order to "bear rule, as other kings do."[41] Edward shook his head, declaring that "I needed not, for I was well enough," yet he registered his uncle's words. When Thomas came to him again that September, he told the child that "ye must take upon you yourself to rule, for ye shall be able enough as well as other kings; and then ye may give your men somewhat; for your uncle is old, and I trust will not live long."[42] Edward chillingly replied: "it were better that he should die." There was little love lost between the monarch and his Lord Protector. Thomas also informed Edward that "ye are but even a beggarly king now," drawing attention to the fact that he had no money with which to play at cards or reward his servants. He told his nephew that he would supply him with the sums he needed.

Somerset's absence in Scotland had had the effect of handing the king to his brother, and Thomas meant to capitalize on it. He trawled through royal records, seeking out precedents to support his bid to become the king's governor, and he openly began to build support at court. He already had three members of Edward's household—Thomas Wroth, John Cheke,* and John Fowler—in his party.[43] Thomas Seymour was, however, incapable of concealing his actions. Word soon reached Somerset that a plot was afoot.[44] The king had shown himself a member of the younger brother's party, declaring that he was happy to take "secret measures" to replace Somerset as governor. This was naturally alarming for the Lord Protector, who, abandoning a promising situation in Scotland, hurried southward to reestablish his authority at court.

The Duke of Somerset kept up the outward appearance of friendship with his younger brother. That month, the Duchess of Somerset sent a freshly killed doe as a present to Catherine.[45] She followed it up, later on, with boxes of marmalade.[46] Thomas returned home to Catherine, thwarted for now—but not beaten.

Thomas Seymour's presence always added excitement to the atmosphere at Catherine's manors of Chelsea, or Hanworth, to where the queen moved in July 1547. The queen was determined to maintain a godly household for "the young damsels" in her care who, as the schoolmaster-cleric Nicholas Udall put it, "instead of cards and other instruments of idle trifling . . . have continually in their hands either psalms or homilies, and other devout meditations, or else Paul's epistles, or some book of Holy Scripture matters, and as familiarly both to read or reason thereof in Greek, Latin, French, or Italian, as in English."[47] The "young virgins" in Catherine's care were reputed to want nothing except their books, abandoning hunting trips, dancing, and games; but this was an exaggeration. While they often studied

* Cheke's involvement is surprising, and he obviously failed to heed the third of his mother's recommendations when he first came to court—that he take care of his God, his soul, and his company (BL Sloane MS 1523 f. 37v).

both early in the morning and late into the evening, there was also time to indulge in "courtly dalliance" as the minstrels played and the ladies danced.[48]

Catherine Parr loved dancing. Her household, while striving for the godly, was also filled with merriment as she sought to make the most of her freedom as a dowager queen. Sometimes, she would go by boat to dine with her friend the Duchess of Suffolk, making a cheerful party as she and her attendants sailed in the summer heat.[49] The duchess, who had once been rumored to be Henry VIII's choice for a seventh wife,* would dance playfully with Seymour, either in her own house or when she returned Catherine's visits.[50] Princess Elizabeth watched the pair with her dark almond-shaped eyes. When the time came and the music changed, she stepped forward shyly, claiming her stepmother's husband as her own for the dance.

As she touched his hand, she would "laugh and pale at it," as though it were a joke, but there was always a clucking Kate Ashley whispering in her ear: "I wis [*sic*] you would not refuse him if the Council would be content thereunto," causing the girl to chase her dancing partner away as quickly as she selected him.[51] Mistress Ashley was as captivated by the dashing Seymour as the others in the household. She, of course, knew that Elizabeth could not now have the married Seymour, even with the Council's consent. Yet, his desirability to the princess was obvious, and Kate teased her. As regards her young and impressionable royal charge, she gave conflicting messages: the person whose role it was to provide a defense of Elizabeth's honor was, simultaneously, nudging her and Thomas together. Kate, more than anyone, knew that the princess, as she approached her fourteenth birthday, was growing up. She took care of Elizabeth's intimate needs, purchasing material for her

* There were already rumors, reported by Ambassador Van der Delft in February 1546, that Henry meant to replace his sixth queen around the time of the heresy accusations with none other than the queen's recently widowed friend Catherine Willoughby, Duchess of Suffolk.

most private garments, including linen cloth to be made into pads for the princess's periods.* The child was nearly a woman.

Somerset, at court, was also aware that Elizabeth was reaching womanhood. He had turned his attention to her marriage by September 1547, when Warwick informed him that an emissary of the Earl of Bothwell—a powerful Scottish divorcé—had suggested a trio of English ladies as potential wives.[52] While the emissary named the youthful Duchess of Suffolk, he was more coy about revealing the names of the other two, but hinted at either Mary or Elizabeth. Warwick kept a poker face, refusing to be drawn on the royal ladies, although he did tell the emissary that he thought the Duchess of Suffolk was his to be won, since she would follow the Protector's commands. Bothwell was not to be thwarted, though. He declared that he would go a-wooing himself in England if he were granted safe conduct, declaring that "if he liked them they would not mislike him."

Somerset might also have considered the nine-year-old son of the Earl of Arran as a potential husband for Elizabeth. He had asked Lord Clinton to kidnap the boy and bring him to London.[53] Such a marriage would help his Scottish negotiations—although such negotiations were always long and drawn-out.

Oblivious to these intrigues, Elizabeth continued to spend many of her daylight hours at Chelsea studying. As the sun waned, even in the long days of early summer, the gathering darkness of late evening made the house feel crowded and dingy. True, there was sometimes the dancing by candlelight. But a dozen candles cost one and a half shillings, which, when the average laborer earned around two or three shillings a week, was a huge expense.[54] There was certainly no sense in lighting all the dark or unnecessary

---

* There is a later reference in Princess Elizabeth's household accounts to Kate purchasing "linen cloth and other necessarys for her grace's use" for 4 shillings (Strangford, p. 32). The small sum, when compared to other purchases of linen cloth, such as one made for 22 shillings 4 pence, suggests that a small quantity of linen was purchased. It seems likely that this would have been for Elizabeth's sanitary protection, or at the very least for underwear.

corners of the manor house. At night, around the princess's bed, the darkness would have been impenetrable.

Nighttime was also the only occasion that Elizabeth was alone. Kate Ashley had always been possessive of her young charge and, toward the end of Lady Troy's tenure as lady mistress, succeeded in taking the old lady's place in sleeping on a small pallet bed beside the princess's own.[55] Sharing Elizabeth's bedchamber, Kate thus acted both as chaperone and confidante, marking her position as a rising star in the household. All this had changed with Lady Troy's retirement. Although her niece Blanche Parry asserted her own claim to sleep beside the girl, she was "put out" by her rival. Kate could not abide anyone else taking her place on the pallet bed; she only reluctantly allowed her maid to sleep there when she was absent from the household.

It caused comment when this arrangement suddenly changed at Chelsea. One day, Kate ordered the removal of the pallet bed from Elizabeth's bedchamber, on the grounds that the room "was so little." (There was, though, room for a reading desk at which the princess could study.) Henceforth, Elizabeth was to lie alone and unchaperoned at nights in her great bed at Chelsea.*

It would leave Elizabeth exposed. For the sake of her virtue, she badly needed protection.

* This was highly unusual. Even as queen, Elizabeth was expected always to be chaperoned (Merton, p. 85).

Chapter Six

GO AWAY, FOR SHAME

Thomas Seymour's first early-morning visit to Elizabeth's bedchamber came within days of his arrival at Chelsea in June 1547. He entered a household that, although still draped in mourning black, was lively and filled with hope for the future. Thrice widowed, the queen had worn too much black in her thirty-five years. No wonder she preferred rich velvets and satins, and favored bright crimson and jewels over dark veils.[1]

Thomas had his own London house, having acquired the residence of the Bishop of Bath soon after Edward's accession.[2] Seymour Place, more palace than house, occupied a pleasant and convenient spot on the Strand, its site sloping down toward the River Thames. Riding into its large courtyard, cobbled with uneven stones, Seymour could dismount while his horse was led away to open stables close to the buttressed chapel.[3] The better rooms faced away from the courtyard, toward the fine ornate gardens that descended in terraces toward the river and a private wharf, which allowed the house's occupants to take to the river at whim.[4]

Jane Grey, having been placed under Thomas's care by her father, the Marquess of Dorset, was at Seymour Place when her guardian's marriage became public knowledge. She spent her days with her head quietly bowed over her books, under the guidance of her tutor Mr. Aylmer. Her mother, Frances Brandon, was on friendly terms with Queen Catherine, whom she had often encountered at court.[5] Both she and her husband were in no way offended by Catherine's marriage when it was publicized; instead, they hoped that their daughter would be transferred to the queen's household, believing that she would learn "good behaviour." They considered that due to her "tender years" the girl required firm instruction lest, "for lack of a bridle," as her mother would later fearsomely put it, she should "take too much the head."[6]

Jane was tiny, even for her age; she would later be dressed in wooden platform shoes to give her some extra *gravitas*. But she was fiercely intelligent and opinionated. It made sense for Thomas to bring Jane—who was, after all, Catherine's great-niece by marriage—with him when he took up residence at Chelsea in June 1547.* Prior to Thomas and Catherine's marriage being publicized, many must have assumed that Jane Grey was at Seymour Place as Thomas's fiancée. Somerset and others at court must have wondered just *whom* it was intended she should marry, if it was not her now-spoken-for guardian. It was better, more proper, that she be transferred to the queen's household.

Jane brought her own servants with her. One gentlewoman, John Astley's sister Elizabeth, was particularly welcome, for she

---

* There is historical dispute about her whereabouts. Some (James, Porter, and de Lisle) consider that she remained, for the most part, at Seymour Place until the household moved to Seymour's castle at Sudeley in the summer of 1548. However, the fact that Elizabeth's later tutor, Roger Ascham, obviously knew Jane and her tutor well suggests that Elizabeth and Jane were sharing a household some time earlier.

resembled her brother in her pleasant manner and her integrity.[7] Princess Elizabeth and Jane Grey shared a similar outlook, and Jane later praised her older cousin as one who "followeth God's word."[8] However, a four-year age gap, while nothing between adults, was still a large gulf between two girls aged nearly ten and nearly fourteen. The girls respected each other, but Jane was not someone in whom Elizabeth could confide once Seymour began his early morning visits. Neither did the princess make many other friends among the household at Chelsea. She seemed "proud and disdainful" to those around her, who misinterpreted her sadness at her father's death and natural reserve as arrogance.[9] And her stepfather's attentions were soon proving alarmingly persistent.

Elizabeth had dressed quickly following Seymour's first visit, as though nothing had happened. She spent her day alone with her tutor at her books and her evening with her ladies. As she retired to bed that night, it must have crossed her mind whether Seymour would return again. The thought was a startling one for the daughter of the disgraced Anne Boleyn. There were many who believed the daughter shared the character defects of the mother executed on accusations of adultery.[10] Elizabeth, though fashionably pale-skinned, resembled her dead mother in most other respects. In particular, both had dark, flashing eyes, which captivated men and made women wary. Princess Mary, who had always tried to show kindness to Elizabeth, nevertheless sometimes looked at her suspiciously, even going so far as to whisper that Elizabeth's conduct made her doubt her half-sister's paternity.[11]

Elizabeth was fascinated by the mother she could not remember, later hiding Anne's portrait in a secret compartment in a ring.* But, as the daughter of "such a mother," Elizabeth was expected by many to behave with her mother's impropriety. Discussing the fate of Anne was taboo to those around Elizabeth, creating a barrier.

---

* In the two recorded instances that Elizabeth spoke of Anne, she portrayed her favorably, in one case asserting that her mother would never have agreed to cohabit with the king except by way of marriage (Cole, p. 4).

Thomas Seymour was the only one bold enough to break the taboo. Indeed, he mocked the embargo to others in the household. "No Words of Boleyn," he sniggered—a punning reaction on being asked about "Boulogne" by Elizabeth's treasurer, Thomas Parry. This was shocking, but it was also liberating for the princess, helping to draw her further toward her unorthodox new stepfather.

Whatever the complexity of Elizabeth's emerging feelings about Seymour, on the next morning following the morning of Seymour's first visit she rose from bed early.* This was a considerable effort of will for her: she was, as she freely admitted, "no morning woman," yet she did not want to be caught by surprise.[12]

Elizabeth's maids slept in a connecting room to her chamber, but they were not with her when the key turned once more in the lock. Elizabeth, though out of bed, was still in her nightdress, which hung loose at the waist. The garment's lining caused heavy drapes of fabric to cling to her legs. Seymour, too, was in a short nightgown, "barelegged in his slippers" as he approached her slowly, again bidding her "good morrow" before asking "how she did."[13] At this, the princess turned to move away, but not before Seymour reached out to smack her on the back and then on her buttocks "familiarly." For a girl who blushed even to brush hands with her stepfather when dancing, this was startling. She fled to her maidens, but Seymour followed, speaking playfully with the girl's attendants as if nothing were amiss.**

Although no longer free to marry Elizabeth, Thomas was undeniably interested in the company of his wife's maturing stepdaughter. There was danger in this. As the author of *The Education of a Christian Woman* put it, "from meetings and conversations with men, love

---

* In one sense, Thomas Seymour might be said to have been doing Elizabeth a favor in causing her to rise earlier, since contemporaries agreed that "the sleep of a virgin should not be long" (Vives, p. 91).

** A. Haynes, in his study of Tudor sexual activity (1999, p. 19), considers that Seymour's conduct was "an eroticised substitute for penetrative sex, an attempt to subordinate her to his will."

affairs rise. In the midst of pleasures, banquets, dances, laughter, and self-indulgence, Venus and her son Cupid reign supreme."[14] For a closeted young princess, whose usual dealings with men were confined to exchanges with servants, Seymour might well have been a dangerously enticing and heady presence.

When Queen Catherine married Thomas Seymour, along with the promise in the conventional marriage vows that she would be "buxom" in bed, she vowed to obey him. The fact of her marriage allowed him dominance over every aspect of her person for, as a married woman, she ceased to exist independently in law. Everything that married women owned, down to the clothes on their backs, passed to their husbands, to whom wives were utterly subject. In autumn 1547 Seymour began to take full advantage of his status, requiring that his wife's officers transfer regular and huge sums of money to him to help support his extravagant lifestyle.[15] In total and "by his commandment" Seymour took over £2,000 from Catherine's coffers in only three months, providing a tangible demonstration of his power over her. When Thomas arrived at Chelsea in the summer of 1547, he arrived as the house's new master. No door was locked against him—he held a key to them all.

Seymour's authority extended over every aspect of the claustrophobic world of Chelsea. The building, which was small, was packed to the rafters.[16] Even though, as dowager queen, Catherine's household had necessarily reduced in size, more than a hundred people accompanied her to Chelsea. Some were boarded out in local houses, but for many there was nightly competition for space in which to unroll beds in the crowded rooms and corridors.[17] As well as accommodating Elizabeth's own household too, Catherine was attended by a number of gentlewomen who brought their own servants, as well as by household officers and other attendants.[18]

To add to the manor's population, Catherine had adopted her little nephew, Edward Herbert, placing him under the care of the same matron who had previously nursed her stepdaughter Margaret Neville.[19] Frustrated by her own failure to bear a child, Catherine lavished attention and money on the boy, buying him necessary items such as his shirts, as well as more extravagant purchases, including a little jacket of damask and velvet obtained that July.[20] By Christmas, he had outgrown it, appearing instead in black and yellow taffeta.[21]

When Henry VIII had acquired the smart brick manor house at Chelsea, directly fronting the street, he had never intended it to be a permanent residence. With its flat façade broken up only with chimney stacks flanking the entrance, Chelsea manor was very far from palatial; but it had served him as a stopping point—a place to stay, with a skeleton household, on his way to summer hunting or other pleasures. As such, it had the character and aspect of a holiday home, a place of escape from the capital when hot weather or plague drove the court toward the countryside. With Catherine Parr's permanent arrival, it became something different—filled with domestic tumult. Fresh rushes were regularly swept over the floor as feet scurried about their duties. There was little privacy in the crowded, plain rooms, but this mattered little to Thomas Seymour. His interest in Elizabeth was becoming common knowledge within the household, but Catherine, for one, resisted seeing it as anything other than a man taking an interest in his wife's child. She would later join in the tickling herself on occasion, as if to show the world—and herself—how innocent it was.

Thomas Seymour had never been conventional, but he was always personable. He was twenty-five years older than Elizabeth, but she was reaching an age enough to be attracted to men. As he was well aware, people found him handsome, with his thick, long, and deeply masculine auburn beard. He always dressed to impress in the latest fashions and cut a fine figure at Chelsea, where he was the only man of rank. Seymour liked it that way.

Catherine was a woman of great passions,[22] but she was under Thomas's thumb, anxious to do nothing to antagonize him even if this meant persuading herself to look the other way. Seymour expected his wife to do as she had promised and obey her husband. He would even start petty quarrels as a means of testing her devotion and her willingness to submit. Once, in the highly charged summer of 1547, he accused her of infidelity after finding the door to Catherine's chamber shut just before a groom emerged, carrying a coal basket. Although he later claimed to be feigning jealousy, Seymour flew into a rage.* He was rumored to be an "oppressor" in his domestic arrangements, and Catherine, though she loved him, dared not vex him. Thomas Seymour, a man ruled by ambition and given to fiery passions, was not someone that any at Chelsea dared to cross.** No one wanted to intervene when he began his morning visits alone to Elizabeth's bedchamber.

The gardens at Chelsea offered their own opportunities for secret dalliances, should anyone have cared to use them. They were beautiful, being the one part of the manor and its grounds on which Henry VIII had been prepared to spend money. Catherine, too, consulted with her gardeners over the "making of the little garden."[23] She even had archery butts set up in the grounds for her amusement.[24] When not at her books, Elizabeth would walk in the gardens with the queen, as might her cousin Jane Grey. With sweet-smelling rosemary and lavender planted low in borders filled with roses and fruit trees, the gardens were idyllic in the summer of 1547.

Ten years earlier, Henry had paid twenty-nine gardeners to plant 64,000 privet plants, which had now grown to create a maze of

---

* As mentioned in Thomas Parry's confession. A. Haynes (1999, p. 11) discusses the close relationships between master/mistress and servants in the household, suggesting that Seymour's concerns need not have been entirely paranoid. In 1556 a Somerset gentlewoman, Mary Stawell, was found to have become besotted with a servant, to her husband's rage.

** In spite of Catherine's considerable number of administrative staff, Seymour also took on a controlling role in relation to her lands (as can be seen at the National Archives in document TNA E163/12/17 f. 1). He had terrified one of Catherine's officers in Hampshire, such that the man protested that he had in no way "misused" his office and pleaded: "I shall be glad and most willing to accomplish in all that I may [which] your lordship determine as well herein as in all other things."

pathways and secret spaces.[25] The privacy afforded by the nooks and crannies had already been appreciated by Catherine and Thomas as they courted earlier in the year, in the moonlight, among the spring-blossomed trees. By June the blossom had given way to budding fruit, but the foliage was as dense as ever. There were, in theory, opportunities for Elizabeth and Seymour to be alone—a chance meeting in the gardens could lead them toward a secluded pathway.

Elizabeth was, though, always watched by Kate Ashley. By day, Thomas Seymour was mostly content to play his games with Elizabeth in public—hiding his behavior in plain sight. Elizabeth looked on Kate as a mother figure, acknowledging that she "hath taken great labour and pain in bringing me up in learning and honesty."[26] To her credit, Elizabeth was as devoted to her lady mistress as Kate was to her, later declaring that "we are more bound to them that bringeth us up well than to our parents, for our parents do that which is natural for them—that is, bringeth us into this world—but our bringers-up are a cause to make us live well in it."[27] Kate only wanted the best for her charge, but she was deeply misguided when it came to Thomas Seymour and, perhaps, more than a little in love with him herself.

Seymour's attentions toward Elizabeth showed no signs of abating as the summer heat increased and the household packed up its trunks, moving westward in July 1547 to Hanworth in Middlesex.[28] This manor, which Henry VIII had also granted to Catherine, was pleasantly situated—close to the village of Hounslow but also within a day's ride of London and the court.[29] The queen regularly took advantage of this proximity, distributing alms to the poor that she met on the route.[30] Hanworth was also close to the Thames and not far from Hampton Court, so that Thomas was able to make his daily visits to the king there by boat during Somerset's absence in Scotland.

The move to Hanworth from the crowded Chelsea manor meant that the latter could now receive a badly needed cleaning. Filthy rushes could be swept from the floor and new straw laid, while walls and surfaces could be scrubbed, and linens cleaned. As the building emptied, such work became easier, since the queen carried much of her personal furniture with her, loaded onto wagons. The royal women rode, unless they were carried in litters, either way avoiding the bone-jarring awfulness of the wagons, which lacked suspension. The journey took the best part of a day.

By 1547, Hanworth was an imposing structure; nestling among cattle pasture and meadows, it dominated the rural landscape. The house itself was situated in the midst of a great park, dissected by the public road that allowed passersby a glimpse of their social betters.[31] Poor women would make the trip along the dried, rutted mud road, bringing small offerings of apples, strawberries, or other home-grown dainties for the queen, while hooves thundered down the lane bringing news from court.[32] Members of the household going hunting would pass the same way. Here, too, Catherine set up archery butts in the grounds that summer for the diversion of her ladies.[33] Entering the house over a drawbridge to the front, visitors passed over a moat that had been "cleansed and scoured" only a few years before.

The house had room for Catherine's vast household of over 120 gentlemen and yeomen, as well as the ladies of her Privy Chamber, maids of honor, and the respective attendants of her husband, stepdaughter Elizabeth, and great-niece Jane Grey.[34] The queen still expected to be treated as the first lady in the land, and many of those that had been sworn to attend her during Henry VIII's lifetime remained in her service afterward.[35] They were sternly warned in her ordinances not to be "pickers of quarrels or sowers of discord and sedition."[36] All required bed and board at Hanworth, where Elizabeth was one of very few occupants to enjoy her own bedchamber. Most members of the establishment laid down beds each night to sleep in the crowded, noisy great hall. And two enormous kitchen fireplaces were well able to feed such a hungry royal household.*

Henry VIII and his father, who had first acquired the manor, had both spent considerable sums in stocking and setting up the park, as well as "cleansing" the ground. It was a pretty house, and one that Elizabeth's grandfather had struggled to purchase. The notoriously cautious Henry VII had so coveted the place that he had already spent considerable sums on building and repairs before the sale was finally completed six years after his death.[37] He had been well known to have "a singular mind, affection and pleasure to resort unto [Hanworth] for the health of his body."[38]

There were reminders everywhere of Elizabeth's mother too. Anne Boleyn had received the house as a present from Henry VIII back in 1532, the year prior to their marriage. Anne had brought her considerable style to the place. The furniture—boxes, cupboards, desks, chests, tables, and even doors—had been selected by her from Hampton Court, newly acquired by Henry after Cardinal Wolsey's fall from favor. She had ordered decorative battens for the roof of her private chapel and a chimney ornamented with painted "antique" scenes. Everything was exquisitely done. Anne had removed "certain antique heads" of terracotta from Greenwich Palace to incorporate them into Hanworth too. These classical busts of long-dead emperors now glared down unsmiling from the walls. They were so important to the decorative scheme that Anne had employed two skilled Italian craftsmen to place them for her.

Hanworth was a Renaissance palace in miniature. Henry VIII had maintained his second wife's work there after Anne's execution, before passing the house to Catherine in 1544. The ghost of Anne Boleyn must have been everywhere for her daughter, as she studied and danced in its lavish rooms.

---

* These were the only parts of the old building to survive into modern times (Dugdale).

Henry's ample expenditure on Hanworth had created "a fine royal seat" that provided "a scene of his pleasures."[39] Now Thomas Seymour was determined to have his pleasure there too.

Kate Ashley had actively encouraged Seymour in his earlier pursuit of Elizabeth, believing his protestations of love in his proposal letter.[40] For Mistress Ashley, a marriage of Elizabeth to Thomas would have offered the possibility of a stable home and status for Henry VIII's illegitimate daughter and, more importantly as far as Kate was concerned, the promise that the girl would remain close to her in England rather than being taken abroad as the bride of some foreign prince. She would later declare that "I would wish her his wife of all men living."[41] With no evidence at all, Kate had somehow gotten it into her head that Henry VIII himself had desired Seymour as a son-in-law. As such, she genuinely believed that Elizabeth was meant for Thomas Seymour and that Catherine had effectively stolen the girl's betrothed.[42]

Yet the fact remained that Thomas's marriage to Catherine meant that he was now, in Kate's eyes, out of bounds. She was therefore deeply concerned when informed of his morning visits to the princess. In spite of her fondness for Seymour and the fact that she considered herself his "friend," Kate's higher loyalty remained with Elizabeth. She was not prepared to let Seymour, through rash behavior, wreck Elizabeth's reputation, and in the autumn of 1547 that was all his attentions seemed to promise for the princess.

Kate resolved to keep a closer eye on her charge, going to her early in the morning. She was sitting in Elizabeth's chamber one morning when Thomas entered to find the princess still asleep in her bed. He must have seen Kate waiting, but merely smiled, ignoring her as he reached once again for the bed curtains. If anything, Kate's presence as an involuntary but powerless chaperone seemed only to serve to inflame the situation, as Seymour entered the bed itself, moving the sheets over his bare knees. Although Elizabeth shrank back, as she did on the previous occasion, there was nowhere for her to go. She held the covers up in an attempt to preserve her modesty, but did not struggle as her visitor reached down to kiss her where she lay. This was too scandalous for Kate, who darted forward, crying "go away for shame": she was ignored. To the maids, with whom Seymour flirted, it was nothing but a playful game between a stepfather and his stepdaughter. How could anyone see anything sinister in his actions? But Kate did see something deeply alarming in Seymour's conduct. She warned her charge not to let herself be placed in such compromising positions.

Elizabeth herself was deeply conflicted. Catherine had offered her the only stable home she had known, but the queen's new husband had been Elizabeth's suitor just months before. Seymour was handsome and she was attracted to him. Nevertheless, she took Mistress Ashley's admonishing to heart, ensuring that she woke before her usual hour the next day. This proved fortunate, since Seymour visited early, intending to beat the disapproving Kate to the room. As his key began to turn in the lock, Elizabeth, "knowing he would come in," leapt from her bed and called her maids from the next room.[43] Together, they hid behind the bed curtains, keeping out of Thomas Seymour's reach. Seymour waited, with growing impatience, but Elizabeth remained where she was, her mounting unease recognized even by the women around her. Seymour's silent presence finally unnerved Elizabeth's gentlewomen too. That day they told Mistress Ashley what had occurred.

For Kate Ashley, Elizabeth's evident alarm proved that Seymour had overstepped the mark. How could it be a friendly childish game if the girl was forced to hide to defend her modesty? Given Thomas's standing, she knew that she had to deal with the matter delicately. She first tried an indirect approach, going to Seymour's servant John Harington, while the queen was again staying at Chelsea.[44] She took him aside, pointing out that while visits to Elizabeth's chamber by Seymour and the queen together were "well taken of everybody," Thomas's visits by himself were "misliked" by some. Kate's subtle approach had no effect; she knew that a more forceful response was required. Steeling herself to confront Thomas himself, Kate marched to the gallery at Hanworth, where she found Seymour alone. Although tiny compared to the athletic Thomas, she squared up to him as she dared to speak to him even in his own house. Her neck craned as she berated him for his conduct, stating that "these things were complained of, and that My Lady was evil spoken of." He was having none of it, however, swearing fiercely "God's precious soul!" before declaring that "he would tell My Lord Protector how it slandered him, and he would not leave it, for he meant no evil."

What disturbed Kate most was the fact that Seymour only seemed interested in pursuing his games with Elizabeth when she was in bed or in a state of undress. Naturally bashful, and under pressure from her lady mistress, Elizabeth continued to make an effort to get ready earlier. Often she would be dressed and reading when Thomas arrived. This certainly had the desired effect. Now Seymour would merely look in at the door and bid her good morning before going on his way. There were no playful spanks or tickles when the princess was up and fully clothed in undergarments, corsets, gowns, bodices, and kirtles.

At night, in the privacy of her own marital bed, Kate Ashley discussed the matter with her husband, running over the events of the day and previous weeks. John Astley, who was himself one of Elizabeth's chief attendants, was as concerned as his wife, warning her "to take heed." He had his own private concerns that he now shared, confiding that "he did fear that the Lady Elizabeth did bear some affection to My Lord Admiral," since "she seemed to be well pleased" with his attentions and "sometimes she would blush when he was spoken of." As a virgin, Elizabeth was not supposed to know anything of sexual intercourse and, still less, desire it.[45] Nonetheless, in spite of her protestations, there are hints that she enjoyed the attention and even reciprocated it. Astley was not the only one to warn his wife that Seymour's affections appeared to be returned.

Kate was uncomfortably aware that she bore some guilt in the matter herself. As the princess herself later confessed, Kate had playfully confided to her not long after Seymour had married Catherine, that if the bridegroom "might have had his own will" he would have had Elizabeth "afore the queen."[46] This piqued the girl's interest. She had asked Kate "how she knew that," to which her lady mistress had replied that "she knew it well enough, both by himself and by others."

Kate must also have been concerned about her own position, since it was she who had removed the pallet bed from Elizabeth's room. Whether that change was motivated by her new married status, or by pressure from Elizabeth to let her sleep alone, either way it did not look good. Yet, in spite of her unease, Kate did not force the girl to be chaperoned again at night. For several hours each night, Elizabeth continued to remain alone, and Thomas Seymour had a key to her room. It would have been a simple matter for him to slip into her chamber at Hanworth, unobserved, just as he had slipped into Catherine's bedchamber at Chelsea some months earlier during his secret nighttime visits.

The queen, in love with her husband but also in thrall to him as her "oppressor," resisted seeing what was in front of her face. That summer and autumn, she was a far from attentive guardian. She had other things on her mind. Sometimes she would be away at court or even at the Protector's house at Sheen, remonstrating with him in his treatment of her and her property.[47] She was also grieving the loss of Lord Parr of Horton, who had raised her. On his death in September 1547, she wrote plaintively that "it hath pleased Almighty God to take unto his mercy my entirely beloved uncle," before remembering her position and substituting the more royal "our beloved uncle."[48]

Despite mixed, confused emotions, Elizabeth was rapidly growing infatuated with her alluring admirer. It was while they were staying together again at Hanworth that events took on a more dramatic turn. As Kate later put it, Thomas Seymour, who had with such little effort won himself a queen, also wanted to possess and "be homely with" the young princess.[49]

Chapter Seven

A DRESS SO TRIMMED

When the court moved to Oatlands Palace, in Surrey, toward the start of autumn 1547, Hanworth proved to be a convenient location for Thomas. Oatlands was another fine house coveted, and then acquired cheaply, by Henry VIII.[1] The palace, which stood near Weybridge, was nearly twenty miles from Chelsea—too far for Seymour to make the journey comfortably from there in a day. Catherine's continuing residence at Hanworth, however, meant just an eight-mile trip to the boy-king's court, allowing Thomas to return home at night if he chose not to make use of his rooms at court.

Catherine visited the court herself in August, but as the months began to turn colder she tended to stay at Hanworth. Unfortunately, she fell ill there in October.[2] While recuperating, she occupied herself instead with her ladies, her gardens, and her intellectual pursuits.[3] She also continued to mother little Edward Herbert, ensuring that he had sufficient shirts to see him through winter and engaging a tailor "for making apparel" and "other necessaries" for him.[4]

Catherine also continued to try to make contact with her royal stepson. While still in his "tender years" and "as yet by age unable to direct his own things," Edward had, as God's anointed, a certain innate authority.[5] Both Catherine and Thomas were therefore keen to "instil into His Grace's head" that he should "take upon himself the government and managing of his own affairs," a position that Protector Somerset considered to be perilous.[6] Catherine and Thomas could see only the benefits in Edward obtaining greater authority. The queen wrote regular lengthy letters to the king. He finally replied in September 1547, informing her that her letters had "been thoroughly enjoyable to me, most noble queen, which you have written to me very recently."[7] This was encouraging; yet Catherine was still not allowed to see her stepson, who was kept cloistered away. Instead, Somerset surrounded him with his wife's family, whom, unlike his brother and Catherine, he trusted absolutely.

Thomas Seymour was jealous of the access afforded to Lady Somerset's stepfather, Sir Richard Page, about whom he complained on a number of occasions. If he could have "the king in his custody as Master Page had he would be glad," as he once assured John Fowler. He disliked the duchess's grasping half-brother Sir Michael Stanhope too, the man who controlled access to the household. Thomas would have been "contented that he [Thomas] should have the governance of him [Edward] as Master Stanhope had," he assured anyone who would listen. Somerset trusted the two men implicitly, seeing them as a line of defense in his attempts to maintain his authority. It was with his support that Stanhope issued orders to the king's household that "if any man should knock at the door after he was abed they should call him up and waken him before they did open the door." The fact that Stanhope had to issue this order three or four times in six months suggests that it was not, though, very effective.

Somerset had other matters to concern himself with, as his glorious Scottish campaign of 1547 began to fade into memory. He was faced with a mountain of hard work. The Protector's government needed money, and the surest way of raising this was through taxation, something that could only be agreed by the Lords and Commons in Parliament.[8] Somerset also needed the consent of the realm for large planned changes in religion and to safeguard his own position as Protector. He carefully sent out summonses to the Lords to attend or send proxies, while ordering county sheriffs to organize elections.

That autumn, a wave of excitement swept the county towns and Parliamentary boroughs as all freeholders worth more than forty shillings assembled to choose their representative. Few had much choice in the matter, since most polls were uncontested. But some elections could be raucous, complete with threats and shouting as the matter proceeded to a vote. Once elected, a new representative could saddle his horse for London, secure in the knowledge that he would be paid a small allowance and expenses, and would enjoy immunity from prosecution until he returned home. For Thomas Seymour too, Parliament looked like an interesting prospect—potentially one in which he could advance his interests.

Interests of a different kind continued to be pursued at Hanworth when Thomas was there. They took a bizarre turn one autumn day, as Elizabeth walked through the neat autumnal gardens, talking comfortably with her stepmother.

The weather was getting colder now, though Elizabeth could not feel it through the warm layers of her dress. The plump strawberries in their cages were all gone—plucked for the queen's table before the frost came.[9] The gardens had been a favorite of the old king's, and Elizabeth could still hear his birds twittering in their aviaries as she walked through the ornate gardens, set close to the house and near the park. It was an idyllic spot. Catherine and Elizabeth often crossed a narrow bridge over the moat to the back of the house, taking their exercise. They could stroll into the orchard if they chose, or even as far as the park, stocked full with deer and other game.

Passing the hedges that were still green, although other plants were beginning to die back in advance of winter, the princess and Catherine saw Thomas approaching them—with his dagger threateningly unsheathed from his belt.[10] The air must have crackled with tension as the princess turned to clutch at her stepmother, who held her tightly. Slashing quickly, Thomas proceeded to cut Elizabeth's dress into a hundred pieces, an action that must have left the princess struggling to preserve her modesty and hold the remains of her garments together amid the debris of cloth now on the ground.[11] Strangely, in clutching her tightly, Catherine was effectively offering her up to Thomas's attentions. Once released from the queen's grip, the princess, with her dress "so trimmed," rushed to her room, where an astonished Kate Ashley beheld her. Kate chided her on seeing her in such a bedraggled state, but Elizabeth pleaded that the queen had held her while "My Lord did so dress it."

The incident was a shocking one, which Kate sought to conceal at the time.* Perhaps it was all intended as a kind of practical joke. Yet, on the face of it, Thomas Seymour had tried to strip away the clothes from Henry VIII's daughter, with the acquiescence of his wife. If Kate was hoping that the queen would be an ally in reining in Seymour's unwanted attentions toward Elizabeth, this incident seemed to suggest she was to be sadly disappointed. In the face of such authority, the powerless Kate could do nothing other than complain to Elizabeth that "I would My Lord would show more reverence to you although he be homely with the queen."

---

* The secret was revealed only later under interrogation, after Catherine's death, in a short deposition which, although written in her own hand, Kate Ashley did not sign.

Although she had participated in some of the romps in which the princess was tickled in bed, Catherine Parr was now becoming deeply troubled by them. Not long after the incident in the gardens, she called Kate Ashley to her.[12] Elizabeth's lady mistress was surprised by the summons, but came at once. Kate found the queen alone and furious. According to Catherine, Thomas Seymour himself had come to her to complain about Elizabeth's conduct. He had been in the house, she reported, when he had happened to glance in at the gallery window, just as Elizabeth "cast her arms about a man's neck" in an embrace. Such a sight was scandalous, and the queen gave Kate a dressing-down for her negligence in chaperoning the girl. Chastened, Kate vowed to get to the bottom of the matter. She marched away from the room, going at once to see Elizabeth.

To her surprise, the princess, who usually confided in her, denied everything. Elizabeth burst into fits of weeping and, with tears running down her face, begged Kate to ask all her women whether it was true. She insisted that it was a lie. Resisting the urge to console her at once, Kate was perplexed. She prided herself on her close relationship to Elizabeth and accounted herself the person with her best interests at heart. She wanted to believe her. Summoning the women, Kate interrogated them. Everyone said the same thing: there was no man in the gallery; the princess had never gone there unchaperoned. By that time, Kate was having considerable doubts herself. It was a crowded household, it was true, but save for Seymour the only other gentleman who had private access to the princess was William Grindal.

For Kate, the idea that Elizabeth could have embraced her scholarly, unworldly schoolmaster in that fashion was so laughable that he could not even be considered a suspect. So, there was no one else—except Thomas Seymour. But Thomas was hardly likely to report himself or risk implicating himself to his wife. Instead, as she mused on the matter in the days that followed, Kate came to the shocking conclusion that the story had been invented by the queen herself, jealous of the palpably deepening relationship between her stepdaughter and her husband. Watching them warily, Catherine must have resolved to act, making up a story in an attempt to get Kate to take better heed "and be as it were in watch betwixt her and the Lord Admiral."

Kate resolved to do just that. It was widely believed that "girls hate their parents and relatives because they stand in the way of their love." Perhaps Elizabeth was also jealous of her stepmother, who possessed Thomas.[13] In an increasingly difficult situation, it was no surprise that Catherine leapt at the upcoming Parliament as a chance to separate her husband and stepdaughter.

After a brief visit to Chelsea in October 1547, Catherine returned to Hanworth in November to supervise the packing of her belongings for London.[14] In time for the opening of Parliament, the queen, along with at least sixty cartloads of furniture and other goods, moved her household to Seymour Place.[15] For the time being, she left Elizabeth behind at Hanworth.

In London, it was less Princess Elizabeth who now occupied Seymour's thoughts than her brother. Although Somerset attempted to control access to Edward, Seymour was able, thanks to the friends he had made in the king's household, to enter with relative ease.

The young king was in his apartments at Westminster early in November 1547 when Thomas came to him, looking more shifty than usual and carrying a piece of paper intended for the Parliamentary session in his own handwriting, which he asked his nephew to copy out for him.[16] When Edward asked what it was, Thomas dismissed it, saying only that it was "none ill thing; it is for the Queen's Majesty." Edward, though young, was nobody's fool and he replied sensibly that "if it were good, the Lords would allow it, if it were ill, I would not write in it." Thomas shook his head, urging the boy to comply, saying (as Edward himself later related) that "they would take it in better part if I would write." The king wanted no part of whatever the mysterious business was, desiring his uncle to leave him alone.

Seymour next went to John Cheke, whom he had paid to favor him with the king. He was carrying a piece of paper when he entered the room, declaring to the tutor that it was a bill that he meant to bring to the House of Lords. Disingenuously, he told Cheke that Edward had agreed to write in favor of this suit and he therefore required the scholar to pass it to his charge "and get it written of the king, as he had promised him to do." The king's schoolmaster scanned his eye over the paper quickly, committing the words to memory. They were written in Thomas's hand, but as if from the king: "My Lords, I pray you favour My Lord Admiral mine uncle's suit, which he will make unto you."[17]

Cheke shook his head, declaring that Paget had already ordered him to ensure that Edward should be permitted to sign no papers. Although Seymour's money was an incentive for the impecunious teacher, Sir William Paget was a force to be reckoned with and Cheke would not directly contravene his orders for anyone. Frowning, Thomas declared to Cheke that he "might do it well enough, seeing that the King's Majesty had promised him: and although he was an ill speaker himself, yet, if he had that bill, he was sure the best speakers in that house would help him to prefer it." Cheke refused vehemently to take the bill, and Seymour eventually retired, defeated.

Edward was also musing on the matter. He raised it with Cheke the next time he saw him. The tutor privately told him that it was "best not to write." This was sage advice, since the king's authority was absolute, even though he had only just passed his tenth birthday. A piece of his writing in the wrong hands could cause real damage. Cheke was therefore relieved when Edward declared "that the Lord Admiral should have no such bill signed nor written of him."[18] For Edward and Cheke, at least, it seemed the end of the matter.

Although Cheke could later recall some of the letter's contents, it is likely that it also contained a request by Edward that Seymour be appointed as his governor—still the main focus of Thomas's ambitions.[19] Thomas intended to take the letter to the Commons himself. His friends were already planted in the Lower House to cause "a broil or tumult and uproar" when the letter was read.[20] He was furious to be thwarted; but he still had plans for the Parliament, as it prepared to assemble.

While lurking in the halls around Westminster, Seymour came across an acquaintance, George Blagge, who had previously been attached to the poet Sir Thomas Wyatt and then to the executed Earl of Surrey. He had hitherto led a life of great rises and falls, having narrowly escaped death on the pyre for heresy in the more conservative atmosphere of 1546. His religious beliefs and his desire to remain safely on the right side of the law had naturally drawn him to the Protector, with whom he had only recently served in Scotland.

Blagge owed his knighthood, and his seat in the Commons, to Somerset, so he was in no mood for plotting.[21] He considered himself to be an intellectual, with literary ambitions, although he was a poor poet. He also bore a grudge, later gleefully recording that "this dog is dead" when he heard of the demise of his former tormentor, Lord Chancellor Wriothesley. Blagge was an experienced Parliamentarian, and his voice carried weight—as well Thomas knew. When Thomas sidled up to him, waggling a paper and declaring that here was a matter that would come before the Houses, Blagge responded: "What is that, My Lord?", his curiosity naturally piqued.[22] "Marry," answered Seymour, "requests to have the king better ordered, and not kept close that no man may see him," before he launched into a rant on the Protector's manner of raising the boy-king, considering that it would raise a fool rather than a monarch.

Blagge, keeping his face neutral, asked Thomas who would dare present such a bill to the Commons? "Myself," answered Seymour.[23] "Why then," retorted his companion, "you make no longer reckoning of your brother's friendship if you purpose to go this way to work." Thomas did not care, declaring that "I will do nothing but that I may abide by." Blagge immediately tried to dissuade Seymour from this course, considering it madness and highly dangerous. His words seemed to be having some effect. With Thomas's mind wavering, Blagge pointed out that the Protector would certainly imprison him if he knew what was happening. But at this Seymour laughed, denying the possibility: "No; by God's precious soul, he will not commit me to ward. No, no, I warrant you." Blagge persisted, declaring that Somerset would send for his brother and lock him away, but Thomas merely shook his head: "If the Council send for me, I will go; he will not be so hasty to send me to prison." Blagge was persistent, though. He repeatedly questioned Thomas on how he hoped to be released if he *were* committed to prison, to which his companion became visibly discontented. They parted on bad terms; Blagge refused to speak to Seymour again.[24]

At around the same time, the Earl of Warwick also heard of Seymour's paper and called him to him.[25] Did he not know, he asked, that if Somerset heard all that he was doing, "he will set the said Lord Admiral fast in the Tower"? It was what *he* would do if he were Lord Protector, he assured Seymour. Swearing "by God's precious soul!" Thomas became incensed with his former naval superior. If anyone tried to lay hands on him to send him to prison, Thomas declared, "I shall thrust my dagger in him."

In such conversations Seymour was bullish, even if his underlying stress was obvious in his explosive temper. In private, though, both Blagge's and Warwick's warnings had an effect on him. He already knew that he was a poor public speaker and likely to stumble over his words in the Commons or the Lords. Without the authority of the king, his letter carried very little weight, so he abandoned it. He continued to try to build support for himself, however, going to his allies on the Council and his friends among the nobility, requiring them to "stick and adhere unto him for the alteration of the state of and order of the realm" and, vaguely, "to attain his other purposes."[26]

Thomas Seymour had already been attempting to build support among the members of the Commons, who were mostly local gentry or the wealthier villagers and townsmen. When in the countryside, he made it his business to seek out the leading men of the villages—the yeomen and franklins. These individuals, who were one step below the gentry, had comfortable houses and lifestyles. Although they tilled the land, they were also senior enough to sit on juries and commissions, and they acted as leaders of their communities in a way that their social betters could never hope to achieve.

In his personable and jovial way, Thomas made much of these men, whom he considered to "be best able to persuade the multitude." He visited their houses, flattering them and carrying a flagon or two of wine so that they could drink together and make merry. He would also bring a pasty of venison—a rare delicacy for those who did not possess carefully stocked parks in which to hunt. For all his failings, Thomas Seymour understood the people better than his elder brother, who deliberately set himself apart from those around him. These lower-ranking countrymen loved him for it, something that, as he later confided to the Marquess of Dorset, ensured that he would have them at his commandment.[27] To demonstrate this, Seymour kept a map of England, which he delighted in displaying, pointing out the areas in which he could count on support as well as indicating just how far his lands stretched.[28] In these, as he would say to William Sharington, "I am in the midst of my friends."

He would also point out the lands of his brother or the Earl of Warwick, "unto whom," Sharington could perceive, "he had no great affection." But Seymour, Somerset, and Warwick were drawn together in the House of Lords that winter.

On Friday 4 November 1547, Thomas dressed himself in his Parliament robes of rich scarlet and ermine.[29] He had spent the night at Seymour Place so had only a short distance to ride, quickly joining the procession of the Lords at Westminster Abbey, with the king himself leading the company. The group made their way to the neighboring Westminster Palace and took their places before their monarch, who sat enthroned. Young Edward surveyed his assembled Lords and the elected Commons, all crammed into the

Parliament chamber.[30] He had just turned ten and was still spare and pale-looking—as his mother had been. He sat in silence as a clerk read out his commission, composed only the previous day. It vested control of the Parliament in his uncle the Protector, although it was written as if it had come direct from the sovereign. That done, the session opened with an oration by Lord Chancellor Richard Rich, Wriothesley's successor, who sat upon the traditional woolsack.[31]

Thomas Seymour was present, but belittled: he was noted in the records as the least significant of all the Council members and officers of state. The snub hurt. Later, on around 11 or 13 December, he was talking with Sir William Sharington at Seymour Place when, in fury, he complained that—unlike his brother—he had been denied a prominent seat in the Lords as one of the king's uncles.[32] But on 4 November he said nothing publicly. With the commission read out, the assembled Parliamentarians departed to spend Saturday and Sunday in their London lodgings. Thomas Seymour had two days to dwell on events and to plot.

The House of Lords reconvened on Monday 7 November. Seymour and his fellow peers were once again in attendance. Unlike members of the Commons, who sat in a smaller chamber, the Lords were permitted to remain in the White Chamber at Westminster Palace. The Lord Chancellor once again took up his ceremonial seat upon a woolsack in front of the empty throne, while the other peers sat on benches around the room. Both Somerset and Seymour attended every session of the Lords during November and the first week of December, allowing them to eye each other warily across the room. It was an important session of Parliament for Somerset, since he hoped to push through his religious changes, central to his policy as Protector, which would propel the country beyond Henry VIII's religious settlement and more clearly on a Protestant course. A bill placing the valuable chantries in the hands of the king was one of the most significant matters on the agenda.* It was to be

* Chantries were chapels that carried endowments, whereby priests said masses for the souls of the dead. Their effective dissolution brought revenues for the state.

accompanied by new legislation allowing the laity to take wine in communion (previously reserved for the clergy) as well as bread, and the repeal of some of Henry's laws.

In spite of the enmity between the Seymour brothers and their wives, the four had reformist religion in common. Catherine was deeply committed to her faith, as her narrow escape from the taint of "heresy" in the last months of Henry VIII's reign had shown. She had raised her younger stepchildren in the tenets of her beliefs.* Having been emboldened by the tenor of the Parliament, by December Catherine's household at Seymour Place was no longer celebrating the mass; the ceremony was also abandoned by the Protector and the Earl of Warwick.[33] Times were changing. Already, the great crucifix that had stood for centuries on the altar in St. Paul's Cathedral had been cast down. Elsewhere, churches were being stripped of their ornaments. As time went on, even where the mass was still being celebrated, parishioners were beginning to sing their psalms in English. For Princess Mary, who remained in her deep depression until the end of the year, this direction in England's religious practices was devastating; for her half-sister Elizabeth, by contrast, it was enlightening.

In Parliament that November, Seymour made a beeline for the Marquess of Dorset.[34] Thomas's lack of public recognition as the king's uncle smarted. Grumbling, he asserted loudly that "if I be thus used, they speak of a black Parliament, by God's precious soul, I will make the blackest Parliament that ever was in England." Lord Clinton was standing behind and heard every word, declaring that "if you speak such words, you shall lose My Lord utterly, and undo yourself." Thomas had not even noticed that Clinton—his deputy in the navy—was there. He turned to face him, stating: "I would you should know, by God's precious soul, I may better live

* For example, in the will of Catherine's stepdaughter Margaret Neville (TNA PROB 11/31/45), who died as a teenager, she said that she looked inwardly into herself and found "nothing but damnation the only goodness within her coming from Christ."

without him, than he without me." It is clear that he was dwelling on his brother—raising him before even his name was mentioned. The two peers thought Thomas paranoid. He certainly seemed it, claiming that he was sure that matters at the session were directed against the queen. In the throng of Westminster Palace, he ranted that "whosoever shall go about to speak evil of the queen, I will take my fist from the first ears to the last." Much of his own status derived from his marriage to a queen.

The Marquess of Dorset was baffled, wondering whether Seymour feared that Catherine's marriage to Henry VIII would be declared invalid. He considered this fear groundless, attempting to soothe Thomas gently: "My Lord, these words needs not, for I think there is no nobleman that would speak evil of her, for he should then speak evil of the king, that dead is." But Seymour continued openly to declare that "he would make the blackest Parliament that ever was in England." His words were heard by many. In a fury, Somerset would later demand of him: "Did you so or no?";[35] but in November 1547 Seymour would heed no advice, not even from his closest ally.

In practical terms, Edward's refusal to support Thomas's letter meant that there was little that Seymour could actually do in the way of mischief during the Parliament. Nonetheless, he tried. Although Somerset's authority had been originally conferred by letters patent in March 1547, the Protector thought it prudent to have his protectorship confirmed by Parliament. This seemed a straightforward proposal, so he was amazed when his brother turned it into "a great matter."[36] For Thomas, this was an opportunity to attack. He whispered in as many ears as he could find that once Somerset's authority was approved by statute, the Protector would (improbably) give English-held Calais to the French as a means of securing an alliance.[37]

His attempts were pernicious but ineffective. Seymour's actual Parliamentary involvement was uneventful in the period leading up to the vote—he missed only two days during the first month of the session, which was a remarkable record given the fact that truancy was rife.* He was also active in the Council during the period, diligently sitting with his brother and peers on 11 December as they debated the orders to be sent to the king's ambassador in Germany.[38] As usual, the document was passed through several members of the Council before it finally reached Thomas's hand for signature, but he made the best of it—marking his name with a signature as large and flourishing as his brother's.

Finally, after sitting through the third reading of the Protector's Bill, the time for the voting arrived. This was the moment that Seymour had been waiting for. On 14 December, as the royal court prepared for Christmas, he answered "nay" as those around them gave their assents.[39] To his consternation, only the Marquess of Dorset joined him in this show of dissent, and the protectorate was confirmed. Thomas had probably grossly overestimated the support he could command in the Lords. Somerset was furious, and Seymour too was irate. As a sign of his discontent, Thomas petulantly objected to a bill concerning instruments used for weights the following day, but this time his dissent was followed only by Lord Cobham.

Thomas made himself scarce from the Lords from 20 December 1547 and did not attend on Christmas Eve, when the king came in person to adjourn the gathering until April. Seymour had probably been warned away by his brother. Unsurprisingly, he received word to attend the Protector to answer for his conduct during the Parliament, but he refused to come.[40] No doubt readying his dagger to run through any who tried to arrest him, he was surprised to find that nothing happened. Somerset, out of lingering affection for his wayward brother, had resolved to show him "leniency,"[41] a lack of consequences that merely inspired Seymour to continue in his "mischievous purpose." He had failed to disrupt the Parliament,

* Absences from Parliament were technically quite serious matters. An absent peer was expected to send his excuse by another member, but if it was not accepted by the Lord Chancellor, then "he is to be blamed by the house as the fault requires" (BL Harley MS 6807 f. 75).

but he still had designs on the governorship of the young king—and on the person of Princess Elizabeth.

Thomas Seymour spent Christmas in London with Catherine, still openly complaining "that it was never seen, that in the minority of a king, where there hath been two brethren, that the one brother should have all rule, and the other none; but if the one were Protector, the other should be Governor." He had, by then, not seen Elizabeth for two months, and instead he focused only on his wife's bed. With Seymour's undivided attention, Catherine, despite being "past middle age" and reputedly "barren," surprised everyone by becoming pregnant.[42]

Chapter Eight

IN A MAIDEN'S CHAMBER

The winter of 1547–48 was bitterly cold and would prove to be a long one. Princess Elizabeth wrapped herself heavily in furs when she ventured outside. The biting weather, bringing chapped lips and red clumsy hands, seemed unremitting. From Denmark and farther afield, there were reports of horses struggling to pull sledges over the frozen ground, when only a few months before they had hauled wagons.[1] The princess spent the Christmas season away from court, although she looked forward eventually to joining Catherine and Thomas in London.

On New Year's Day 1548, Edward VI went publicly to mass at Hampton Court, which was celebrated in the usual way.[2] He spent the best part of a month at this palace, where he was born.[3] His and Somerset's reign had, by that time, lasted very nearly a year, although the boy continued to resent his overbearing uncle. Whenever he was permitted to see his subjects, which was rarely, Edward complained that "my uncle of Somerset dealeth very hardly with me, and keepeth me so straight, that I cannot have money at my will. But My Lord Admiral both sends me money and gives me money."[4] Such reports pleased Seymour, and he continued to send funds to the child. In spite of his anger at Cheke's failure to support him during the Parliament, Thomas paid money to the tutor when the king asked him to, as well as a bookbinder at the request of Edward's French master.[5] He made so many payments on the young king's behalf that Edward—less than a year later—was unable to recall them all. Edward made a poor show as king on account of his poverty, Seymour informed him. At the same time, John Fowler was always making sure to praise Seymour when he spoke to Edward. "Ye must thank My Lord Admiral for gentleness that he showed you, and for his money," he enjoined his master, hoping to keep the flow of coins from the admiral coming.

To outsiders in the know, it looked very much as though Seymour was using his wealth to "corrupt" the Privy Chamber, encouraging its habitués "to persuade the King's Majesty to have a credit towards him," with the intent that Thomas could "use the king's highness for an instrument to his purpose."[6] He almost certainly was. As far as Seymour was concerned, the governorship of the king was his birthright as Edward's younger uncle.

Elizabeth, who was another instrument to Seymour's purpose, was finally able to throw off her mourning clothes that January. She still often chose to wear black, however, which suited her pale face and reddish-blond hair, ensuring that she cut a striking figure in the household. Unlike her stepmother and Princess Mary, she liked to dress in a plain style rather than following "showy" fashions; she had a particular "contempt of gold and head-dresses." Having turned fourteen on 7 September 1547, she had reached an age when she could expect to be married. Since her brother Edward appeared to be in robust health, and would surely himself marry in a few years and beget children, Elizabeth appeared to have little hope of the throne herself. At Christmas 1547, as she spent her time with her music, her books, and her tutor, she waited to hear who might be arranged for her as a husband.[7]

William Grindal, while being—as far as Kate Ashley was concerned—an unlikely lover of the princess, was a kindly man, beloved of everyone who knew him. It was therefore a shock for everyone when, in the early weeks of January 1548, Elizabeth's tutor sickened. The cause of his illness was alarming, since it was the terrifying bubonic plague, which had wiped out a third of Europe's population two hundred years before. The outbreak in 1548 was, fortunately, small and largely confined to London and surrounding areas; but its eruption in the middle of Elizabeth's household struck those around Grindal with terror.[8] His case did not, in the end, lead to an epidemic in the house, but Grindal failed to recover, dying later that month—and leaving Elizabeth without a tutor.

Roger Ascham was devastated when he heard the news of his dear friend's death. It came in the midst of a difficult time for the scholar. Disputes in which he was involved were reaching a boiling point at Cambridge. On 5 January, Ascham wrote to the Protector's secretary, William Cecil, to raise the issue of one such dispute in his college—St. John's—concerning the mass.[9] The arguments had gotten so out of hand that the university's vice chancellor, John Madew, had stepped in, ordering an immediate cessation. Ascham, however, who was an argumentative fellow at the best of times, could not desist, informing Cecil that he and his fellows had written a book on the matter, which they greatly desired to present to the Protector. Ascham had also acquired a copy of Catherine Parr's *Lamentations of a Sinner* as soon as it was published, reading with interest "the most holy confessions of our queen"—although, as he told Cecil, he preferred the secretary's prologue with its "beauty and eloquence." There was no such praise for Catherine's writing. He was, however, deeply interested in her stepdaughter.

With a heavy heart, Roger Ascham sat down to write a letter to Princess Elizabeth on 22 January. He spoke of their common grief "at the death of our friend Grindal."[10] But he hesitated to offer his condolences, for fear "that reminding you of it would rather increase than assuage your sorrow, if I did not clearly understand your great prudence, strengthened by the counsels of Mistress Katherine Astley and the precepts of my dear Grindal himself." In spite of his anguish, Ascham was aware that his friend's death left a highly prestigious opening—and one that could get him away from the turmoils of Cambridge. He suggested, tentatively, that Elizabeth should consider "that other Grindal" (William Grindal's kinsman, Edmund) as her new tutor; but really he was already lobbying for himself. He spoke of the goodwill that he was sure the princess had for him, asking only that "your former favour may rest on the opinion which Grindal has so long held about me, and not be referred to the judgment of anyone else; for though I have lost him, I do not wish to lose the benefit of his good opinion." What better character reference could he have than the testimony of "his Grindal"?

Ascham offered the princess his service and obedience, while skirting around his obvious desire that she should think of him as a new tutor. He certainly needed to absent himself from Cambridge, where the master of his college had recently written him such a letter that it "plunged us, not into a disturbance, but into the great sorrow" and which provoked Ascham to protest that "we have done nothing to merit so bitter a letter."[11] As the dispute over the mass rumbled on at Cambridge, Grindal's death—for all its dolefulness—must have seemed providential.

In lobbying for the position, Ascham became aware that he had a rival. Catherine and Thomas, as Elizabeth's guardians, had the final say in the matter, and they wanted Francis Goldsmith. They knew him well, since he had been a member of Catherine's household for years. Moreover, his skill in Latin was formidable. He was also not averse to performing a little flattery, playfully referring to his mistress as the Queen of Sheba or "the most pious Queen Esther" and assuring her of as glorious a reputation in years to come.[12] All he desired, he insisted, was to "be able to distinguish myself as worthy in some degree of your highness, in the condition of a servant." He was obsequious, but Catherine was nevertheless flattered and resolved to give him the coveted post. While Goldsmith lobbied for preferment with the guardian, however, Ascham was going straight to the pupil.

By 1548, Ascham—hirsute and plump-cheeked—was approaching his mid-thirties.[13] A Yorkshireman by birth, he had enjoyed an idyllic childhood with his parents, whose marriage lasted a devoted forty-seven years and who even passed away together, dying on the same day. He was the star of the family, going south to Cambridge while still a teenager and taking his degree at the age of sixteen. Nearly penniless, he was hungry for patronage. His native county was proud of him: the Archbishop of York diligently sent a pension to Yorkshire's favorite son.[14] Ascham was a man of strong feelings; despite the hothouse of Cambridge keeping him from his parents for years on end, he was devastated at their deaths in 1544.[15] Although Ascham was a self-promoter and highly ambitious, he was to be often brought low by grief. He later found himself unable to sleep after the death of his infant son (a "sweet babe"),[16] an event that caused him to question the very nature of life, in which he "found nothing but sorrow and care, which very much did vex and trouble me."

Ascham was an undeniably complex character—convinced that his career was in the doldrums and that he was overlooked in favor of lesser men, but also given to moments of feverish excitability, as when, on one occasion, he was shown a pelican in Germany. This marvel, he recorded, was a great "milk-white" creature, well able to swallow an English penny loaf, while its eyes were "as red as fire, and, as they say, an hundred years old."[17] He could be slippery, too: his father's dying request was that he leave Cambridge and its disputes behind and take himself "to some honest course of life." He had no desire to leave and, later, confided in John Cheke that if "peace and unanimity can be fully restored, I shall then think that I have virtually left Cambridge, according to my father's advice."[18] Possessing one of the keenest intellects of his day, Ascham was prepared to leave nothing to chance regarding Elizabeth. He had already taken the time to write to Kate Ashley personally as his "very loving friend," recognizing her influence in the household.[19] He praised her for the work she had done in the education of "that noble imp," as well as sending her a silver pen as a very extravagant token. As a way of currying favor with the princess, he also sent Elizabeth an Italian book and a prayer book. He had heard, he wrote, that the princess's own silver pen had been broken and offered to mend it at his expense, if Mistress Ashley would only send it to him. Kate did as she was bid, with Ascham hurrying to fix the pen and send it back, together with a personal note to Elizabeth.[20]

The scholar also resolved to visit Elizabeth personally. Saddling his horse, he rushed over to Hanworth in the first week of February 1548. Catherine and Thomas were both still away in London, and Elizabeth gave Ascham an audience. He was intrigued by her poise; it also turned out that he had no need to lobby further for his appointment. Elizabeth ignored his attempt "to make any bargain." Could he confirm that he "was ready to obey her orders," she asked? When he confirmed that he could, she revealed that she had already begun to seek his employment with the queen and Seymour. Sadly, the girl informed him that she knew of Goldsmith's candidacy. Downcast, Ascham "advised her to comply" with her guardians before praising Goldsmith and advising her to "follow their judgment in such a matter."[21]

Ascham had not ridden so far to be beaten, though. With calculated flattery, Elizabeth's guest "prayed her not to think of any good to be got by me, but to let nothing stand in the way of her bringing to perfection that singular learning of which Grindal had sown the seeds." Although seeming to bow out gracefully, Ascham stayed for several days, while Elizabeth showcased her language skills. He approved, while also intimating that (as he said) "although I am foolish and in fact nobody in almost everything, yet that I can be of use to her in teaching her Greek and Latin and in performing the duties of her secretary." As far as Elizabeth and Ascham were concerned, it was settled. As the princess was packing up to join her stepmother and stepfather in London, she was preparing to persuade them of the wisdom of her choice. For good measure, Ascham also wrote to John Cheke in London for his support for his suit: Goldsmith may have won the support of the queen and Seymour, but Ascham had the upper hand with the royal pupil. Joyfully for him, he was soon ensconced as part of Elizabeth's household.

Once Elizabeth had joined Thomas and Catherine in London, in February 1548, she found a stepfather still embroiled in the ramifications of his recent actions. Protector Somerset appeared prepared to ignore Thomas's conduct in Parliament, and hoped that Thomas's plotting had now ended. He was, in any event, absorbed by the concerns of state, as the war in Scotland continued to rumble on, while news from France was hardly encouraging. As ever, Somerset presented a friendly, but circumspect, face to Imperial Ambassador Van der Delft, who was determined to get the latest information from him, going in person to see him on 23 February 1548. The ambassador asked Somerset bluntly "whether it was true that the King of France had a force of cavalry ready to ship and send to the assistance of the Scots."[22] Somerset agreed that he had been informed that this was the case, although at that time Henry II of France was appearing better disposed toward England than before. Somerset explained patiently to the ambassador that the French king was conflicted, wanting both to comply with his treaty of peace with England and his promise to aid the Scots. His words sounded almost as though he were trying to convince himself of the truth of them.

The death of Henry VIII's old sparring partner, Francis I of France, in 1547 had led to the accession of his son Henry, a man determined to revenge the English capture of Boulogne. While technically England and France were at peace, Somerset and everyone else knew that the French were aiding the Scots. It looked to everyone as though England's ancient continental enemy was preparing for direct military action too. In Paris that spring, talk was of war and the reclaiming of Boulogne.[23] To compound things, there were rumors that a French painter, who had spent time in England, had been commissioned by Henry II to produce pictures of all the ports in England, for the use of the French navy.[24]

Earlier in February, Dr. Wotton, English ambassador in Paris, sent details of the large-scale naval preparations to the Protector.[25] At the same time, four English ships carrying wine for Edward VI's own table were captured by France's Scottish allies. To Wotton, all the signs pointed to an imminent war. As late as spring 1548, he was met only with evasive answers and delays when he attempted to obtain compensation for the captured English vessels.[26] In an attempt to avoid war, the Council issued a commission to meet with the French to settle the boundaries of English territory around Boulogne. Thomas Seymour was one of the signatories present when the Council decided on this course.[27] It looked to everyone, though, that a war on two fronts was imminent. And it was a prospect that England's Lord Admiral—who still saw himself as a navy hero—rather relished.

That spring, as relations soured with France, Somerset wrote to Thomas to request that he use his authority to help some London merchants, who had unfortunately chosen to ship their goods to Rouen and Dieppe using French vessels.[28] Predictably, they had met with a fleet of Englishmen who, not knowing the provenance of the goods, had boarded and captured the ships, appropriating everything on board. When the merchants complained to Somerset, he passed the matter to his brother, commanding him to remedy it. In light of this "detestable robbery and spoil," Thomas wrote at once to order his officers to search for the ships, and to seize the goods, if they found them, on his behalf.

Little, if anything, of the merchandise made its way back to the rightful owners, however, since Thomas had already begun using the navy for his own personal profit. For some months, he had been extorting money from merchant ships intent on landing in England. He had also begun to take bribes from ships before they sailed, "contrary to the liberties of this realm and to the great discouragement and destruction of the navy of the same"—as was the accusation later laid against him.[29] Although Seymour had a sizable income when coupled with his wife's dower, he wanted more. He turned his attention to the goods of foreign merchant ships that, being "with wind and weather broken," yet came "unwrecked to the shore."[30] He ignored direct orders from the Council to return the goods—orders that had actually been signed by him in the Council chamber. Instead, as the Council would later charge him, "you have not only given contrary commandment to your officers, but as a pirate have written lines to some of your friends to gather them as much of those goods as they could should be conveyed away secretly by night further off, upon hope that if the same goods were assured, the owners make no more labour for them, and then you might have enjoyed them." Such conduct was "contrary to justice and your honour."

Seymour, however, did not care. By the spring of 1548, he had effectively turned pirate. Many of his seafaring friends were on the wrong side of the law. When a pirate was taken, Thomas would often wade in, freeing the man and confiscating the goods and ships, which rightly belonged to the individuals who had captured them from the pirate. To add insult to injury, he came down firmly on the side of the pirates, sometimes even imprisoning their captors to create a very effective deterrent to would-be pirate-takers.[31] In fact, Thomas Seymour had so embraced piracy that his houses were soon stuffed with stolen goods, from both foreign and English merchants.[32] Much of the evidence was hearsay, or could be put down to poor judgment or incompetence, but it was notable that Thomas kept the Scilly Isles in his own hands.[33] The Protector, for one, heard a whisper that his brother was accounted the "chief pirate" in the waters around England.[34] The best that could be said of him was that he failed to "guard the seas better against the robbers."[35]

Thomas Seymour continued to direct his energies to buying support for his cause. In early 1548, he decided to approach his brother-in-law William Parr, Marquess of Northampton, one of the highest-ranking peers in England. Northampton was a few years younger than Catherine, but had been the darling of the Parr family. His widowed mother had indebted herself to buy his marriage to Anne Bourchier, heiress to the Earl of Essex. Northampton had, eventually, acquired his wife's earldom, but the marriage proved a disaster. Both partners took lovers, and Anne bore at least one illegitimate child.[36] Perhaps emboldened by Somerset's repudiation of his own adulterous first wife, Northampton petitioned for divorce in April 1547. Unwilling to wait on the glacial pace of proceedings, Northampton secretly married his mistress Elizabeth Brooke at the persuasion—it was rumored—of Catherine and the Duchess of Suffolk.[37]

This move was a miscalculation. In late February 1548 he was commanded by the Council to abandon Elizabeth Brooke and never speak to her again on pain of death. Northampton was outraged at what he saw as the Protector's duplicity, as was the queen, who showed her support by bringing Brooke into her household. It was a simple matter then for Seymour to bring the disaffected marquess over to his own party. As the storm broke, Seymour approached his brother-in-law, telling him that he perceived he was not contented or pleased.[38] He advised Northampton to set up his household in the north, in the midst of his lands and support, since, "being well beloved there" of his friends and tenants, he "should be the more strong, and more able to serve the King's Majesty." Northampton would also be better able to serve his brother-in-law's interests.

For Princess Elizabeth, the arrival of the beautiful—if scandalous—Elizabeth Brooke in the household was enlivening. The princess also supported and recognized the couple's marriage, and the two women would later be close.

Elizabeth continued to spend most of her time at her studies, however, enjoying the rigorous curriculum implemented by her new tutor. The scholar was particularly noted for his fine italic hand, which he now took pains to teach to his young pupil, as well as ensuring that she could write in Greek.[39] During their time together, Elizabeth and Ascham progressed slowly through the works of Cicero, as well as much of Titus Livius's monumental history of Rome. The daily routine was familiar. The princess worked on the New Testament in Greek during the morning, before tackling Classical works in the afternoon, including the tragedies of Sophocles. Each work was carefully selected, Ascham hoping that "from those sources she might gain purity of style, and her mind derive instruction that would be of value to her to meet every contingency of life." More daringly, he added Philip Melanchthon's *Commonplaces in Theology*, which was a Lutheran text published less than thirty years before, and which he considered "best suited, after the Holy Scriptures, to teach her the foundations of religion, together with elegant language and sound doctrine."

Elizabeth learned quickly and was attentive, asking for guidance on words that she thought had "a doubtful or curious meaning." Under Ascham's tutelage she quickly developed sophisticated tastes, as when she told her teacher that she could not abide writers who imitated the great Erasmus who "tied up the Latin tongue in those wretched fetters of proverbs." Elizabeth knew what she liked, and this was "a style that grows out of their subject; chaste because it is suitable, and beautiful because it is clear." As Ascham noted, "she very much admires modest metaphors, and comparisons of contraries well put together and contrasting felicitously with one another." She had a good ear and excellent judgment, attributes that greatly assisted her abilities in Greek, Latin, and English composition. In her English compositions, she had a very concise writing style.

Elizabeth's writing reached a wider audience that spring when she found that she had become a published author. Somehow, the reformist firebrand John Bale, who had been exiled under Henry VIII, managed to acquire a copy of her translation of the *Mirror of the Christian Soul*, which she had finished some months before.[40]

For Bale, it was manna from Heaven. Although Protestant in his convictions, his publications while in exile were too critical of the political regime to find favor with Somerset. By late 1547 Bale was a man cast adrift and badly in need of a patron, as someone in Catherine's household—with access to Elizabeth's manuscript—was all too aware. His works were still banned in England. Catherine herself disliked him, for during Henry's reign Bale had printed the names of some of her ladies in connection with the Protestant martyr Anne Askew, placing them in danger.[41] It seems most unlikely that Elizabeth voluntarily published with Bale, who was as far from the mainstream as it was possible to be; it would have been more straightforward, had Elizabeth wanted to publish, to use Catherine's publishing channels rather than relying on the exile. But if not Elizabeth, who did send out the manuscript? Only her tutor or her closest ladies are likely to have had access to her personal writings, and few would have dared offend her by actually *stealing* them. Perhaps it was, after all, an act of youthful rebellion against the authority of her stepmother, whom she knew would be offended by any contact with Bale.

John Bale certainly believed that Elizabeth had sent him the work in the hope that others might profit from its "consolation in spirit." As he flicked through the manuscript with glee, he began to prepare it for publication, addressing it "to the right virtuous and Christianly learned young lady Elizabeth, the noble daughter of our late sovereign King Henry VIII." Bale had been informed that the princess worked chiefly to improve her studies, although she also wanted the "spiritual exercise of her inner soul with God." He was impressed with her work, which was "neither to be reckoned childish nor babyish though she were a babe in years." The girl's youth charmed him; he praised her royal blood too. He wanted her to be his patron.* The book, which was printed in April 1548, depicted Elizabeth as she then showed herself to

---

* Elizabeth would indeed later show him favor.

the world, in its woodcut on the title page: a young girl wearing an elaborate embroidered dress with fine necklaces, kneeling in prayer.[42]

Quite different from Bale's, or even Ascham's, interest in the fourteen-year-old princess was Thomas's continued fascination. Queen Catherine had doubtless hoped that the distance between Hanworth and London in the autumn and winter of 1547–48 would dull her husband's interest. This proved not to be the case. He made his intentions very plain the morning after the princess's arrival at Seymour Place. On that morning, and on every one afterward, he appeared in his loose-fitting nightgown (which reached only to his knees), his legs bare and his feet slippered.[43] Elizabeth had been expecting this. Concerned for her reputation, she made sure that she was up and reading her book at her desk. Disappointed, Seymour merely looked into the bedchamber and wished her "good morrow," before going on his way, resolving privately to try again the following day, and the next. Finally, Kate Ashley roundly berated Thomas, informing him that "it was an unseemly sight to come so bare legged to a maiden's chamber." Seymour, who had been grooming those around Elizabeth for some time, was angry to be crossed, but left.

Yet the Protector's brother was undaunted. Seymour's early morning visits continued.

Chapter Nine

THE QUEEN'S DISPLEASURE

Longer days of sunshine brought the gardens at Hanworth back to life as spring 1548 approached, casting off the bitter, cold winter. Catherine's household returned there in the early spring. Throwing off her furs, the queen could once again stroll through its leafy grounds. She had been married for more than a year, she was now pregnant, and the child had already quickened, stirring in her womb. She should have been content, but her mind was troubled. Casting her eye over Bible verses, which she diligently copied, she prayed that she would "be swift to hear, and slow in giving answer." She asked herself to "be not a privy accuser as long as thou livest, and use no slander with thy tongue."[1] She had to be certain before she accused those closest to her. That certainty soon came. At Hanworth, in the early summer, the scales finally fell from Catherine's eyes.

The revelation came as the household servants busied themselves with preparations for the birth of what was hoped would be Catherine and Thomas's "little man."[2] To Catherine, her pregnancy after so many years of barrenness seemed a reward for her piety. She firmly believed—as she wrote in a letter—that children were gifts from God, that "He" had comforted her "with such a gift" of a "jewel."[3] Just as she had once seen God's silence as proof of his divine plan for her when she married Henry, she now saw the impending birth as her reward. As her pregnancy advanced, the queen joyfully added an extra panel to the front of her gowns, allowing room for her belly to expand. God's providence did not, however, extend to easing the discomforts of pregnancy. The queen suffered with morning sickness into the later months of her pregnancy, appearing "so sickly" to those around her.[4]

Catherine, as a first-time mother, was fascinated by the development of her baby. When Thomas was away, she called upon Mary Odell, who was one of her chamberers, to share her bed. As they lay together, Catherine would guide her friend's hand to her stomach, so that she could feel the "little knave" kick.[5] Thomas, too, was excited at the prospect of an heir, particularly enjoying Catherine's reports that the "baby doth shake his pole."[6] For the child's father, however, he hoped this evidence of vigor would ensure that the baby was strong enough to continue his quarrel with the Protector into the next generation and (as he wrote to Catherine) "revenge such wrongs as neither you nor I can at present."[7]

While for Catherine maternity was a new and mostly delightful experience, she was anxious to ensure her child's health, taking advice on diet and taking long walks in the fresh air.[8] She stayed fit and lean, hoping for an easier birth thereby, while Thomas joked that with all Catherine's good efforts the baby "may be so small that he may creep out of a mousehole." The couple had good reason to be anxious. After all, women of Catherine's age were more usually first-time grandmothers than new mothers. They had both known many younger women die either during childbirth or shortly after it—as Thomas's own sister had done. By becoming pregnant at all, Catherine was facing the greatest danger that she had ever known.

Keeping such thoughts out of her mind, she threw herself into preparations for a baby who would be an almost-prince. There was the nursery furniture to be purchased and staff to engage. In particular, the wet nurse would be supremely important. Although some women of Catherine's class breastfed, it was considered unusual.[9] Instead, a healthy and respectable local mother would be engaged to succor the newborn child, imparting—it was believed—something of her character in her milk.

With Catherine preoccupied by impending motherhood, Seymour continued to try to extend his influence over the king. That Easter, which fell on 4 April, Thomas was again at court attempting to gain access to Edward. As always, he could rely on John Fowler for assistance, and the pair talked together, finding a quiet corner while the court was at Greenwich. Thomas still keenly resented the influence of the Duchess of Somerset's stepfather, Sir Richard Page, over Edward's household. As he so often did, he lamented his lack of official role with the king, telling Fowler that he would be glad to have the king in his custody in the manner that Page enjoyed.[10] Fowler had heard this, or something similar, many times before, but this time there was something new.

Thomas lowered his voice, ensuring that no one else could hear. He whispered that he believed he could take the king. He could bring him through the gallery to his chamber, he thought, before anyone noticed and then spirit him away by horse to Seymour Place. For Thomas, this may have seemed the natural culmination of his ambitions: he wanted to be the king's governor, so this was one means of obtaining physical possession of the boy. To Seymour's surprise, Fowler was aghast. Backtracking, Seymour tried to laugh it off. He had spoken only merrily, he assured the attendant, and meant no harm; but a plot to kidnap the king was arguably treason, even if the king's uncle did not intend to hurt him. Fowler accepted the comments as the joke that Seymour claimed they were. Thomas was prone to wild claims, and Fowler viewed him, as others did, as a man "fierce in courage, courtly in fashion, in personage stately, in voice magnificent, but somewhat empty of matter."[11] He put Thomas's words out of his mind and forgot them. Seymour, however, had been deadly serious. Seymour recalled this "merry speech" nearly a year later, when pressed.

It was no surprise that Seymour began to consider more radical measures in spring 1548. Relations with his brother were getting worse. Catherine was still unable to secure the return of her jewelry, and she was growing increasingly furious. As far as she was concerned, she had deposited the jewelry in the Tower for safekeeping and its detention was unlawful. This was also the view that Seymour took. That April, he acquired a new servant, who was immediately tasked with assisting in the recovery of the queen's jewels. Sir Anthony Browne, who had helped Somerset secure his protectorship back at Enfield in the cold January of 1547, died on 28 April 1548. He had been a leading conservative at court and one of the men courted by Thomas during the Parliament of 1547. At the same time, Seymour had noted William Wightman, a thirty-year-old Coventry man who had risen from his humble roots as the son of a capper.[12] Wightman had been a particular favorite of Browne, owing his seat in Parliament to his patron's good graces. In late April, though, he was a man cast adrift by Browne's death—and grateful of an offer of employment by so great a figure as Thomas Seymour.

Seymour was determined to make use of the clever young gentleman. Two or three days after Wightman entered his employment, Seymour called for him, ordering him to write to potential witnesses to Henry VIII's gifts to Catherine.[13] Wightman made careful note of his instructions, anxious to please his brand-new employer. He was specifically to ask whether the jewels had come to the queen by gift or loan, in the hope that the answers would support Catherine's case. In particular, he should implore the witnesses "as near as they could to make him advertisement of the very words His Majesty spake at the sending of such jewels or household stuff unto her." Wightman was assisted in his task by one of Thomas's lawyers, Richard Weston, and the pair composed the letters together. William Wightman was not, however, to be privy to the replies. Weston took those secretly to his master.

All the lawyers that Thomas consulted said the same thing: that if he could prove that Henry VIII had made a gift of the jewels to Catherine, then they were hers. Yet he struggled to prove it. Seymour also lamented the loss of the jewels to his friend Sir William Sharington, declaring that he disliked his brother for it and that he had obtained five legal opinions of learned counsel, all in his support.[14] They did him little good. Catherine's jewels just formed another front in Thomas's war with his brother. Musing with his devoted servant John Harington one day, he stated: "Some doth think, that there is something that I cannot bear at My Lord Protector's hands; and indeed I have some occasion to think unkindness in him, if I would so take it; for he keepeth away the queen's jewels, the which I might attempt to recover by the law, if I would; for the law hath power of him, as well upon other of the Council; but I had rather they were on fire, then I would attempt it."[15]

A few weeks later, though, at Catherine's urging, he did attempt it, securing an interview with his brother. Thanks to his position on the Council, Seymour was regularly in London. He was at Westminster on 10 May 1548, from where he wrote a letter to his vice admirals on navy business.[16] He was also present in the Council chamber on 5 June, carefully adding his signature to a letter urging the county justices to prepare for war with France.[17] He remained in London for the next few days, in order to find an opportunity to speak to his brother.

Thomas found Somerset calm but indecisive, giving him little hope of the jewels' return while not leaving him entirely in despair.[18] The matter of the jewels was a point of pride for Thomas, but also a highly personal matter. Among the confiscated items was jewelry bequeathed to her by her beloved mother. Thomas knew how much it meant to her, writing to Catherine after his meeting that he had broken with his brother "for your mother's gift." Catherine wanted her queenly jewels, as was her right, but she also wanted to possess, hold, and wear the few sentimental trinkets that she had received from her mother. Somerset himself acknowledged this but gave no firm answers. As Seymour stood, attempting to cajole him, the Protector promised that once matters had been resolved, the queen would either receive those jewels that were found to belong to her or be compensated. It was the best that Thomas could achieve, but it smarted. At Hanworth, the queen was livid, writing to her husband that she had become disillusioned, since she had "supposed My Lord Protector would have used no delay with his friend and natural brother in a matter which is upright and just, as I take it." She firmly believed that Somerset retained her jewels out of greed.

She was far from the only person to hold such an opinion of the Protector, whose lavish building projects were already causing comment. Somerset, who publicly bemoaned the king's empty treasury, seemed to have unlimited funds for his own projects. From April 1548, while construction of his great Thames-side mansion of Somerset Place was in full swing, he paid out over £10,000 to craftsmen and laborers. The pace of building was relentless, and the palace was almost finished within three years. Its classical façade exuded wealth and power,[19] outstripping other buildings in the area, including Seymour Place, which appeared insignificant in comparison. Although Seymour Place was a great house, Somerset Place, with its great gallery and withdrawing chamber, was a seat from which England could be governed.*

Vast sums passed through the hands of the Protector's cofferer, John Pickarell, who would dutifully take his account books to be "subscribed with the hand" of the duke's auditor.[20] (Even Elizabeth's officers did business with him, receiving on 12 May a payment of £4 30 shillings 16 pence for her own coffers.) Somerset and his family lived lavishly and ostentatious, his banners resplendent

* Today's Somerset House dates from the late eighteenth century. It was built on the site of the Protector's palace, which was demolished.

in gold and silver. By 1548, he was appearing in fine velvet and silks, while his heir, the young Earl of Hertford, looked similarly magnificent. The Duchess of Somerset could purchase her own finery, helped in no small part by the allowance of £400 per year paid to her by her husband. It must have seemed petty, in the extreme, to his brother that Somerset insisted on retaining Catherine's trinkets, particularly since—as Thomas himself complained—"one is her [royal] wedding ring."[21]

Thomas and Catherine had always planned that their baby should be born at Sudeley, in Gloucestershire, in the castle intended to stand as their ancestral seat. There was also a more practical reason to leave for the country that summer: London and its environs were riven by plague. By July 1548 the king and the Council had fled London to avoid the pestilence, moving to the cleaner air of Hampton Court.[22]

In early June 1548, therefore, Catherine's vast household of servants and retainers were already busying themselves in packing up her possessions. It was to be a major operation, with curtains stripped from the windows and carpets from the floors, before being carefully stowed alongside the furniture to adorn the new residence. The Tudor nobility never traveled lightly and queens even less so, preferring the familiar comforts of their own things, even against a frequently changing backdrop as they moved residences—and even when so many of the coffers remained unopened.[23] Although the bulk of Catherine's jewels were still in the Protector's grasping custody, she had managed to retain many fine items, including gold rings set with diamonds or rubies. Catherine packed indiscriminately, taking everything with her, including several fine jewelry boxes and broken, worn favorites, such as her seventeen little buttons of gold garnished with small pearls (many of the pearls being lost) or the damaged ruby ring stored away for repair at some later date or to be made into something new.

Her prayer books and psalm books came as well, as did a little pair of silver tweezers used for plucking hair and twenty-eight hair-nets of gold and silver. She brought her inkwell, too, to allow her to stay in touch with family and friends. The household servants all had to stow carefully their own possessions in trunks. It was thus no surprise that those first days of June 1548 were bustling, busy ones at Hanworth as everyone struggled to be ready to take the road to Sudeley.

Although Catherine was a seasoned traveler, having lived with her first two husbands in the north and endured annual progresses with King Henry, she must have balked at the hundred-mile journey northwest to Sudeley. A rider might cover that distance in two to three days, but a train encumbered by wagons, and in which the queen was carried in a litter, would take much longer, requiring frequent stops along the road.

Unsurprisingly, the queen wanted her husband with her and feared any delay to their journey. But Thomas was at court as the household packed, tying up the loose ends of his business in the Council and the Admiralty. There were concerns that he might have to postpone his journey, since rumors were rife that the French were planning to attack the English coast. Catherine was "very sorry," she wrote on 9 June, to hear this, telling her husband that "I pray God it be not a let to our journey."[24] She was worried and could not "be very quiet" until she heard one way or the other. Thomas was anxious to ensure that his wife was upset no more and replied immediately. He had already informed his brother, he said, that they would be leaving on Wednesday 13 June as arranged. While the Protector was "very sorry" to hear this, Catherine's husband bowed to no persuasions. He agreed only to remain at Westminster for one more day, "to hear what the Frenchmen will do," before leaving on the Monday for Hanworth. He would be there in time for dinner, served mid-morning, he promised.

As admiral, Seymour's place was with his navy in the face of such a crisis, but he was determined it would be no "let" to the journey. He put a positive slant on it, spreading it abroad that, with regard to his wife, "his devotion was such that he would not leave her palace."[25] Already, at Westminster, his thoughts were far from any proposed invasion. On the Monday morning, 11 June, he went over to the court, but instead of seeing his brother he called only for John Fowler.[26] The gentleman heeded the summons, coming quickly to Thomas's chamber.

On Fowler's arrival, he found Seymour alone and in a confident mood. Thomas told him: "Mr. Fowler as I would do nothing but I would the King's Majesty should be privy of it, I pray you tell His Grace I will be a suiter to My Lord my brother for certain jewels which the king that dead is did give the queen." He assured Fowler that he had the law on his side, but his ally only shook his head, saying: "alas My Lord that the jewels or the muck of the world should make you to begin a new matter between My Lord's Grace and you." "Nay," replied Seymour dismissively, "there will be no business for this matter for I trust My Lord my brother will be content." He said nothing more on the topic, merely calling for his boat, which was ready to take him to Hanworth and his dinner. As he stepped aboard, he turned once again to Fowler, bidding him to send only to him if the king lacked anything, as well as ensuring that the boy-king remained in "remembrance of him" in his absence. Seymour was ever terrified that the monarch might "forget him."[27]

Someone in no danger of forgetting Thomas was the king's half-sister. Elizabeth met few men of substance for, being a minor, she had little access to the court or to the Protector. At Hanworth, as always, she spent her time immersed in her studies. She found Ascham a gentle, dedicated schoolmaster and thrived under his care. His approach was enlightened, informed by the belief that "there is no such whetstone, to sharpen a good wit and encourage a will to learning, as is praise."[28] He did not believe in punishments for simple mistakes, instead encouraging Elizabeth to come to him when she was uncertain. He wanted to inspire a love of learning in his charge. He was successful, since Elizabeth often chose to read Greek for pleasure, as well as Latin, Italian, French, and Spanish.

It made sense for the princess to discuss her studies with her young cousin, Jane Grey, who was herself becoming highly proficient in Greek under the guidance of her own tutor, Dr. Aylmer. The ten-year-old would soon be reading Plato for her amusement. Ascham was fascinated by Jane too, striving to become very "intimate" with her during their time together in Catherine's household.[29] He found a friend in Dr. Aylmer, whom he adopted as something of a protégé, calling him "my Aylmer" when he wrote to Jane. Aylmer was a man whom Elizabeth's tutor trusted, one into whose "bosom shall abundantly pour all my sorrows." The two men, bringing their pupils together at times, shared notes on their curricula. Ascham lauded his fellow's young charge, telling her: "O happy Aylmer to have such a pupil, and much happier you to have him for a tutor!"[30] Such occasions were some of the only opportunities that Elizabeth had to speak with anyone of her own rank, save Catherine and Thomas.

For Elizabeth, Thomas remained a constant but complex source of fascination. It was clear even to her less intimate servants that there was "good will between the Lord Admiral and Her Grace."[31] When Catherine asked Elizabeth to arrange a messenger to carry the sealed letter of 9 June to Thomas at court, the princess—perhaps emboldened by Thomas's physical absence from the house—decided to add her own message on the reverse. Taking up her quill, she pointedly inscribed the letter with the words "Thou, touch me not" in Latin, before deleting the phrase and substituting "let him not touch me."[32] Even though attracted to Seymour, she knew that his intimate behavior was unacceptable, and she was now all but ordering him to stay away. Her first, erased phrase was bluntly addressed direct to Thomas; her second was almost a plea for someone else to relieve her of Seymour's overfamiliar attentions. The truth was, she did not really know how the situation should be handled. Either way, Thomas Seymour had no intention of staying away from her. He ignored Elizabeth's note.

Catherine Parr loved her husband with a great passion, in spite of his own jealousies and his frequent absences. She could understand jealousy, for she felt it herself. After warning Kate to be more watchful of Elizabeth, the queen had continued to observe, growing daily more suspicious of what she saw. Whenever Thomas was present at Hanworth, his eye was caught by Elizabeth and his attention drawn to her. It was obvious that—as Elizabeth's cofferer, Thomas Parry, would later put it—he "loved her but too well, and had so done a good while."[33] As Catherine approached motherhood, her belly growing larger by the day, she had watched anxiously and with increasing anger. Jealous of, and confused by, both her husband and her stepdaughter, she was more alert than ever to reasons as to why her worries might be justified, "suspecting the often access of the Admiral to the Lady Elizabeth's Grace."[34]

After Seymour returned to Hanworth on 11 June, following his meeting with Fowler and having pondered Elizabeth's note, he pulled the girl aside. The queen, noticing that they had disappeared, went to seek them out. She came upon her stepdaughter in her husband's arms, alone together, embracing in an otherwise empty room.[35] She was devastated by the sight, and her initial reaction was to rant and rave at the pair, falling out with them both in her fury. Such confirmation of her fears was brutal: this could not be construed as playful tickling or adolescent hijinks. Neither Thomas nor Elizabeth, pulling away from the embrace, had much to say, since their actions spoke louder than words. Although Elizabeth had tried to save her stepmother's feelings and had commanded Seymour to stay away, ultimately she could do little to resist him in his own house; and Thomas was too dangerously attracted to Elizabeth, for her youth and beauty and for her position as second in line to the throne. Catherine's actual words to Elizabeth and Thomas were not recorded. Perhaps Thomas sought to blame Elizabeth, reminding his wife of Anne Boleyn's reputation.[36] It took considerable effort on Catherine's part to regain her composure.

Catherine's ire also turned on Kate Ashley, who had entirely failed to watch her young charge. The queen called for her at once, telling her exactly what she thought of the matter and venting her "displeasure." For all Catherine knew, the pair might already have been sleeping together; she certainly feared what they had been doing when they were alone. After venting her spleen with Kate, Catherine dismissed Elizabeth's lady mistress from her presence.

Elizabeth must have been filled with dread as to the consequences. Catherine had to think quickly of just what to do with her stepdaughter, now that preparations for the move to Sudeley were almost complete. She knew with certainty that she could not allow the girl to stay in her household, given the danger that Elizabeth posed both to the queen's marriage and to her own reputation. The princess needed a new guardian.

The queen therefore decided to send Elizabeth to stay at Cheshunt, Hertfordshire, in the house of Sir Anthony Denny and his wife, Joan. When they were first mentioned, the couple must have seemed a surprising choice for the girl, since they were very close to Kate Ashley and her husband. Joan and Kate were sisters, and although of very different characters the two couples moved in the same social circles. Nonetheless, the queen knew that she could rely on the couple to be discreet and watchful.*

Elizabeth's new host was a serious-minded man in late middle age. He was a scholar, having been given a fine humanist education at St. Paul's School in London, before studying at Cambridge. He had been an early friend of Elizabeth's father, and was the only man

* It is possible that the embrace witnessed by Catherine occurred earlier than the afternoon of 11 June, with Elizabeth's departure for Cheshunt already planned before Catherine's letter of 9 June was written. On the balance of probabilities, though, the sequence set out here seems more likely, particularly given Catherine's friendly tone in the letter.

brave enough to inform the old king that his end was approaching in January 1547. Sir Anthony's father, who had spent much of his time in London, had been a staunchly religious man, asking for masses to be said for his soul to speed him through Purgatory.[37] It was Anthony who made the family's fortune, far eclipsing his father as he also turned away from the traditional faith.[38] He was a straight-talking, honest man, zealous in religion, and he was well matched with his forceful, pious wife.

Joan Denny was a practical, no-nonsense woman who trod a more conventional path than her sister.[39] She liked fine things, though, possessing several gold tablets decorated with diamonds, which she looked on as family heirlooms and hoped to pass down to her daughters. To show her piety, she wore a beautiful gold cross, garnished with five diamonds, which sparkled against her sober clothing, while at her wrists were gold bracelets. As a sign of the trust between husband and wife, Sir Anthony bequeathed her his personal gold chain—his most precious possession—which she diligently later passed to their eldest son, who was named "Henry" after Elizabeth's father.

The couple was blessed with sons and daughters surviving to adulthood. The sons, who were around the same age as Elizabeth, were still at home when the princess arrived. They were, like their parents, ardent Protestants. The eldest three—Henry, Anthony, and Charles—were all clever boys, interested in learning; their parents were preparing them for university education and, in due course, the law.[40]

As far as Catherine was concerned, the Dennys would make excellent guardians. She immediately sent them a message, asking them to invite Elizabeth into their home. Catherine then summoned her stepdaughter to her, as the girl's servants packed up her things. The queen—who had known Elizabeth for only five years but loved her like her own child—had decided to be kind. She was unwell, but left her sickbed for a private interview with her stepdaughter, who was "replete with sorrow to depart."[41] Elizabeth, red-eyed and tearful, stood in near silence. Catherine, who remembered Anne Boleyn as much as everyone did, had much to say. She was fearful for the girl's reputation and promised to warn her of "all evils" that she should hear of Elizabeth, something that she rather feared would happen. The princess, at least, took this as a sign of Catherine's good opinion. At the end of their meeting, as the pair prepared to part, Catherine offered friendship to her. In spite of her hurt and anger, the heavily pregnant queen was determined that they would not part on bad terms. She informed the girl that she believed her when she promised that she and Thomas had gone no further than an embrace. This was a relief to the girl, who was already uncomfortably aware of rumors both within the household and without, in which "all men judge the contrary."[42] They might judge and whisper, but it was Catherine's support that Elizabeth wanted. The princess's clothes and personal items were now carefully stored in wooden coffers before being loaded onto wagons. She left hurriedly, probably on 12 June 1548.

The reason for Elizabeth's departure was kept deliberately vague; indeed, her own servants were uncertain of the cause. Thomas Parry, who dealt with the expenses of the move, could not remember whether his mistress "went of herself, or was sent away."[43] Setting her own feelings to one side, the queen allowed her husband to escort the girl at least part of the way toward Cheshunt.* It was better for everyone if no hint was given that the princess went in disgrace. Nonetheless, Kate Ashley—chastened—kept a close watch on Seymour, speaking with him on the road, although the older woman always refused to divulge what was said.[44] She did not, though, break with the Lord Admiral. She still held considerable admiration for him and desired his friendship. She was certainly prepared to risk much for Thomas Seymour.

* In her later confession, Kate attributed Elizabeth's departure to the week after Whitsun (the last week of May 1548), but Elizabeth's inscription on Catherine's letter to Thomas—dated to 9 June (or at the latest, 10 June)—throws this into doubt as it indicates her presence in the household. Since Thomas only returned to Hanworth on the morning of 11 June and left for Sudeley on 13 June, then 12 June is really the only plausible date on which Elizabeth could have left her stepmother. Seymour is known to have accompanied her at least part of the way toward Cheshunt.

The journey to Cheshunt from Hanworth was a long one, taking most of the day on horseback. The princess was tired when she arrived on a fine early summer evening. Coming from the west, she passed the common, which, with its leafy fruit trees, made up much of the large parish.[45] Three church spires rose up over the little town. It was a pleasant green settlement, its streets lined with small houses attached to market gardens. Elizabeth rode past the old manor house at Cheshunt, which, as with Hanworth, was circled by a picturesque moat. Sir Anthony Denny's father had obtained control of a manor in the parish when he was just a boy. Sir Anthony himself had once been a landless younger son. But ten years ago he had acquired the keepership of Cheshunt Park, allowing him to control hunting in the area. It must have felt like a homecoming. He secured the grant of Cheshunt nunnery following its dissolution under Henry VIII, allowing him to move his family into the building, which quickly took on a higgledy-piggledy character as rooms were fitted out for habitation.[46] The family worshipped in the church at Cheshunt, a chilly stone space where Sir Anthony's brother, two decades before, had asked to be buried under "a picture of death," reciting the chilling legend "as I am so shall ye be."[47]

It was in the courtyard of the old nunnery that Elizabeth finally dismounted, as servants hurried to take the reins of her horse and show her to her rooms. The house was welcoming. Kate was relieved to be away from Catherine's hostility and in the company of her sister. Roger Ascham was also not displeased to move to Cheshunt, since he knew Sir Anthony Denny and had earlier sought his patronage.[48] As the men conversed after dinner, there were opportunities for him to secure influence and, perhaps, a pension. The relocation also brought Ascham closer to his beloved Cambridge—though he would struggle to obtain permission from Elizabeth for a trip to the university, since (as he lamented) "she never lets me go away anywhere."[49] As whispers spread about the coquettish daughter of Anne Boleyn, Princess Elizabeth wanted her friends around her.

Chapter Ten

A CHILD BORN AND MISERABLY DESTROYED

At Cheshunt, Kate Ashley was able to spend enjoyable hours with her sister and her family, but she was also anxious. She already knew that Elizabeth was "evil spoken of," but hoped that with time and with her separation from Seymour this would come to an end. It did not. The rumors, once established, grew—almost with a life of their own.

To compound Elizabeth's problems, her health took a downward turn. She had suffered from teething problems as an infant but had otherwise been remarkably healthy.[1] This all changed in 1548 after she left Catherine's household. At Cheshunt, she almost immediately took to her bed with the first of a series of illnesses that would affect her teenage years. She was unwell throughout the summer of 1548 and into the autumn. Her symptoms, which included migraines, headaches, digestive problems, jaundice, and irregular menstrual cycles, have been identified as being stress-induced. Might there have been more to them?[2] Many of her symptoms could also be attributed to pregnancy.

More than fifty years later, an old lady—almost Elizabeth's exact contemporary—sat down with her servant to tell her story. Jane Dormer, the great and noble Duchess of Feria, had spent decades in her adopted homeland of Spain, but she did not forget the red-haired princess she had once known at court. The aged noblewoman, who hailed from Wing in Buckinghamshire, was familiar with the Seymour family. Indeed, her father had very nearly married Jane Seymour before Henry VIII claimed her. Jane was ardently Catholic, which might be why her dislike of Elizabeth began to color her recollections. She told her story to her servant Henry Clifford, who diligently recorded it for the benefit of her English family.

Jane Dormer considered herself well acquainted with the relationship between the princess and the Lord Admiral. Thinking back over the decades, she recalled that there was a rumor, spread around, "of a child born and miserably destroyed, but could not be discovered whose it was." She did not know the details of this murdered baby, only that there was "the report of the midwife, who was brought from her house blindfold thither, and so returned, saw nothing in the house while she was there, but candle light; only she said, it was the child of a very fair young lady."

The midwife did not know whom she attended, and neither did the authorities when they investigated the matter. But, as Jane recalled, "there was a muttering of the Admiral and this lady, who was then between fifteen and sixteen years of age." She could not say that Elizabeth was certainly the child's mother, but "if it were so, it was the judgment of God upon the Admiral; and upon her, to make her ever after incapable of children."[3] To add to the authenticity of her source, Jane Dormer believed that "the cuckold," as she called Somerset thanks to the disaster of his first marriage, "then made no great reckoning of the Lady Elizabeth," actively showing his disapproval at court.[4]

Jane Dormer's account, given before 1612 (when she died), is the earliest telling of a story that has passed into legend and has been considerably embellished over the years. In May 1616, a very similar story emerged in Flanders, where it was related by Ambassador Sir Dudley Carleston to his friend John Chamberlain, in England.[5] In this version, two men came in visors to a midwife's house and carried her away. She was led to a masked woman in labor in a great house. When the child was born, it was cast into the fire. On seeing this, the mother cried out at the cruelty, declaring that this was the fifth time that this had been done. The story carried an anti-Catholic message: the writer commented on the "barbarous" men and the unfortunate woman—"I expect before long to hear your Catholic gentlewomen put into the number of saints." No mention was made of Elizabeth, though, and indeed the setting was entirely changed; but the essence of the story was the same.

The tale, in its most famous form, was related by the antiquary John Aubrey, in the mid-seventeenth century, a hundred years after the events it was supposed to describe. Aubrey believed that one Sir John Darrell of Littlecote Manor, in Wiltshire, had impregnated his wife's waiting woman, causing an understandable scandal in the household.[6] Rather than turning the girl out of doors, Darrell ensured that she was cared for in his manor. When the time came for her confinement, a servant was sent with a horse to fetch a midwife and bring her blindfolded to the house. The child was delivered and brought to Darrell, who immediately murdered it and threw the body into the fire.

The midwife was then given a large reward and sent home again, with a heavy heart. She continued to reflect on what had happened for some time, considering how far they could have ridden and the fact that the room in which she was shown had a ceiling twelve feet high. She then went to a magistrate and a search was made, with suspicion immediately falling on Darrell. He was tried, but he bribed the judge—Sir John Popham ("a huge, heavy, ugly man")—with a gift of his house and lands. Aubrey's purpose in writing was an attack on Popham, whom he considered "lived like a hog" in spite of his vast wealth. But both Popham and the Lord of Littlecote were long dead by the time that Aubrey wrote—so why did he record the story and write of their involvement?

The story cropped up yet again at the end of the eighteenth century, when it was set "in a county verging on London" and dated to the past hundred years.[7] According to the writer, it concerned a "family of great opulence," although now banished from the neighborhood and now "in a continual state of decay." As the story ran, a young lawyer, at the beginning of his career, was called at short notice to hear a case "of the highest importance to the reputation, the happiness, not to say, the existence, of the ancient family alluded to." Worse was to come when he learned the circumstance of the crime. It was murder, the accused being "no other than the daughter of an ancient baronet, one of the most beautiful young women of that day" and her two relatives.

The facts were almost identical to earlier versions of the story. A midwife had just returned home tired from a birth. When strangers arrived to attempt to engage her, she tried to send her assistant, but they had come specifically for her. In the face of her refusals, they bundled her onto a horse, with a handkerchief over her eyes, while informing her that "a lady of the first quality in that part of the country waited her help." With the blindfolded midwife clutching the waist of her abductor, they traveled "at a smart trot." She was terrified but could sense that, during their journey of an hour and a half, they rode through fields, away from the main road. In ever-increasing alarm, she heard the horses' hooves clatter into a courtyard, where she dismounted. She was then conducted to a chamber with a lady in labor, where she was forced to perform her office still blindfolded. The midwife was sure that the mother was "a very young lady," but could discover no other details. Unseeing, she delivered a boy and passed it to a female attendant. Only then was she permitted to rest, although she was soon disturbed by "a very uncommon and burning smell." After her return home, she came to realize that the terrible stench had been the body of the poor murdered infant.

The story crops up again, bizarrely, in a twenty-first-century collection of ghost stories set in the U.S. state of Maine. Here, it concerns a phantom fiery infant said to haunt the father who so cruelly threw him in the fireplace.[8] His birth is once again mysterious, and a midwife is brought blindfolded to a house. There, she finds a "lovely young woman" about to give birth, but with no wedding ring in sight. Close by, ominously, is the child's father, intent on doing harm.

At first glance, the story, in all its incarnations, appears to be nothing more than a macabre fairy tale or folk legend—a figment of the writers' imaginations. Unless the world was awash with blindfolded midwives and charred babies, the tales must ultimately have the same origin, dating to at least the mid-sixteenth century. Those writers that retold it for their own time did so with particular aims in mind: Dormer to damage Elizabeth's reputation, Carleston to attack Catholics, and Aubrey to smear Popham. It could be left at that—except that, surprisingly, these events really *did* occur in the mid-sixteenth century, while Elizabeth was young.

One evening, in 1577, the magistrate Sir Anthony Bridges was called to Great Shefford in Berkshire to attend the deathbed of a local woman, Mother Barnes, whose family was well known in the village and had lived there for generations.[9] Bridges was a busy man. He did not usually rouse himself to witness the dying of old ladies, but he had been informed that the woman, who had served for many years as the community's midwife, had a confession that she needed to make. This revelation concerned murder.[10]

Bridges was ushered into the old woman's small village home. He found her in bed, where she was ready finally to unload her burden.[11] The events she described had happened a number of years before, she told him.

She was already an experienced midwife at the time of the events, well respected in the local area and often traveling some distance to tend to the ladies of quality who required her service. One evening, as she rested in her house, she heard riders approach. Glancing out of the window, she saw two men, dressed like servants in black frieze coats. They approached her door after dismounting from fine, expensive horses.

Intrigued, Mother Barnes hurried out to them. They informed her that they were employed by the respectable Mrs. Knyvett, wife of Sir Henry Knyvett, who lived thirty miles away at Charlton.[12] Their mistress prayed the midwife "of all loves to come unto her forthwith at her promise," since she had already engaged Mrs. Barnes to attend her in her expected labor. Mrs. Knyvett was an excellent client for Mother Barnes, so she was anxious to do a good job, immediately gathering her things and mounting a horse behind one of the two men.

To her surprise, they did not go in the direction of Mrs. Knyvett's house—and to her considerable alarm, it soon became clear that the men were not who they said they were. Instead, with thundering steps, the horses raced through the night, covering the miles through the inky blackness as the midwife clung precariously to the waist of her abductor. It was almost daylight when they finally arrived at "a fair house," which the midwife did not recognize.

She was hustled from the horse and toward a door, at which a tall, slender gentleman appeared, wearing a fine long gown of black velvet. He carried a candle and beckoned her inside, shutting the door on those who had brought her and leading the midwife in silence up the stairs. Mother Barnes was thoroughly alarmed, but followed the gentleman, finding herself in "a fair and large great chamber, being hanged all about with arras." A great fire was burning in the grate and she was taken through to another room of a similar size, also richly hung with tapestry and lit by a fire burning. She again passed through, entering a third room as rich as the others. There, she found a "richly and gorgeously furnished" bed, around which the curtains were firmly drawn. The man stooped low to her, whispering in her ear: "Lo, in yonder bed lieth the gentlewoman that you are sent for to come unto, go unto her and see that you do your uttermost endeavour towards her, and if she be safely delivered, you shall not fail of great reward, but if she miscarry in her travail, you shall die."

Mother Barnes stood for a moment amazed, before moving to the bedside and drawing back the curtains tentatively. Inside, she found a gentlewoman, her body arched with pain, but lying in luxury on the bed in fine nightclothes. To the midwife's surprise, the woman's face was covered with a mask, although she did not note it in detail, later being unable to recall whether it was a visor or a caul. The birth proved to be quick. The midwife delivered a baby boy, wrapping him in her apron since she was surprised to find no clothes had been provided. She then picked up the baby and walked into one of the bigger chambers, where she found the gentleman waiting. He turned to her and demanded to know whether the woman had been safely delivered "or no." She had, she said, proffering up the baby proudly and asking that some clothes be provided for him. The man made no attempt to take the child.

Mother Barnes moved closer to the fire, where the gentleman was standing. She held the baby out to him as the flames crackled in the grate, but he would not look at her bundle. Persisting, the midwife was silenced by a sudden command to cast the baby into the fire. This was the horrifying moment when Mother Barnes realized that the man's concern was only for the mother's safety, not the child's. She fell to her knees, begging that "he would not seek to destroy it, but rather give it unto her." She promised to raise the boy as her own child, if only he would not murder him. Yet the man had no intention of allowing the child to live. Eventually, the tiny wriggling bundle was thrust into the flames. Mother Barnes was then commanded to go back to the mother and tend to her, where she remained for the rest of the day.

When night finally fell, the exhausted midwife was led outside, and the same two men who had brought her to the house helped her onto a horse. Although it was dark, she was determined to note the route they took, recognizing Donnington Park on her right-hand side. They crossed a great and long bridge, which she supposed must be over the Thames, lying some miles from her house. Once home, she kept her secret, although it lay heavy on her mind. Many years passed—although how many was not clear. Finally, as she felt her end approaching, she unburdened herself of her tale. As far as she was concerned, the events of that night were real—as they seemed to the magistrate to whom she spoke. There had been a masked lady, there had been a birth, and there had been a child cruelly destroyed. But who was the mother?

Great Shefford lies only six miles from Littlecote Hall, on which John Aubrey later fixed the tale, his florid touches little masking the fact that he recounted Mother Barnes's story. The magistrate who sat with the old woman as she breathed out her words also had some connection to Littlecote. Sir Anthony Bridges was a friend of Sir William Darrell, who owned the manor. After his own cursory investigation, Sir Anthony passed the papers to Darrell the following July at the same time as those relating to another murder, requesting that he consider them both as a magistrate and landowner in the local area. Neither matter was particularly urgent, Bridges informed his "good cousin," beginning his covering letter with a reminder about £20 that his kinsman owed him. With the formalities out of the way, Sir Anthony complained that he had "been of late amongst crafty crowders" who took up his time and meant that he was unable to attend to business. There was no indication that anything was out of the ordinary or that either murder was connected to Darrell other than in his professional capacity as justice of the peace. Indeed, Bridges simply wanted to share the administrative work of keeping justice in the local area, inviting a colleague to assist him with matters.

"Wild" Will Darrell was, though, a far from suitable figure to administer justice. Born in 1539, he was a troublesome man and a difficult neighbor. He was often a party in local disputes, finding himself imprisoned in 1587 for a misdemeanor.[13] John Aubrey certainly believed that he was the father of the murdered baby, and it is clear that he did indeed have a connection to Sir Anthony Popham, who took over the Littlecote estate after his death. Darrell must have spent a good deal of time with the future judge, who served as one of his lawyers, since at one point he was simultaneously involved in twelve legal cases.

In later life, having bargained away his inheritance to pay his legal expenses, Wild Will spent much time in London, although he was visiting Littlecote when he died in October 1589. Legend claims that his end came while he was out riding too fast on his estates, at a place that came to be called "Darrell's Leap." Leap he did, but not successfully. When his horse failed to jump at the last moment, the middle-aged reprobate fell, breaking his neck. By the nineteenth century, there were rumors that the horse had started on seeing the ghost of the burned infant out to wreak revenge.*

Darrell was never charged, but as one writer later said, he became "stuck with the murder."[14] But there was nothing contemporary to pin the murder on him. Mother Barnes laid no accusations against him. It may even be the case that his enemies seized on the stories to tarnish him.[15] The story was not commonly told at Littlecote in the late sixteenth century when the antiquarian William Camden passed through, since he did not record it when he wrote of both Popham and the Darrells.[16] Interestingly, Elizabeth I's arms appear in one of the bedrooms in Littlecote Manor—although these were carved toward the end of her life, in 1601, when she proposed to visit there.[17]

If the baby was indeed Darrell's, then the mother was most likely Anne Hungerford, who was his mistress. She was divorced from her husband in around 1569 because of the affair, and she retired to Louvain, living there until her death in 1603.[18] The couple had been deeply in love. Anne called her paramour "dear Dorrell" and signed herself "all yours during life" even as her divorce case was being heard.[19] She also begged him: "for the love of God my

* The mother, too, is traditionally believed to haunt Littlecote.

good Will be careful for me in this matter" (meaning her divorce), before asking him to establish an alibi. Yet, although the couple tried to prove that they were slandered, in private Lady Hungerford swore an oath on scripture promising to marry Darrell if only "Sir Walter Hungerford, my husband, now living do depart out of this life."[20] There were claims that she meant to hasten that happy day: Sir Walter accused her of trying to poison him in 1570, while also denouncing her affair, which he claimed had lasted the best part of a decade.[21]

Anne was not only the subject of a scandal—she was also the beloved sister of Jane Dormer, who would hear nothing unkind said about her. In Jane's eyes, Anne had lived a blamelessly Catholic life in England, until her religion earned her the wrath of a husband who "albeit nobly descended, yet by his base covetousness and disordered sensual living much blemished his person and worth."[22] Finally, Anne was able to persuade him to allow her to leave England, "where she might have liberty of conscience and serve God freely." She lived in the Low Countries for thirty-two years "with great example of true nobility and Christianity, much honoured for her rare parts of valour, and discretion."[23]

Anne's sister insisted that she lived a charitable, respectable life in Flanders, instead accusing her husband of adultery.[24] Anne died in December 1603, "full of good works." This was the picture of Anne Hungerford that her sister wanted to present to the world, but it was very much at odds with Anne's dangerous passion for Wild Will Darrell. Jane Dormer, who had lived in the local area herself, must have been recounting the rumors of Mother Barnes's story to Henry Clifford—but she had no desire in doing so to cast any blame on her sister. Perhaps she meant to remove suspicion from her sister by smearing Elizabeth. More likely, since she was unlikely to record a scandalous story in which her sister's name risked being mentioned, there was simply no known connection to Littlecote, Wild Will Darrell, or Anne Hungerford until John Aubrey set down his scurrilous tale. If not Anne, who was the mother of the murdered child?

Mother Barnes, a woman who knew the local area and who lived just six miles from Littlecote, is unlikely to have been fooled, even if she was led by a roundabout route to the house in the dark.[25] There are other problems with the identification too. The journey from Littlecote back to Great Shefford does not pass Donnington Park on the right—the one location the midwife was largely certain about. Interestingly, however, until Mother Barnes's deposition came to light in the nineteenth century, tradition held that the midwife had been summoned from Great Bedwyn in Wiltshire, a place that, if one takes a circuitous route via Donnington Park, is thirty miles from Great Shefford, a distance that would take much of the night to ride.

Clearly, Mother Barnes did not come from Great Bedwyn; but perhaps she was going there. It has long been suggested that the river she crossed, which she believed was the Thames, might have been the Kennet at Hungerford, which is particularly broad at that point. This diversion makes no sense on a journey from Great Shefford to Littlecote, but was necessary if a party intended to travel from the midwife's house to Great Bedwyn—the home parish of the Seymours.[26]

Edward Seymour—the future Protector—had inherited Wolf Hall on his father's death, but it remained the ancestral home. Both the old Sir John Seymour and his eldest son, John, were commemorated by tombs in Great Bedwyn Church following the destruction of their first—monastic—burial place.[27] In the nineteenth century Sir Walter Scott publicized the story, including it in his poem "Rokeby": it had been drawn to his attention by Lord Webb Seymour, who was aware of the local tradition.[28]

The identity of the mother cannot be proved. But the evidence suggests that the murdered infant might have been a Seymour baby, just as Jane Dormer suggested, born illegitimate at Wolf Hall to one of the Seymour women or a mistress of one of their men. This does not mean that the mother was Elizabeth, since there is no evidence that she visited Thomas Seymour's childhood home or even the local area. If she was pregnant when she left Catherine's household in June 1548, her baby was not the child thrown on the fire.

Nevertheless, Jane Dormer's story was not the only one to suggest that Elizabeth was no virgin when she left Hanworth. In 1594, the thinly veiled narrative poem "Willobie His Avisa" had the young Avisa, who can be convincingly interpreted as Elizabeth, defending her honor with a knife.[29] A nobleman of "ripe years" has apparently tried to force himself upon Avisa, forcing the girl to snatch the dagger from his belt. The courtship, tantalizing and dangerous, was considered by the late sixteenth century to be "a warning to all young maids of every degree, that they beware of the alluring enticements of great men."[30] In this fictionalized account of the courtship, the nobleman declares to the girl: "Ah silly wench, take not a pride, though thou my raging fancy move thy betters far, if they were tried, would fain accept my proffered love; T'was for thy good, if thou hadst wist, for I may have whom ere I list." The nobleman of the poem belittles the girl when she tries to reject his advances, asking: "Art thou preciser than a queen?" He offers her everything he can—"my house, my heart, my land, my life, my credit to thy care I give." In reality, while Catherine lived, Seymour could hardly offer Elizabeth honor.

In the summer of 1548, ill in her bed, Elizabeth was aware of the rumors circulating around her. They made her furious. She remained so poorly that word reached the Protector, who wrote inquiring about her health, as well as sending a royal physician, Dr. Thomas Bille, to attend her.[31] It was no surprise that Elizabeth was reluctant to hazard her health to a local physician: the medical profession was not held in high repute, even by some of its own members,* and Elizabeth always insisted on being treated by royal doctors.[32]

* Even a century later, a Fellow of the Royal College of Physicians and the Royal Society published a damning indictment of the London medical profession (see Goddard). Behind the scenes, "raw and slovenly apprentices" did the work of preparing the prescriptions, with such creatures being "no ways capable of discovering his secrets, but only fit to kindle fires, tend a still or furnace, beat a mortar."

Thomas Bille was a Cambridge man who had joined the College of Physicians in the early 1540s, and who had served both Henry VIII and Edward VI.[33] He was trusted, taking great "diligence and pains" with the princess, placing her back on the road to recovery. In September, the princess sat down to write her thanks to the Protector, asking that the physician be rewarded. She hesitated, though, to put in writing just what had ailed her, instead informing Somerset that Bille "can ascertain you of mine estate of health wherefore I will not write it." She was grateful for Somerset's support "in this time of my sickness." Just what exactly this sickness was is unknown, which helped to fuel the rumors.

In the case of expectant mothers, it was usual for royal ladies to be attended in their confinements by doctors rather than midwives, as Queen Catherine would be that same September. It was not impossible that in Elizabeth's case a cover-up occurred and a child was born. Pregnancies could be—and were—hidden, even in the full glare of the court.* If such a child existed, however, it was very well concealed and the truth was never discovered. But the fact that Catherine sent her stepdaughter away, and that Elizabeth then took to her bed at Cheshunt, did little to hinder the rumor mill.

* Elizabeth's own mother was several months pregnant before her marriage was announced. Her cousin, Catherine Grey, was close to full term when she finally confessed her pregnancy at Elizabeth's court.

Chapter Eleven

THE LITTLE KNAVE

By the time that Elizabeth left Hanworth in June 1548, Catherine was six months pregnant. The queen would place her hand on the tiny life in her womb, "to feel it stir," and speak soothingly to her unborn child.[1] The baby kicked "like an honest man" both in the morning and in the evening, delighting its mother, who was reassured by each fluttering movement. Only days earlier, Catherine had been happily sharing these experiences with Thomas, telling him that "when ye come it will make you some pastime." Yet her husband had instead looked for his pastime with Elizabeth, and although the queen could not upbraid him in public she dwelled on that fact.

They set out for Sudeley on 13 June, as planned. Moving slowly down dry, rutted roads, the household looked more like a procession, snaking its way through villages and into the countryside as it left the environs of London far behind. The queen, naturally enough, attracted attention wherever she went. She was glad finally to arrive at the place where her baby was to be born. The castle was visible for miles from the high London road, lying in a wooded valley close to the town of Winchcombe in Gloucestershire.[2]

The idea of Sudeley was a romantic one for Thomas. Although a manor house had long stood on the site, whose outline was still visible in the grass of the park, the castle was only a hundred years old. It appealed to Seymour that it had been constructed on naval gold. Ralph Boteler, the first Lord Sudeley, had become rich as an admiral in the French wars of Henry V and Henry VI.[3] That one of the towers was named after a French ship captured and ransomed by his famous predecessor captured Thomas's imagination.

The first Lord Sudeley had built a palace rather than a fortress, with blue-green beryl used in place of glass in the round windows of the great hall. It was opulent and splendid. Dark rumors of treason also hung over the castle. It was later reported that Boteler, on riding to London to make his peace with the Yorkist King Edward IV, had looked back at his mansion and declared: "Sudeley Castle, thou art a traitor, not I," before passing it to the king in return for his freedom. For Thomas, there was this added frisson of rebelliousness in the place, Boteler having earlier been one of the leading advisers to the young Lancastrian King Henry VI.

Sudeley Castle had been in a poor state when Seymour acquired it in February 1547, but he had then made it fit for his and Catherine's quasi-royal dynasty.[4] In this effort, Thomas had acquired the help of his friend and second cousin by marriage Sir William Sharington, who was a Norfolk man by birth and nearly twenty years his kinsman's senior.* Sharington had heavily lidded and

* Sharington's first wife was Ursula, an illegitimate daughter of John Bourchier, the 2nd Lord Berners. Bourchier was the son of Elizabeth Tylney, Countess of Surrey, who was the half-sister of Thomas's maternal grandmother, Anne Say. Sharington's father-in-law and Seymour's mother were therefore first cousins.

uneven eyes and arching thick eyebrows, surmounting a broad, round face, which was lengthened slightly by a bushy brown beard. This last he kept trimmed back below his mouth before allowing it to grow curly over his neck.[5] He habitually dressed plainly. His one great passion in life was building, on which he spent lavishly.

Sharington had secured the grant of Lacock Abbey in Bedfordshire following Henry VIII's dissolution of the monasteries, at first taking up residence in the abbess's house while he made a plan of works.[6] With the help of the builder John Chapman, who had previously been employed in the king's works, he set about transforming his new residence into a building that rivaled even the ambitions of Somerset Place on the Strand.[7] Broad-shouldered Sharington was always a contradiction: plain-living, yet overseeing the most ornate house in England; quiet in his tastes, yet marrying three times; a pillar of the local community and yet—beneath the veneer—a common thief, for the funds for his extravagant building works were not acquired honestly. Sharington was cunning. He was just the kind of fellow Seymour, with his underhanded schemes, needed, and Thomas was drawn to his older kinsman.

Lacock Abbey, with its French-inspired classical detailing, was an exorbitantly expensive marvel. Its Cotswold stone and large windows spoke to the world of their owner's exquisite taste.[8] Sharington's renovations began in the southern range close to the wall of the destroyed abbey church. He wanted to build a modern home, producing his own characteristically "Sharingtonian" style, with its fine gable-coping, square-headed doorways, and transomed windows with panes dividing into four large panels.[9] His approach was unique and tasteful, and Sharington was much in demand as a designer.

Early in 1547, Thomas had engaged Sharington to make the sixty-mile journey to Sudeley to oversee the fine alterations planned there. Seymour trusted him so much that he gave him nearly £3,000 to spend on works at both Sudeley and his other house at Bromham. Others, too, hoped to engage Seymour's friend for their own projects. He had been kept busy for over a year, and he was now present in the West Country as Seymour and Catherine made their way toward Sudeley in June 1548.

The castle that greeted Thomas and Catherine was also a Cotswold stone building, set amid pretty parkland and ornate gardens. Sharington had been busy on Thomas's behalf, his hand visible in the fine augmentation of the east range, which sat in the inner courtyard of the castle close to its very heart.* The rooms there were palatial, as visitors would discover after being led through the elaborate outer wall of the castle into the newly remodeled grand apartments. The queen could enter through a small corridor from the ground floor, where she would find herself in a compact outer chamber leading into the large principal room. It was dominated by a great bay window, looking out on the courtyard and onto anyone approaching the building.

In the winter this room could be heated by the great fireplace; in the summer, guests could note the view of the lush green gardens from three ornate windows on the opposite side of the room to the bay window. Up a narrow spiral staircase there was a fine presence chamber, where Catherine could receive visitors. The ceiling rose two stories high, and light flooded the room through a huge window. Additional windows stretched from floor to ceiling, giving the impression almost of being out in the open. At one end of this chamber was a private room, where occupants could retire alone, for peace. At the other end was a private chapel, so minute that to reach it, visitors had to squeeze past a fireplace built precariously next to a doorway, clutching their clothing close to avoid the spluttering flames.

---

* Emery identifies the east range, which was heavily altered, to be the richest part of Sudeley Castle. He suggests that these changes can be linked to royalty. Although he identifies Richard III as the likely instigator, it seems more probable that the changes were made for Catherine Parr at Thomas Seymour's behest. The design of the windows is similar to that at Lacock, and this, coupled with the fact that Seymour paid £1,100 to Sharington to rebuild Sudeley, means that it is likely the changes were newly made in 1548.

These rooms at Sudeley were all fine ones, yet Catherine did not choose them for her own residence. Instead, she selected a more intimate suite almost in the center of the castle, behind a comfortable anteroom in which she could sit with her ladies. The queen, who was always conscious of her royal status, wanted both privacy and comfort as the time of her confinement neared.

For company, Catherine had many of those she loved around her. Her beloved sister made the journey to be with her, as did her friend Elizabeth Tyrwhitt, who shared her radical religious views. Although the absence of Princess Elizabeth left a gap in the household, it could partially be filled by Jane Grey, who was approaching eleven years old and who was now the only other royal lady in Catherine's household. Catherine was coming to rely on Jane as her closest companion, while Jane truly loved and admired her guardian, honoring her memory to the end of her own brief life.* She flourished under Catherine and Thomas's care, enjoying, as she put it, the "great goodness" that they had shown her "from time to time."[10] For her, Seymour had "been towards me a loving and kind father," while Catherine became a second mother. Jane recognized the great benefits that they had heaped upon her and was "ready to obey" their "godly monitions and good instructions" as any grateful daughter should. She was not and could never be, however, Catherine's daughter. As her own baby stirred in the womb, the queen's thoughts turned once again to her royal stepchildren.

Catherine had not seen Princess Mary for more than a year by the time she arrived at Sudeley. She had made overtures of friendship before, but was aware that the wound caused by her seemingly hasty marriage to Seymour was still open.[11] Already in her late thirties, Catherine feared the risks of her confinement and she

* Jane received Catherine's prayer book on the queen's death. When Jane was in the Tower awaiting execution in 1554, she passed the book to her sister, also named Catherine, informing her that "I have here sent you, good sister Katherine, a book, which although it be not outwardly trimmed with gold, yet inwardly it is more worth than precious stones" (*Harleian Miscellany*, Vol. I, p. 372).

knew that there was a chance that she would not survive the birth. She therefore reached out again to Mary that summer in letters. To her satisfaction, the princess, who missed Catherine, happily replied, indicating that she was once again Catherine's "humble and assured loving daughter."[12] Longing to be a mother herself, Mary was pleased for her stepmother and wrote, trusting "to hear good success of Your Grace's great belly."* She was relieved, she said, "to hear of your health, which I pray almighty God to continue and increase to His pleasure, as much as your own heart can desire." As well as agreeing to act as godmother for the expected baby, Mary went so far as to ask Catherine "to take the pain to make my commendations to My Lord Admiral." Letters such as this were joyful to Catherine, but they must also have helped to bring home the fact that she was separated from Elizabeth—to whom she had more fully been a mother.

Elizabeth was still on her sickbed at Cheshunt when she plucked up the courage to write to her stepmother. She agonized over doing so, aware of the damage that had been done to the relationship and that Catherine, who was both unwell and emotional, was "not quiet to read."[13] Nonetheless, she hoped to salvage the relationship, as she had done when she had previously been left behind at Hanworth in the autumn of 1547. She was grateful for the queen's efforts to preserve her reputation in not publishing the reason for her departure, even if the rumors still circulated. The girl sounded truly remorseful in her letter, continuing: "but what may I more say than thank God for providing such friends to me, desiring God to enrich me with their long life, and me grace to be in heart no less thankful to receive it than I now am glad in writing to show it." It was a tentative letter. She must have worried about just how it would be received.

---

* The princess, fond of her stepmother, later took mementos from Catherine's personal possessions when she became queen herself. Carley (pp. 141–142) notes that Mary acquired most of Catherine's books, including her religious works: in spite of their differences in belief, Mary remembered Catherine as a "spiritual mentor."

Catherine did not herself respond to the letter. In early July, however, Elizabeth received an unexpected letter from Seymour, who apologized for not corresponding sooner.[14] She was polite—even friendly—in her reply, declaring that he "needed not to send an excuse to me" and confirming that she recognized his "goodwill" toward her. She could not consider him unkind, she said, assuring him "for I am a friend not won with trifles, nor lost with the like." Although she assured Thomas of her continuing goodwill, it was Catherine who was on her mind. Could he please humbly commend her to his wife, to whom she had not yet dared to write again? She was, she promised him, his "assured friend to my little power."

The correspondence between the pair was most likely a test, Elizabeth's conventional—and appropriate—response a key to Catherine admitting her once again as a daughter. The queen wanted to heal the rift before her confinement. This letter opened the floodgates to the affection between stepmother and daughter, with Catherine writing several letters to Elizabeth over the following weeks. The princess was ecstatic, admitting that each missive was "most joyful to me in absence yet, considering what pain it is to you to write, Your Grace being so great with child, and so sickly, your commendation were enough in My Lord's letter."[15]

In spite of their rapprochement, there was still much that remained unsaid as messengers hurried between Sudeley and Cheshunt. Catherine kept her letters to safe subjects, writing of her health and her newfound love of the countryside around Sudeley. She also missed the teenage girl deeply, speaking of her longing to have her with her again, although she did not dare to send for her. Reassured and gratified, Elizabeth assured Catherine that she would never leave her company voluntarily, even should residence at Sudeley begin to feel stale to her (something Catherine had feared might happen, had Elizabeth stayed in the household). Elizabeth wished she could be there to assist the queen during her impending confinement. When the queen wrote proudly of the child's somersaults in the womb, Elizabeth replied that if she could only attend "his" birth she would "see him beaten, for the trouble he hath put you to."

The tone of the correspondence was jovial and affectionate. Elizabeth was so certain of Catherine's forgiveness that she even dared mention Kate Ashley, to whom the queen ascribed the lion's share of the blame for the preceding events. Both Elizabeth's lady mistress and the Dennys sent their prayers for "a most lucky deliverance," she assured her stepmother. Basking in Catherine's forgiveness, Elizabeth almost forgot Seymour, asking only that he keep her informed "from time to time" of "how his busy child doth" when the queen was unable to write. She might have found Thomas both fascinating and attractive, but it was her stepmother who provided the emotional warmth on which she thrived. Catherine's "humble daughter" looked hopefully toward a return to the maternal fold once the birth was safely out of the way.

Catherine still had one other royal stepchild left with whom she longed for direct contact, as did Thomas. Although now far from Hampton Court, Thomas retained a strong influence with young Edward, thanks to the good offices of John Fowler. Seymour kept the flow of money steadily trickling toward the gentleman, who repaid him by regularly nagging the king to thank Seymour for the gentleness that he showed him and "for his money."[16] Fowler was always praising the admiral in the boy's presence.

Thomas wrote to Fowler on 15 July 1548, soliciting a letter from Edward for the queen, who missed her stepson.[17] Fowler showed the letter to Edward, who felt sufficiently guilty for his lack of contact with his "dear mother" that he purloined a tiny scrap of paper and scribbled a note to his uncle, declaring: "My Lord thank you and pray you to have me recommended to the queen," before dating it from Hampton Court on 18 July and signing it "Edward."[18] His motives were, perhaps, not solely affectionate, since he had come to rely on his uncle's largesse to make the financial gifts expected of a king to his servants. On another scrap the young king also scribbled: "My Lord send me for Latimer* as much as ye think good and deliver it to Fowler. Edward."[19] Nonetheless, since Somerset closely monitored both Edward's visitors and his access to pen and paper, these two scraps were a considerable victory. The boy spent so little time alone that, although he protested that he would like to write more fully to the queen, he never had even half an hour to himself. And Catherine was certainly not on his approved list of correspondents.

John Fowler kept Edward's notes hidden away overnight, before writing a more fulsome letter to his patron the next day, proudly enclosing the two "small lines of recommendation" written with the king's "own hand." There was little else for him to report in a court that had largely closed for business in the summer heat and plague-affected city. There were some concerns over the campaign in Scotland, but this was of little import to Thomas, immersed in domesticity at Sudeley.

At the same time, Fowler passed on the news that the Duchess of Somerset "is brought to bed of a goodly boy" and, diplomatically, trusted "in Almighty God the Queen's Grace shall have another." It was a testament to the frosty relationship between the Seymour brothers that no official announcement was made to Thomas of his nephew's birth. Somerset took the opportunity of his brother's absence to try to break into his network of connections. He promised the mercenary Fowler that he could have his choice of the keepership of various Sussex parks. The atmosphere at court was hostile enough toward the admiral that Fowler implored Thomas to keep his letter secret, to ensure that it "shall tell no more tales after your reading; for now I write at length to Your Lordship, because I am promised of a trusty messenger." Their dealings were furtive

* This was Bishop Hugh Latimer, who served as one of Edward's chaplains and whom the king wished to reward for preaching before him. The fanatically Protestant churchman, who proved no friend to Seymour, would be burned in 1555, during the reign of Mary.

that summer, as Thomas attempted from Sudeley to keep his hold on the young king's affections.

Both Catherine and Seymour were pleased with Edward's notes, taking the time to discuss the boy, whose growth into manhood they both looked forward to. As at Hanworth, the queen walked in the gardens each day in an attempt to keep her weight down and her body healthy. In summer's bloom, the grounds were lush. Catherine could wander out to the little chapel, some distance from the castle, or walk along the graveled paths or dew wet grass.

One day, Catherine was strolling with her kinsman Sir Robert Tyrwhitt in the park. He was one of her highest-ranking officers, who ensured the smooth running of her household and payments to her servants, and whom she could trust with her money.[20] She was fond of the dour household officer and his wife, both of whom shared her reformist religious beliefs. That day, as they ambled through the grass, she spoke plainly with him, criticizing the Protector's habit of granting away Crown lands to his supporters. When the king comes of age, she said, she was certain that "he will call his lands again, as fast as they be now given from him."[21] Tyrwhitt, who had the castle in view as he walked, raised an eyebrow to this. Surely, he commented, Sudeley would also be taken back from Thomas? Catherine and her husband had already discussed such a possibility, and now she laughed: "marry, I do assure you, he intends to offer them to the king, and give them freely to him at that time." Since they were busily (and expensively) trying to establish the fine building as their baronial seat, such a willing gift to the king was unlikely. But they probably hoped that making the gesture would be enough to ensure continuing royal favor should Somerset's regime begin to unravel. Thomas had been granted several properties from the king's lands and he cannot have truly desired to return them when the boy reached eighteen.

Supporting Catherine's royal household took money, as did the regular bribes to the king and his servants, so Thomas expected his manors to earn their keep. He was, accordingly, interested in the smooth running of his estates. There were deer to be driven in the parks and livestock to be sold. His sheep were diligently stamped with the letter "S" as a demonstration of his ownership.[22] Seymour was enterprising, employing twenty-three men on one Sussex manor to keep his furnaces going to cast raw iron, before sending it to London to fetch a good price.[23] He had great money-making schemes. In 1547 he had already pushed his friend Sharington into Parliament, for Sussex, to assist in his scheme to build a town in the county, on forest land that had belonged to Sele Priory.[24] Seymour handled the negotiations himself and also fixed upon the site—although the town, like so many of his plans, never came to fruition.

Thomas continued, however, to be involved in Sharington's ambitions of a more criminal nature. By 1548, Sharington was dividing his time between Lacock, Sudeley—and Bristol, where he had the official position as Under-Treasurer of the Mint.[25] Since the boy-king was officially the treasurer at Bristol, the under-treasurer effectively controlled the mint at Bristol, the only mint outside London authorized to strike gold as well as silver coins. Sharington did so in great numbers, much of his coinage destined to be shipped to Ireland to line purses there. These were the official issue; but he was determined to profit himself from his position.

In the spring of 1548, Sharington began minting testoons—silver shilling pieces—bearing his own initials "WS" and the mark of the Bristol mint as well as a bust of Henry VIII. These small coins were worth three times as much as the more common groat. Sharington's issue looked entirely official, but it was not. He had already received an official command from Sir Edmund Peckam, High Treasurer of the Mints in England, to cease production of the official issue of the coins, which were relatively new additions to the currency. Yet Sharington needed the cash—as he later confessed—to have "more money in my hands" to spend at the St. James's Day fair at Bristol.[26] He wanted to buy silver at this two-week event, which began on 25 July and was the highlight of Bristol's civic calendar. His testoons, minted in 1548, were therefore counterfeits.

Sharington was able to mint at least £300 worth of testoons after the order to cease production, without anyone in authority noticing, while at the same time he kept the mint busy with an official issue of groats for Ireland. Thomas Seymour was already well aware of Sharington's activities in Bristol. Not long after the old king had died, he had sent a servant carrying £500 of silver groats to the coiner as a favor to his kinsman. As Thomas knew, Sharington required silver to melt down, and Sharington paid for it with £500 in other coin. The admiral also promised to send him some of his own silver plate to melt down, intending to enter into a business relationship with Sharington.[27]

Thomas was very interested in his friend's ability to produce counterfeits. One day during the summer of 1548, he was walking with Sharington when he turned to him and asked "what money he could make him [i.e., Sharington] if need were?"[28] Thinking for a moment, Sharington suggested about £400. "Tush," said Thomas dismissively, "that is but a little; but what could you make me?" This was a different matter entirely since Seymour, with his plate and access to silver, could provide a very ready source of the raw materials for coining. Sharington considered before answering that at short notice it would be hard for him to make the admiral much more than that, "but if you give me a little warning, I shall be able to make you so much as I have stuff to make it." This was what Seymour wanted to hear, and he asked his friend to begin collecting together into his hands as much coinage as he could. Sharington's secret operation was going to get considerably more busy, since Seymour firmly believed that with a "mass of money ready" a man "might do somewhat withal."

Although absent from London, Seymour continued to dwell on the wrongs he believed his brother had done him. His lawyer, Richard Weston, had tried to arrange a meeting of lawyers to discuss the case of Catherine's jewels. But there was plague in the Temple—the legal heart of London—and many of the lawyers that Thomas's servants had sounded out about the case were out of town and unavailable. In July 1548 Weston wrote to Seymour, asking if the matter could wait until Thomas returned to London, so that he too could escape the diseased air of the capital.[29] With nothing resolved, the Seymour brothers spent the summer sniping at each other by letter, while Catherine awaited the birth of her baby.

Chapter Twelve

LET ME BE NO MORE

For royal women, the last month of pregnancy was spent in the quiet of their chamber. Queen Catherine retired to hers, at Sudeley, in early August 1548. Many years before, Edward's great-grandmother, the domineering Margaret Beaufort, had set down a set of ordinances by which she expected royal mothers to live. Catherine—anxious to preserve her status—would not have deviated from them. Thus, her male household officers were replaced by female ones as she rested and waited to bear her expected son.

While Catherine ceased to appear in public during that long dry summer at Sudeley, a near constant stream of messengers to the castle ensured that Thomas was kept occupied.* That July, the

* The summer of 1548 was notable for a "great drought for lack of rain" (Wriothesley, Vol. II., p. 5).

Protector had been troubled by the news of a French army off the coast of Scotland. On 7 July, the five-year-old Mary, Queen of Scots, was betrothed to the French dauphin: the "rough wooing" to bring about a marriage between Edward and Mary seemed to have failed. There were now at least eighteen French galleys, sailing with nearly two hundred other ships, all sitting low in the water, carrying a force of seven thousand armed men.[1] Hurriedly, Somerset ordered a royal fleet of eighty ships to be prepared. Once again, he preferred Lord Clinton as commander to his brother.[2] The English fleet, with its modern galleasses—paid for with the funds lavished on the navy by Henry VIII—was a force to be reckoned, so Lord Clinton had reasons to be confident. The difficulty would come with actually locating the French, who were rumored to be planning a quick landing in Scotland to spirit Queen Mary away to France. While the English fleet was smaller, Clinton, with his brash, seafaring air, was "extremely confident," since his ships were so well fitted out. It was just the sort of mission that Seymour would have appreciated; but he was excluded from it.[3]

Nonetheless, his office kept him busy in other ways, and Thomas continued, while at Sudeley, to take an active interest in ships and their cargoes. On 19 July 1548 he wrote to the Mayor of Waterford to order him to deliver a captured pirate ship into his servant's custody.[4] He took great pains to ensure that the vessel and a smaller boat should be delivered "with all the goods in them," and that they should then be conveyed to him along with "all such men as were in them both at the time your first stay of them." On 23 July 1548 he wrote again to the mayor, having heard that two ships—one Portuguese and one Spanish—had been captured by pirates, before being retaken when they attempted to dock at Waterford.[5] He sent his servant, Thomas Woodlock, to obtain the two ships, as well as their captains, taking the thieves and their booty into his own hands. In return for the compliance of the mayor (his "loving friend"), Seymour offered his goodwill and aid in any private matter.

Earlier, in June, Seymour was also enriched with £200 from the profits of his ironworks in Sussex—a sum that testified to the success of his enterprises there.[6] He also continued to try to build support, sending Lord Russell warrants to take two bucks from Enfield Chase as a gift, to which the peer gave "hearty thanks."[7]

Yet outside problems also kept intruding on the summer domesticity at Sudeley. On 16 July, Seymour sent a terse note to a correspondent demanding payment of a debt owed to the queen.[8] The previous month, he found himself dragged into an unfortunate dispute following his sale of Yanworth manor in Gloucestershire to a man named Bush.[9] Although Seymour sold the manor as his own, he was astounded to hear that another gentleman, Thomas Culpeper, claimed it. With time on his hands, Seymour did some digging around, finding out that several manors had been settled on Culpeper's kinsman Thomas Culpeper the Younger in remainder.* These had been forfeited to the Crown when the young man was found to have been involved in an adulterous relationship with Henry's fifth wife, Catherine Howard. As far as Thomas was concerned, the manors were rightfully his own to sell. He wrote to his brother's secretary, William Cecil, to so "use the matter so that I have no cause to be further troubled to sue for any recompense on behalf of Bush."

Thomas had parted from his brother on poor terms. Their relations remained ice-cold, even though their written conversations were as hot as the sweltering August sun. The Lord Protector stayed at Hampton Court into the first week of August, finishing up business before he sailed upriver for Sheen.[10] Somerset—honoring his brother's title of Lord Admiral if not the authority that went with it—kept him scrupulously informed of military events. He wrote in August that the loss of life they had expected in Scotland was

* "remainder"—a trust. One individual was entitled to the profits of the manor for life, with another entitled "in remainder" (i.e., receiving the manor after the life tenant's death).

not as great as feared.[11] He was pleased to see from Thomas's letter that his brother showed a "good bearing of the last evil chance in Scotland which in deed is nothing so evil as we first thought."[12] Nonetheless, the war with Scotland was not going well. The French, still insisting that "they break no peace" with England, yet offered considerable provocation that August when they fired on the pier at English-held Boulogne.[13]

Somerset, along with the rest of the Council, now wished Seymour to marshal his ships in Devon and Cornwall to go to sea against the French. Seymour immediately wrote to his vice admirals, informing them that it was better to take the initiative "with such suspicious friends rather than to suffer injuries and sustain costs."[14]

Nonetheless, the idea of his navy taking preemptive action against the French pleased Seymour. He was all for it, condemning them for their "open enmity at sea and their feigned profession of friendship since communication between Your Grace and their ambassadors and our ambassador and the French king." He wrote to his brother and the Council on 11 August to confirm that his ships intended to "distress their fleet of Newfoundland fish": French ships had been returning from the New World with fish for market. Thomas, like his brother, hoped that the fish—packed in ice to keep them fresh—would soon be sold in markets along the English coast, rather than destined for French tables.[15] His vice admirals were quickly writing of their good success in tackling the French, reports that contrasted pleasingly for Seymour with his rival Clinton's failure in Scotland:* That summer, almost under the noses of the English, the little Queen of Scots landed in France, accompanied by "a great number of ladies and gentlemen."[16] Thomas's own fleet was not entirely successful, however—it failed to find the fish.

Even when the Seymour brothers were in agreement about naval matters, they could not resist sniping at each other, with each

* Although the talk among the English garrison in Calais was that "the Lord Admiral and Lord Clinton were chiefly to blame for the French galleys getting back to France from Scotland without molestation" (Gruffydd, p. 59).

determined to be the true master of the Admiralty. An opportunity arrived for Somerset in the complaint of a seasoned ship's captain, one Matthew Hull.[17] Ordinarily the Protector, immersed in his war against the Scots and quarrels with the French, would pass such matters to a subordinate. But he was usually ready to hear the worst against his brother, as many knew. Now, sitting at his writing desk at Sheen on 16 August 1548, Somerset surveyed Hull, standing before him, who was waiting to carry a letter.

Hull had a sad tale to tell. He owned a ship, available for hire, with good space for merchandise to be stowed beneath the heaving decks. Standing before Somerset, he swore to him that he had had no reason to be suspicious about the men who had come to him looking for a ship to carry their cargo. What Hull did not know, he assured the Protector, was that the men had insured their goods for four times what they were actually worth. The men were intending that the ship, and the goods, should be lost at sea, so that *he* would suffer but they would gain very substantially.

Hull was rather vague on the details of exactly how this plot had been discovered by Thomas Seymour's men, but he was furious when *both* the goods and the ship were impounded and declared forfeited to the Admiralty. Hull's specific complaint was that "not only his furnishings is detained from him but also that he is troubled in the Admiralty court alleging that he would have taken away his own ship with the goods in the same." This was hardly an unreasonable belief for the court to hold, given the facts of the case: it was rather hard to wreck a ship without the collusion of the captain and crew.

Thomas's own deputy, Anthony Hussey, believed that Hull had agreed to spirit away the cargo and the ship, keeping them both, while his co-conspirators would claim for their goods on the insurance. He intended to prosecute Hull for this in court. But Somerset believed Hull's story. Arousing Thomas's anger, he turned the matter into an attack on Seymour's loyal deputy, the Protector complaining that Hussey "hath not behaved himself uprightly now or other matters also wherein we may charge him unto you." In Somerset's judgment, Matthew Hull was wronged, and Hussey's conduct in the "troubling of this poor man" amounted to little more than harassment.

Sealing his letter, Somerset passed it to Hull and bid him ride to Sudeley to deliver it in person. Matters would soon be straightened out, he assured him, since the Protector "required" his brother to write to Hussey "commanding him without further delay to see that the said Matthew Hull may be answered for his freight." He signed his command "your loving brother," but there was nothing but contempt in the missive's contents. If Thomas were going to continue to allow his Admiralty to wrong men such as Hull, Somerset would step in. It perhaps did not occur to Somerset that Hull's keen interest in the freight—which did not belong to him—rather than just his ship suggested more guilt in the matter than he would admit to.

Matthew Hull's complaint had already touched on another point of contention between the two brothers. A few days earlier, Seymour had written on behalf of Francis Agarde, one of his servants.[18] Agarde had found himself embroiled in murky goings-on between a man named Leche and his father. There had been a disagreement over the "lewd life of Leche's wife," which had placed the patrimony in danger. Doubtful of his daughter in law's honor, the older Leche had determined "to part with the land rather than bastards should be his heirs." Agarde, on hearing of this, had rushed in to bargain for the property; but there were attempts made by the Leche family—on reflection—to set the contract aside.

On 13 August, Somerset responded, patronizingly declaring to his younger brother that Agarde "hath abused you," before dismissing the man's concerns.[19] He wrote that he had examined the matter personally and found in favor of the plaintiff, content that he would not look into the private life of Leche and his wife in such a matter. The response infuriated Thomas, who stewed over the matter for some days—and then received the surprise of Somerset's imperious commands regarding Matthew Hull. It was not until 19 August that Seymour felt able to write his sniffy reply, informing his brother that, in spite of the lawfulness of Agarde's position, "I shall make no further importune to Your Grace therewith but only admit therefore that this man at whose request I wrote is surely honest." He was hurt. Somerset would not even bend slightly to favor a servant of his brother in one simple matter. Indeed, he actively favored those who set themselves in opposition to the Admiral and his servants. In an age where nepotism was positively encouraged, this was hardly the action of a "loving brother," as the Protector persisted in describing himself.

Thomas Seymour was also angered at his brother's refusal to see his own opinions as anything other than infallible. Reading through Somerset's letter of 16 August, Thomas was surprised to see that it was meant to have been carried by Matthew Hull himself: yet this "named bearer" had been nowhere in sight.[20] For Thomas, this was proof of Hull's guilt. The man was obviously too ashamed to appear before him. Unlike the Protector, Seymour had come across Hull before and knew considerably more about his dabbles in piracy than his brother, thanks to a confession he had received from a notorious pirate named Kelley. Indeed, as Seymour admonished Somerset, his brother should have known that, since he had himself traveled up to Chelsea the previous summer to examine that matter in Catherine's gardens there.

Intent on proving that Hull had fooled his brother, Seymour carried out his own investigation at Sudeley. Within only three or four days, he was gleefully able to inform Somerset that Hull was both "the principal in the piracy" and deeply involved with Kelley. Indeed, he had the evidence to prove it. As far as Seymour was concerned, his brother was out of touch with the Admiralty.* Thomas would follow the letter of his brother's commands but go no further. He also asked the Protector to be fair to Hussey in such

* Somerset's correspondence incorrectly identified Seymour's chief naval officers. Anthony Hussey was Minister of the Admiralty, and, as Seymour happily pointed out to his brother, it was Dr. Griffin Lyson who served as his chief judge. Seymour informed his brother that he had asked Hussey to be just in his dealings, as Somerset requested; but he did not take the initiative and contact Lyson regarding the matter.

a case where "a dishonest man is his accuser in an unjust suit," thus openly criticizing his brother's misguided belief in Matthew Hull.

For a few days at least, Thomas Seymour satisfied himself that he held the upper hand in his poisonous correspondence with his brother. It was to be a small victory, though. Somerset, in his next letter, forced himself to agree that there might just be some truth in the accusations against Hull. Indeed, he thought it best that Seymour "give such order that the said goods be put in safe custody till it be further known whether it be pirate goods or no."[21] Most likely, though, as far as the Protector was concerned, Hull and his fellow sailors had been deceived by the "false and crafty" men who had sought to rob their insurers.

A steady stream of messages continued to flow between the brothers over the summer. On 27 August, bursting with fury, Thomas finally set out his complaints on paper, snarling that Somerset always seemed to take everyone else's side. It took Somerset some days to feel cool enough to reply.

Thomas Seymour's emotional state was not helped by the tense wait for news of his wife's labor. It was the same for Elizabeth, whose health continued to be poor at Cheshunt, although she was beginning to build a friendship with her host, Lady Denny.* Elizabeth last wrote to Catherine on 31 July, before her stepmother retired for her month of rest and waiting. The princess looked forward to news of what she hoped would be "a most lucky deliverance," resulting in the birth of a healthy little stepbrother.[22]

* The pair were close enough that, in her only surviving accounts from the period, Elizabeth gave Lady Denny the substantial sum of £100 on 12 July 1552, with the record of the payment tucked away between gifts to servants and payments for the bringing of New Year's gifts. Noticeably, payments of the same period to Elizabeth's ladies, such as Blanche Parry, were in shillings rather than pounds—the payment to Lady Denny was a considerable one (Strangford, p. 37).

The queen's impending labor was discussed at Cheshunt by Elizabeth and the ladies around her. Everyone was hopeful. Elizabeth had considerable confidence in Catherine's doctor, Robert Huicke, who had served for some years as a royal physician and in whom she had been happy to entrust her own care when ill.[23] Catherine was also pleased to bring Huicke with her to Sudeley—by then, he had served her dutifully for several years.[24] The doctor had his own reasons for welcoming the change of scene. He had only recently been the subject of a famous divorce case, where he had been censured for his cruelty toward his entirely blameless wife. Despite the gossip on that score, he was renowned for his skill in medicine and had been one of the physicians admitted to the old king's deathbed. Huicke was admired in Catherine's household. Now he consulted with her, as the birth drew near.

The child who had been so active in Catherine's womb finally entered the world on 30 August 1548, in the privacy of the queen's darkened bedchamber at Sudeley. The birth, attended by doctors and female household members, went well. There was no hint that the parents were in any way disappointed to discover that their "little knave" was a girl. They delighted in the child, naming her "Mary" in honor of her eldest royal stepsister, who was to be her godmother.

The day of the birth was hectic, with Seymour rushing in to meet his daughter as the queen tried to speak to Dr. Huicke about her recovery. It was the action of an excited first-time father—but in shooing away the doctor, Thomas later laid himself open to criticism. Catherine had not dared to speak up then, but later, as Elizabeth Tyrwhitt remembered, she plaintively told her husband: "My Lord, I would have given a thousand marks to have had my full talk with Huicke the first day I was delivered. But I durst not, for displeasing of you."[25] Thomas, who—like Catherine—was old to be a first-time parent, just wanted to see his child, pushing all obstacles out of his path. He was besotted with the tiny infant, who lay in her cradle of crimson and gold.[26] She was so pretty, he wrote to his brother, while the queen, too, was doing well. The Protector was still his brother and the first person to whom he wanted to tell his good news. He dispatched his letter posthaste.

Somerset had just dispatched one of his own angry letters to his brother on 1 September, when Thomas's letter announcing the birth arrived later the same day. Fatherhood was far from new to Somerset, and his brother's gushing description of his daughter must have made him smile. Putting aside the pervasive ill feeling, he wrote to congratulate Thomas on his becoming "the father of so pretty a daughter."[27] He was glad, he said, that the queen had enjoyed a "happy hour" and was past danger, although even then, at the moment of Thomas's great happiness, he could not resist a criticism. "It would have been, both to us and, as we suppose, also to you, a more joy and comfort if it had been—this, the first—a son." He himself was already the father of several fine sons, one of whom had been born only weeks earlier.[28] Somerset was sure, however, that, in subsequent pregnancies Catherine would fulfill her dynastic duty.

For Catherine, lying exhausted in her bed on 30 August, the idea that this birth was but the prelude to what Somerset described as "a great sort of happy sons" might have seemed less appealing than her brother-in-law supposed. After decades of barren marriages, she must have felt a sense of achievement as she looked at her tiny daughter, sleeping in her cradle, the daughter of a queen. Catherine felt surprisingly well after the birth. It was confidently reported that she had escaped all danger and that she would soon be up and about.[29] Such reports, however, were quickly revealed to be premature.

On the morning of 3 September, Elizabeth Tyrwhitt came to her friend in the dark, stuffy bedchamber, where only one small window remained uncovered, allowing a glint of sunlight. There she found Catherine sweating with fever in the great bed in the center of the room, and attended by Thomas, who held tightly on to her hand. By now, the cradle had been moved to the nursery. Elizabeth Tyrwhitt entered quietly, so as not to disturb her friend.[30] Yet the queen called out to her, asking where she had been for so long. Before giving Lady Tyrwhitt time to answer, Catherine whispered that "she did fear such things in herself, that she was sure she could not live." She was burning with fever and in pain, ignoring her friend's assurance that she "saw no likelihood of death in her."

Thomas's presence seemed to confirm his concern for his wife, but Catherine's mind was troubled by him. Without glancing at her friend, she breathed: "My Lady Tyrwhitt, I am not well handled, for those that be about me careth not for me, but standeth laughing at my grief. And the more good I will to them, the less good they will to me." She seemed delirious, but Thomas took her words seriously, conscious that he was not the only one to hear them. "Why, sweetheart, I would you no hurt," he answered, sitting at her side. But Catherine, speaking more loudly, declared: "No, My Lord, I think so." He leaned closer to her, perhaps hoping to silence her accusations, and the queen whispered hoarsely—yet audibly—in her husband's ear: "But, My Lord, you have given me many shrewd taunts."

Elizabeth Tyrwhitt heard everything and considered Catherine's words, spoken "very sharply and earnestly," to be the mark of a mind that was "unquieted." It might have been the fever, since the queen was probably by now delirious; but her friend believed she spoke with "good memory." Certainly, Catherine was aware enough to know that she was dying. Lady Tyrwhitt and those around Catherine knew of Thomas's jealousy and possessiveness over his wife, and many in the household knew of the former goings-on with Elizabeth.

Glancing around, Thomas, concerned that Catherine's friend had heard what the queen said, pulled her aside and asked her to repeat it. Lady Tyrwhitt, who had little time for Seymour, "declared it plainly to him," to Seymour's discomfiture. Nonetheless, his main concern was with Catherine, and he asked Lady Tyrwhitt what he should do to ease his wife's suffering. He thought that he might lie down beside her on the bed "to look if he could pacify her unquietness with gentle communication." Catherine's friend, aware of the genuine passion that had also existed between the couple, believed that this might be helpful. Seymour climbed into the great bed beside his wife, whose body gave off the burning heat of her fever.

He spoke soothingly to her, but Catherine shushed him after only three or four words, complaining that he had prevented her from speaking to her doctor and all but accusing him of wanting her dead. She continued to rant against her husband for an hour as Seymour tried to quieten and soothe her. Lady Tyrwhitt, who loved the queen, "perceived her trouble to be so great that my heart would serve me to hear no more"; yet she did not think the words were only the ravings of fever. Perhaps for the first time, *in extremis* Catherine dared to speak her furious mind to Seymour; although she was not heard to make any specific mention of his relationship with her stepdaughter, perhaps it was one of the "shrewd taunts" with which she charged him.

Catherine's illness drew out over the days that followed her daughter's birth. The queen's symptoms were alarming.* There was little that the doctors could do but wait and hope that their patient would recover. Thomas was often with her, tired, emotional, and grieving. It was unfortunate that, as the queen lay on her deathbed, Somerset's two letters dated 1 September arrived at Sudeley. The first, which answered Seymour's peeved letter of 27 August, undid all the good work of Thomas's friendly birth announcement. In this letter, Somerset coldly declared that he had received his brother's letter of 27 August, but that "to the particularities whereof at this present we are not minded to answer, because it requireth more leisure than at this time we have."[31] They would speak about it when they were next together. The letter should have ended there, but it did not. The anger crackled from Somerset's carefully composed lines as he complained—using the royal "we" to denote his elevated situation—that "we cannot but marvel that you note the way to be so open for complaints to enter in against you, and that they be so well received." It was hardly his fault, he considered, if

* There was little understanding of the causes of infection and, of course, as yet there were no antibiotics. Catherine was probably suffering from puerperal fever.

Thomas "do so behave yourself amongst your poor neighbours, and others the king's subjects, that they may have easily just cause to complain upon you." He was very sorry, he said, if these complaints came to him, but it was his brother's fault that the men had such just and valid complaints to make in the first place. He continued, saying that he "would wish very heartily it were otherwise; which were both more honour for you, and quiet and joy and comfort for us." Yet, if the complaints came, he would hear them. It was his "duty and office so to do," particularly where they came from those "that findeth or thinketh themselves injured or grieved." He was not going to make allowances for anyone since, "though you be our brother, yet we may not refuse it upon you." As far as Somerset was concerned, the whole sorry business could be remedied if his brother meekly followed his lead in all things.

There had indeed been many complaints about Seymour's behavior that summer as he sought to gain authority over the country around Sudeley. Somerset considered that his brother should try to make friends with his neighbors and "obtain your desire by some other gentle means, rather than by seeking that which is either plain injury, or else the rigour and extremity of the law." He cited the complaints from one neighbor, Sir John Briggs, which he particularly required Thomas to remedy, before signing his letter "your loving brother." It was very bad luck that this letter crossed with Seymour's more emollient letter.

Somerset's championing of Briggs's cause hit a particularly raw nerve. Thomas's servant William Wightman was present when his master received the letter during a break in his vigil over Catherine. He watched as Seymour's face reddened into a "great heat" of fury.[32] Thomas ranted for some time, swearing his customary oath "by God's precious soul!" before declaring that "My Lord, my brother is wondrous hot in helping every man to his right, saving me." His mind turned once again to Catherine's confiscated jewels, complaining that "he maketh a great matter to let me have the queen's jewels, which, you see, by the whole opinion of all the lawyers, ought to belong unto me and all under pretence that he would not the king should lose so much,—as who say it were a loss to the king to let me have mine own?" It seemed so terribly unfair, particularly since, as Seymour roared, his brother "maketh nothing of the loss that the King's Majesty hath by him," declaring that in Somerset's poor dealing with Crown property he had lost Edward at least £10,000 a year.

It seemed like persecution—in Somerset's eyes, Thomas could do no right. Wightman, aware of the dangerous nature of the conversation, jumped in, declaring that he thought the royal lands so lost were "by all men's guesses, far under that sum." Thomas, however, was having none of it, answering: "Well, well, they are at this point now that there can neither bishopric, deanery, nor prebend fall void, but one or other of them will have a fleece of it." Wightman nodded. What Thomas said was largely true, and Wightman agreed that the Deanery of Wells and the Bishopric of Lincoln "had been sore plucked at."

Seymour was placing all his hopes on his nephew. Calming down as suddenly as he had risen to fury, he said: "It maketh no matter, it will come in again when the king cometh to his years, as he beginneth to grow lustily. By God's precious soul! I would not be in some of their coats for five marks when he shall hear of these matters. For mine own part, I will not have a penny after that rate, nor they shall not all be able to charge me with the value of a farthing." Wightman had the last word, cautioning his master that his "evil waiting and slackness in service in this time of the King's Majesty's tender years" did not look good for him, "when one day's service is worth a whole year's." Could he not just do his duty quietly and wait for better times?

Against the background of Somerset's first letter, the second written on 1 September—in which he gave thanks for Catherine's "happy hour"—must have seemed insincere or mocking when Thomas received it, on 3 or 4 September.

By 5 September, the queen, weakened with fever, was declining; everyone knew that she could not live long. She was calmer, though, and had already asked Thomas for his consent to her making a will.* Early that morning, in the presence only of Dr. Huicke and her chaplain John Parkhurst, who prayed with her, she made her will, declaring that she was "lying on her deathbed, sick in body, but of good mind, perfect memory and discretion."[33] Perhaps the fog in her mind had cleared; more likely, she had never been delirious. Still conscious of her status, she called herself "Queen of England, France and Ireland" and "late the wife of Henry VIII, that prince of famous memory." She also referred to Thomas as her current husband, proudly setting his titles alongside those of her previous husband.

Catherine's will shows signs of revision and alteration. It was not admitted to probate until three months after her death, and the surviving document may not accurately reflect the queen's true wishes.[34] If the will was forged, then Thomas, who was the executor who proved the will, was the most likely culprit. On the face of it, the document demonstrated Catherine's enduring love for her husband, the scribe recording that "the said most noble queen, by permission, consent, and assent aforesaid, did not only, with all her heart and desire, frankly and freely give, will, and bequeath to the said Lord Seymour, Lord High Admiral of England, her married espouse and husband, all the goods, chattels, and debts that she then had, or of right ought to have in all the world, wishing them to be a thousand times more in value than they were or been."

Yet, as a wife, Catherine legally owned nothing. The will was largely pointless as a means of conveying property. It was, however, a useful record of her *wishes*, particularly since anything that she "of right ought to have in all the world" potentially included her disputed jewels, still languishing in the royal treasury. Given Dr. Huicke's somewhat dubious character, he might have been persuaded to help in the forgery of a will that made little legal

* A husband's consent was required for a married woman to make her own will since, legally, all property owned by a married couple belonged to the husband.

difference anyway. Thomas did not absolutely *need* the testament; but it was helpful. Since Thomas would not have consented to a will in which he was not the chief beneficiary, it is unlikely that Catherine's original wishes differed substantially from what was written, although the sentiments toward her jealous, possessive, and wayward husband may well have been expressed in different words.

Thomas remained at Catherine's side, holding the hand of a wife who had once wished him "better to fare than myself."[35] There was no final message for Elizabeth, waiting for news at Cheshunt. Instead, the queen spent her last hours praying with Jane Grey, to whom she passed her personal prayer book as a memento. Catherine had continued to write in the tiny book up until her sickness overcame her, breaking off abruptly halfway through a prayer redolent of one in adversity: "all mine hope and whole affiance, most pitiful Lord, have I cast on Thee. Let me be no more, [I pray] Thee, shake off, for [that] were sore to my rebuke [and] shame among [my] enemies. Deliver [and] succour me of Thy [justice]. . . ."[36]

On 5 September 1548, less than a week after she had given birth to her daughter, Catherine Parr slipped quietly away, her auburn hair lying disheveled on her fever-stained pillows. For Thomas Seymour, the death of his wife threw him into a state of grief and confusion. It also changed everything for him. At a stroke, he was once more England's most eligible bachelor. All his plans were suddenly altered.

Part Three

THE SCANDAL UNVEILED

January 1549. In the crisp winter morning, Thomas Seymour pulled his horse in beside that of the elderly Lord Russell, as they rode together the short distance to Parliament. "Father Russell, you are very suspicious of me," he said. "I pray you tell me why?" "My Lord," replied Russell, "I shall earnestly advise you to make no suit for marriage." But surely, mused Seymour, it was better that princesses Mary and Elizabeth "were married within the realm than in any foreign place and without the realm, and why might not I or another made by the king their father marry one of them?"

To the horrorstruck Russell, such a marriage must surely undo anyone, and Thomas Seymour "especially above all others, being of so near alliance to the King's Majesty." How so? asked Thomas. Lord Russell, a man who was a generation older than Seymour, had the weight of history behind him. Because, he said, the king's father and grandfather had both been suspicious princes and "wherefore it may be possible, yea, it is not unlikely but that the King's Majesty following therein the nature of his father and grandfather may be also suspicious."

The Lord Privy Seal was simply saying what everyone thought—that a marriage to a princess would look dangerously as if Thomas Seymour wanted to become king. Furthermore, it would be an unsupportable provocation to a fraternal relationship strained almost beyond endurance.

Chapter Thirteen

HE THAT HATH FRIENDS

Thomas Seymour was hit hard by Catherine's death. He found himself "so amazed" that, as he put it, "I had small regard either to myself or to my doings."[1] In the days following, he could not think straight, although he ordered a fine Protestant funeral for her. On 7 September 1548, in the dying days of summer, the queen was buried, her body carefully embalmed before interment in a lead coffin.[2] She was carried through the leafy gardens to Sudeley's small chapel, its interior now draped in black cloth. By convention, Thomas, being Catherine's husband, was absent from proceedings—although he could have watched the procession from the castle windows. Instead, Jane Grey attended as chief mourner, standing solemnly as the coffin was laid onto trestles surrounded by tapers.

Jane's official role in the funeral would have been Elizabeth's, had she been there. Instead, Elizabeth was still sick in bed at Cheshunt. "Madam, now you may have your husband that was appointed you at the death of the king," announced Elizabeth's lady mistress, breaking the news of Catherine's death with no thought as to the girl's feelings. As for marriage to her stepmother's widower, "nay," declared Elizabeth, shocked, but Kate Ashley continued: "Yes, if all the Council did agree, why not? For he is the noblest man unmarried in this land." It was a cold calculation; but for the moment the princess shied away from any thought of marriage. She refused Kate's earnest request that she write to Thomas, to help "comfort him in his sorrow."[3] "It needs not," Elizabeth insisted. Kate cajoled her—Seymour would find such a missive very kind. Kate's tongue was not stopped, and a blushing Elizabeth reaffirmed that she would not write, for if she did she "should be thought to woo him."[4] She would not write; but Kate wrote, letting the admiral know that he was remembered at Cheshunt.*

Catherine's death left Sudeley swathed in a pall of grief heavier than any of the black hangings in the chapel. The household was in limbo while its future was decided. Not long afterward, Thomas's servant William Wightman sat down at Sudeley with the queen's first cousin, Nicholas Throckmorton. It was a companionable meeting, in which they debated the "great loss" Seymour had suffered in the death of "so notable a wife." Throckmorton hoped that the death would bring about a reconciliation at court and "make him more humble in heart and stomach towards My Lord Protector's Grace." The gentleman, whose mother had been Catherine's

* The lady wooing a gentleman was not the way Tudor marriage negotiations were expected to proceed. There is an excellent study of sixteenth-century courtship in O'Hara (2000).

aunt, believed that the breach with the Protector's wife could also be healed, now that the chief cause of their rivalry was gone. He dearly hoped that Seymour would "alter his manners, for the world beginneth to talk very evil favourably of him, both for his slothfulness to serve, and for his greediness to get." Seymour was, he said, "one of the most covetous men living."[5]

Throckmorton was not the only person to have noticed Seymour's idleness. William Sharington once asked him why he "gave himself no better to serve, seeing that every other man did do willingly offer to serve."[6] "Hold thy peace, man!" was Thomas's response. Sharington had a point, though—Seymour's predecessors as Lord Admiral had known the names of every man on their ships, but Thomas shirked his duties.[7]

As they sat together at Sudeley, Throckmorton was pleased to see Wightman so closely in agreement with him. He continued, saying that Seymour "is thought to be a very ambitious man of honour" and "it may so happen that, now the queen is gone, he will be desirous for the advancement to match with one of the king's sisters."[8] Wightman agreed, assuring him that if Thomas seemed to court either princess, "I will do all that I can to break the dance otherwise; for although he is my lord and master, I had much rather he were in his grave, than ever he should make any such attempt. Which must needs every way be his utter ruin and destruction."[9] Wightman, being a lawyer, knew that to marry one of the princesses without royal consent was dangerous. Surprisingly, Throckmorton actually rather liked Thomas, considering him "hardy, wise, and liberal," but it was "his climbing high, disdained by his peers" that he believed would lead Seymour to his ruin.[10]

In the days following the funeral, however, Thomas appeared to have no plans. He remained directionless and "heavy," thinking only that his "great loss" would force him to break up his household and lead a bachelor's life once more.[11] He was not immediately thinking of his next marriage, while all thought of wedding Jane Grey to the king was abandoned. In his depression, he wrote to her father, telling him that he considered their agreement dissolved.

He would send her home, he said, to those he "thought would be most tender on her."

Thomas's shock did not last for long, though, and he quickly changed his mind. After being "better advised of myself, and having more deeply digested whereunto my power would extend," he thought that he would keep his household together, allowing him to continue to live in regal splendor. He therefore began calling back those that he had sent away, and kept on the gentlewomen of Catherine's Privy Chamber, as well as the maids who had waited on her and the other women who had lived with her. In addition, he reemployed the 120 gentlemen and yeomen who had previously served the queen. In order to bring many of them back, he offered favorable terms, promising some of them a month's holiday to see their friends and family before they returned to him. Keeping Catherine's queenly household together suggested only one thing: that he had decided to take a second royal bride.

Seymour now wanted to hold on to Jane Grey too, writing on 17 September 1548 to her father that "I mind now to keep her, until I shall next speak with your lordship." Indeed, unless he heard Dorset's "express mind to the contrary" he would retain her. For a chaperone, he would bring his own mother, the elderly Margery Seymour, to become (he doubted not) "as dear unto her, as though she were her own daughter." Whether Margery was a suitable guardian for the royal Jane was an open question: she was past seventy, and only two years later would write that she was "both of ill mind and ill in body."* But, already living in Thomas's house at Bromham in Wiltshire, where she had been since before the death of Henry VIII, she was conveniently close at hand—and available.[12] It was a simple matter for her youngest son to persuade her, and for her few attendant gentlewomen to pack their bags for Sudeley. For his own part, Seymour intended to continue as Jane's "half father

* PROB 11/33/458. Margery Seymour's memory was failing by March 1550, when she struggled to set out her last will; if this was dementia, it may be that she had been suffering from fading recollection for some time.

and more," assuring her actual father that all his household would care for her diligently.

Thomas's letter was sent quickly to Bradgate in Leicestershire, where the marquess's family was spending the summer. Jane's father knew very well that the widowed Seymour was not now, either politically or socially, the man he had been only a few weeks before. After discussing the letter with his wife, Dorset replied on 19 September. He was full of superficial courtesy, noting the offer of a home for his daughter, as well as acknowledging Seymour's "most friendly affection towards me and her." Yet, all things considered, he felt that the best person to continue her upbringing was his own wife. Jane's mother, with a combination of "fear and duty," could ensure she was "framed towards virtue." He assured the admiral that he did not mean to withdraw any part of his earlier promise, confirming that he would still be consulted in the arrangements for Jane's marriage. Yet he felt that she really should be back with her mother where she could address her mind "to humility, soberness and obedience." He appealed to Seymour's "fatherly affection" to see the wisdom of this.

The Marchioness of Dorset—Henry VIII's formidable niece, Frances Brandon—also wrote to Thomas that day, thanking him heartily for his offer to keep Jane with him.[13] However, she also declined his offer, promising only that she would be ready at all times "to account for the ordering of your dear niece; but also to use your counsel and advice in the bestowing of her, whensoever it shall happen." The couple must have wondered whether Seymour's attempts to retain Jane, and the recall of Catherine's household, were a prelude to his engagement to their daughter. Frances's own father had taken a child ward as his final bride, and such practices were common. But they had bigger plans for Jane than marriage to Thomas Seymour; indeed, already the marquess was in discussion with the Protector about a match with Somerset's heir.[14]

Dorset's letter cannot have been a surprise to Thomas. He had already offered to visit Bradgate to discuss the matter further, hoping to arrive by 20 or 21 September. Unfortunately, as he prepared to set out, he was forced to postpone the trip in order to journey to London instead. It was less than three weeks after his wife's death, but his presence was urgently required at court with regard to his own affairs.[15] He hoped that Jane's living arrangements could wait for the moment.

Seymour arrived in London around 20 September. Still feeling the loss of his wife, he stayed at Chelsea.[16] There, he found Catherine's sister, the witty and charming Anne Herbert, who had moved there following the queen's death. She was beginning preparations for handing the house back to the Crown. The manor, as so much of Catherine's property, had only been the queen's for life; but, as the place where he wooed her only the year before, it was filled with memories for the widower. This was Thomas Seymour's last visit to the house.

While at Chelsea, Seymour received a visit from Mary Cheke, wife of the king's tutor. She had been sent by the Duchess of Somerset, who was staying at Syon. As Nicholas Throckmorton had predicted, it was the queen rather than Thomas who had been the focus of the duchess's dislike, and she now sent a message to Seymour to "comfort him for the queen's death." The Protector's wife was effectively putting out private feelers for a reconciliation—in public everyone insisted that Lady Cheke was coming to see Anne Herbert. Thomas, however, was in no mood to make friends again with his brother or his wife.

On his way to court, Seymour called on his brother-in-law, William Parr, Marquess of Northampton, who was as disenchanted with the regime as he was.[17] The pair talked at length about the suits that Thomas had to pursue with the Protector, regarding the queen's servants, her jewels, and other objects that he was claiming had belonged to her. Thomas told Northampton that if these suits proceeded well, he would remain at court; but that if they did not, he would immediately return home to the countryside, "the which life he said he liked well." Thomas was jovial and friendly with his brother-in-law, promising to lend him money or anything else if he ever needed it, as well as giving him a few valuable trinkets as gifts. Seymour showed Northampton "much friendship and kindness."

As summer's fruitfulness gave way to autumn, much of the court began to return to London. Even Princess Mary left her estates in East Anglia and headed toward her brother's capital.[18] The plague was still raging, however, so many chose to stay on the outskirts of town, where the cleaner air was believed to protect against disease. The Protector traveled to Oatlands Palace to see the king later that month, bringing the French ambassador with him.[19] Most of the time, he insisted that the Council meet at his house in the pleasant rural meadows of Syon, close to the village of Isleworth and the Thames. It was there that he met his brother in late September 1548, and—like his wife—he looked for a reconciliation. He had hoped that Catherine's demise had removed the cause of their disagreements, and he spoke to his brother at length. Seymour was far from abandoning his ambitions, however, and he boldly stated that Princesses Mary and Elizabeth should be allowed to marry in order to settle the succession.[20] Somerset would have been a fool not to understand that his brother was putting himself forward as bridegroom, and he angrily dismissed him. Nothing satisfactory was concluded, with Thomas walking away shaking his head. He later said that he would be very wary of how he trusted his brother.[21]

The rivalry remained as heated as ever. Thomas was still not offered the preference he was convinced was his due. He was heard to say, the next time he saw William Sharington, "that it will be strange to some when my daughter comes of age. She shall take place above My Lady of Somerset for then she shall be taken as a queen's daughter, not as my daughter."[22] He was also still determined to secure Catherine's jewels, writing to Princess Mary that autumn to request her assistance. His wife had always told him that Mary "knew and could right well testify" that the jewels had been given as gifts. Would she now condescend to writing a few lines as a witness statement?[23] She appears to have refused, no doubt wanting to stay well away from a dispute that was tearing apart the brothers' relationship.

As Seymour had predicted to Northampton, he did not tarry following his heated meeting with the Protector. He was already formulating plans for the future. As he set out westward, he decided to stop at Mortlake Park, which lay on the river a little farther west than Chelsea. There, he found Sir Robert Tyrwhitt and his wife, Elizabeth, who, like Anne Herbert, had left Sudeley following the queen's death.[24] Now Thomas hoped to win the support of these two close former friends of Catherine to his cause. After discussing Divinity with the upright Lady Tyrwhitt over dinner, before calling over her husband Seymour informed Sir Robert that he had spoken to his brother on the subject of the princesses' marriages. "That was divinity indeed," said Tyrwhitt, "for whosoever married one of them, without the consent of the King's Majesty, and them whom he put in trust for the same, I would not wish me in his place." "Why so?" queried Thomas icily. "I put case, I had married one of them, were it not surety for the king? Am not I made by the king? Have not I all that I have by the king? Am not I most bounded to serve him truly?" His exasperation was clear. Surely they must see—as he did—that it was logical for him to marry one of the princesses?[25]

Sir Robert, who, like his wife, in reality hated Thomas, did not think it logical at all. He warned sharply that whoever married one of the princesses without consent, "let him be stronger then they [the Council] be, if they catch hold of him they will set him up." Thomas said nothing, spending the night as an unwelcome guest with the Tyrwhitts before riding swiftly home for Sudeley. Although he knew he could not count on their support, he took Sir Robert's words to heart. If he wanted to marry Elizabeth, he needed either his brother's consent or strength enough to oppose him. And for the latter, he needed an army.

Thomas arrived back at Sudeley in the last week of September to find himself in the midst of a domestic drama. Undeterred by his written persuasions regarding Jane Seymour, the Marquess of Dorset had made the journey south from Leicestershire to collect his daughter while Seymour was carrying out his business at court.[26]

Jane, who had thrived under Catherine's care, was probably not best pleased to see her father, whom she would later accuse of cruelty toward her.[27] Nonetheless, she was compelled to set out on the eighty-mile journey to Bradgate, since he was "fully determined" that she should no longer live with Seymour.[28]

In Thomas's absence, the best that his servants could do was to provide Jane with an honorable retinue as she made her slow progress northward. Significantly, John Harington, who had been so successful the previous year in obtaining Jane, went with them.[29] But Harington, the gentlemen, and the maids were all under Seymour's strict instructions, when he was informed of events, not to hurry home, in the hope that they should soon be charged with bringing the marquess's daughter back down the road toward Sudeley. Harington well knew Thomas's plans for the girl, since Seymour had told him more than once "that she should not be married until such time as she should be able to bear a child, and her husband able to get one."[30] Clearly, the intended bridegroom was not Thomas Seymour.

Harington met with some success in his attempts to persuade the suggestible Dorset to reconsider. So too did the letters from Thomas, which hurried after Jane and her father, and for which the girl wrote to thank him on 1 October.[31] She was grateful, she said, for his goodness toward her and confirmed that she was willing to obey Seymour again as her "father." It was a short note, but it signified the agreement of the Dorsets to once again allow Seymour a guiding hand in Jane's life. The following day Jane's mother also wrote.[32] She considered herself "most bounded to you, for that you are so desirous for to have her continue with you." At their next meeting—already arranged—she promised that they would speak further and she was sure that she could leave Thomas "satisfied," while she herself was "contented." She looked forward to seeing him again at Bradgate House.

Seymour set out for Bradgate in the first week of October 1548. He rode quickly, gathering up Sir William Sharington, who was still lurking close to Sudeley, to accompany him on the route. Although he had reached a tentative agreement with the Dorsets, he was not on such good terms with them yet that he was invited to stay. Instead, he rested overnight at the dowager Countess of Rutland's house in Leicester, before riding the remaining ten miles to Bradgate in the company of Sharington and her son the following morning.*

Thomas had known the countess since their days at court under Henry VIII. He was fond, too, of her son Henry Manners, the 2nd Earl of Rutland, whom he jovially informed was his "friend" as they rode together. The young earl recalled that Seymour told him he "would be glad to do me what pleasure he could." The earl had only just turned twenty-two and was flattered by Seymour's attention, thanking him for his friendship and informing him of his own goodwill. He had a favor to ask: he begged Thomas to assist in securing his place in the House of Lords that autumn since, when the writs for the Parliament had been issued the previous year, he had still not quite reached his twenty-first birthday, and so had not been summoned. Seymour was doubtful of the earl's chances, since that autumn's sessions were to be attended only by those that had been summoned in 1547. He told Rutland that he had better ask the Council—although (as the earl related) "he was glad that I should be of the House, for that he trusted to have my voice with him." Rutland, who was shrewd beyond his years, said that he had told Seymour he "was content in what my conscience would serve me." Nonetheless, he did indeed take his seat that autumn, perhaps with Seymour's assistance—he certainly sought Thomas out as soon as he arrived in London.

Once the pair's amity had been established, as they rode together, Thomas began, typically, to question Rutland about his lands and estates. He asked him how much support he could muster in the local

---

* The Earl of Rutland's later confession (S. Haynes, p. 81) refers to this visit. It has proved difficult to locate the Countess of Rutland's house. The family's main seat—Belvoir Castle—was more than thirty miles to the northeast of Bradgate and can be discounted, as can the other manors included in the countess's dower (as mentioned in the will of her husband in *Testamenta Vetusta*, Vol. II, p. 720). The family is known to have owned property in Leicester, and this seems the most likely location of her house in 1548. The identification is, however, tentative.

area, before boasting of the "great number of his friends, and also how he was banded in the countries." More pointedly—showing that he had already done his research—Seymour asked Rutland to confirm that he was indeed, as he thought, so well liked in the area that he was able to match the power of the Earl of Shrewsbury. Rutland merely demurred, saying: "I could not tell; howbeit, I thought My Lord would do me no wrong." Thomas then told Rutland to "make much" of the gentlemen of the local area, especially the honest and wealthy yeomen, who were "ringleaders in good towns." He considered, he confided, that gentlemen could not be trusted, but that, of the lower sort of folk, by "making much of them, and sometimes dining like a good fellow in one of their houses," one could have their good wills to go with them, wherever he should lead them. He was already considering how to build support against his brother.

Rutland was far from convinced, telling Seymour that he judged the admiral's power to be much diminished by the death of the queen. Seymour, however, made light of this, telling him "judge, judge, the Council never feared him so much as they do now." Rutland was still not persuaded, but Seymour then burst into praise of the king. The boy was, he said, "now of some discretion" and he wished that he should have the rule of his own affairs "and not as that is now; for that which now is done, the king's highness beareth the charges, and my brother receiveth the honour thereof." He assured Rutland that "I would not desire My Lord my brother's hurt, marry, I would wish he should rule, but as a chief counsellor." Rutland made no comment to this, merely inquiring as to Thomas's relations with his brother. The earl was surprised by the conversation and glad when they reached Bradgate, allowing him to depart.

Dorset's country house was a fine brick mansion, built on high ground overlooking his park. From its large windows, the family could easily see their visitors' approach. On arrival, Seymour and Sharington were shown into the marquess and marchioness's presence. The Lord Admiral marshalled all his considerable charm and greeted Dorset as an old friend, speaking earnestly and insistently and refusing to take "no" for an answer from either the marquess or his wife.[33] Eventually, the couple began to concede, with Seymour renewing his promise that Jane would marry the king, saying that, as the marquess remembered, "if he might once get the king at liberty, he durst warrant me that His Majesty would marry my daughter."

This was Sharington's cue to speak persuasively to Frances, taking her aside while Thomas continued to urge the marquess. Seymour was dashingly plausible, so much so that Dorset, "seduced and availed," promised him that—excepting only the king—"he would spend his life and blood in the said Lord Admiral's part against all men." He did not love Seymour enough to send his daughter for no charge, however. The always impecunious Dorset gratefully received £900 in cash, which had been minted and carried by Sharington as a down payment on Jane's wardship.[34] In addition to this, Seymour promised the marquess a "loan" of £2,000, quickly sending the first £500 of it when he arrived home at Sudeley. Jane's father, who had expressed himself so keen to be involved in raising her himself only two weeks before, was now happy enough to use her as a security for the debt.

While Jane's guardian and father discussed her future, Thomas also turned his attention to Dorset's military power. He advised him to move his household to Warwickshire, which "was a country full of men" to be won to his cause.[35] Dorset insisted that his house there—Astley Castle—was crumbling and that he had no funds to repair it, to which Seymour replied that he would send his own builders before Christmas to take charge. Dorset still refused, saying that his provisions were at Bradgate, but even this was no obstacle as far as Seymour was concerned. He asked how far away the two houses were from each other. On hearing that it was sixteen miles, he laughed: "why, that is nothing," it would be an easy matter for everything to be moved to Warwickshire. Just as Seymour wanted the Earl of Rutland to stand in opposition to the Earl of Shrewsbury in Leicestershire, so he wanted Dorset to oppose the Earl of Warwick in Warwickshire, where the two were rivals for control of the county.[36] During the course of the meeting, he declared dangerously that "he loved not the Protector, and would not have any Protector."

He confided to Dorset his plans. Within three years, he promised, he would have the king at his liberty, with Somerset relegated to mere head of the Council. To the Dorsets, this seemed plausible. "After long debating and much sticking on our sides," as they later claimed, they sent Jane back with the Lord Admiral to Sudeley.

Thomas and Sharington rode together as they wended their way back through rolling countryside and falling leaves. As their horses clip-clopped along the uneven mud roads, they spoke quietly together, making sure that they were not overheard. Thomas, who had previously contented himself with showing his friend a map of England to demonstrate his areas of influence, now pointed out places, commenting: "All that be in these parts be my friends." He told Sharington that he had a great number of gentlemen that loved him and, candidly, that he thought even more loved him than loved the Protector. He was, he said, "happy that hath friends in this world, whatsoever should chance." More significantly, he also pointed out that of his own tenants and servants he could muster 10,000 armed men.[37]

Not long after Seymour returned to Gloucestershire, he considered that figure again, asking Sharington how much money would serve to pay and ration 10,000 men for a month.[38] Sharington thought for a moment, before coming up with the amount of sixpence per day for a man. When Thomas heard this, he commented only that it was good "to have always a good mass of money ready, for if a man have money, he may build at all times." He then asked: "God's faith, Sharington, if we had £10,000 in ready money; that were well, could not you be able to make so much money? I trust we should not lack it." Sharington promised that "if the mint did stand at Bristol" he would make the counterfeits, although when he asked specifically what Thomas wanted the money for, his friend was—for once—circumspect. Later, when Seymour told Sharington that the Earl of Warwick wanted to purchase his lands at Stratford-upon-Avon, he informed him that he would not give them up, since "it was a pretty town, and would make a good many men."

Thomas Seymour's preparations to build an army were already under way.

Chapter Fourteen

BEWARE WHOM YOU TRUST

In the early autumn of 1548, as Thomas Seymour cast off his grief for Catherine and his thoughts turned to ways of achieving power, he had not forgotten the essential ingredient in his plans—a new wife for himself. One day, speaking to William Sharington in the company of his serving man Pigot, he whispered that "I will wear black for this twelvemonth. After that I know where to have a wife."[1] And at that moment, she was living at Cheshunt.

On 7 September 1548, Princess Elizabeth celebrated her fifteenth birthday. She was still weak with sickness, and her condition, combined with the queen's death, meant that no one felt like celebrating. Yet it was another step toward womanhood. She was already a year past what was considered to be a marriageable age. Girls she knew from her childhood were married and had become mothers already. As the princess's health began to improve over the autumn, she began to discuss the possibility of moving to a house of her own.

Thomas retained his close interest in Elizabeth. The idea of her leaving the Dennys' supervision appealed, but nonetheless the expense of such a move was high, since the princess would require additional servants and furnishings. Elizabeth had independent means, but Thomas was keen for her to reduce her household charges, perhaps reasoning that he already had a household of servants fit for a royal woman. Why go to so much expense if, as he hoped, she would soon be his bride? To this end, he sent William Wightman to Uxbridge that autumn to see Lady Browne, the widow of Wightman's former patron.

Lady Browne, the twenty-one-year-old formerly known as Elizabeth Fitzgerald—and poetically as "the Fair Geraldine"—was youthful and vibrant.* She was also well known to Princess Elizabeth, whom she had served as a childhood companion. Bizarrely, Thomas's message asked that she break up her household and move in with Princess Elizabeth, so that they could both save household charges. To sweeten the widow to his schemes, he hinted that he would give her 500 marks. He had recently looked over his old will, while going through his papers at Hanworth, and had noticed that he had bequeathed this sum to her. If he died at any point, "she should have been no loser by him."[2] Thomas had more to tell Lady Browne. The next time he was in London he tried earnestly to see her, but she avoided him, instead sending a message that she was going to visit Elizabeth the next morning.

---

* The Earl of Surrey, who was the last person to be executed on the orders of Henry VIII, described Elizabeth Fitzgerald as the "Fair Geraldine" in his poem "The Geraldine," written when she was only ten years old. She would eventually be married twice, first to Sir Anthony Browne in 1543, at the age of only sixteen, and when he was already middle-aged and a father of eight children.

The object of Thomas Seymour's matrimonial advances had little interest, too, in sharing a household and was busy preparing to leave Cheshunt that autumn. But where to go? In London, the plague still "reigned sore," unhampered by the drought that had lasted for all the hot summer, and which had turned roadways to dust and left parched brown earth in the parklands and fields.[3] There was little cheer to be had in the narrow streets within the city, or even in the settlements clustered on its edges. That October, a calf with two heads (both with "white faces") and eight legs provided some diversion for Londoners, with crowds braving the pestilence to pay to view its carcass in Newgate market: the spectacle remained for some time until, alarmed by the potentially infectious mob and the stinking of the fetid cadaver, the lord mayor called for the carcass to be hurriedly buried in the fields outside the city's bounds.[4] On 28 September the Protector issued a proclamation banning even preaching in the town in an attempt to root out the sickness.[5] The next month, some of his own household died from the disease. On 25 October 1548, Parliament, which had been adjourned months before, was postponed for a further month, in the hope that London's streets would then finally be free of plague.[6]

Deciding against the capital, Elizabeth consulted Sir Anthony Denny in her choice of residence. He suggested Hatfield, in Hertfordshire, which had been under his charge since 1542. He could assure her that it was comfortable, having overseen extensive repairs only the previous year, when the chamber of presence and other rooms were updated.[7] It was also only a short ride of ten miles from Cheshunt, while also close enough to visit London with ease.

Elizabeth had first stayed at Hatfield when she was only a few months old. She was fond of the place and knew it well, enjoying reading in the park even in winter and exploring its labyrinthine rooms. The house, once home to the Bishop of Ely, was built in russet-colored brick toward the end of the previous century.[8] It was a contradiction: modern in its construction materials, but retaining much of the medieval gothic so familiar to the princess in the churches and chapels in which she worshipped.[9]

While Elizabeth was asking Denny's advice, Thomas was ensuring that he was kept informed of the princess's movements. He sent at least one servant, a man named Edward, to attend on the princess for the move. Kate Ashley made a point of speaking to him as the horses were being saddled and the last of Elizabeth's possessions were loaded onto wagons: she later recalled that he had told her of the Lord Admiral being heavy in his grief for the queen.[10] Also arriving to escort the princess on the journey was young John Seymour, the Protector's eldest son by his first marriage. He pulled Kate aside, saying that he had been sent by his uncle to inquire of Elizabeth "whether her great buttocks were grown any less or no?" Kate's response is unrecorded.

By autumn 1548, Thomas Seymour's finances had become hopelessly entwined with William Sharington's. In the summer, the coiner had lent £2,000 to Sir William Herbert, which was likely to have been at Thomas's urging.[11] This was not the only debt owed to Sharington, who kept the names of his debtors safe in a bill of remembrance; it even included the Protector himself, who had tapped Sharington for a loan of £500. In return, Sharington owed £300 to Seymour, but the bulk of the debt flowed the other way, with Thomas owing him around £2,800 for the counterfeit coins and for the building work that the tasteful Sharington had undertaken on his behalf. Such a sum was enormous and—if it had been known—would have drawn government attention to the Bristol mint.

Sharington was a man bowed low under the pressure of his wrongdoing, living every month in fear that he would be undone "by so often melting of the money" for his own financial gain.[12] He had cause to worry, since even a cursory glance at his finances suggested fraud. By his own reckoning, the amount he had spent on his house at Lacock had outstripped his income every year for the last three.[13] He was a man of relatively modest means, with an annual income of approximately £630.[14] On top of that, he maintained houses in Bristol and London and was deeply in debt, owing £3,000 to the king. Every moment he feared detection, aware that his early attempts at coining—before he had perfected the art—were so "evil made" that discovery was inevitable. At least he had the vast sum of £4,000 squirreled away, ready to finance his escape or to bribe the relevant parties when the inevitable happened.

Sharington's mint was vital to Thomas's plans, so his friend's increasing instability was a worry. The pair agreed that, in order to cloak matters, they should turn the debt around. Instead of acknowledging Thomas as the debtor, Sharington agreed to pretend that he had borrowed the £2,800. Seymour then approached both his brother and the Council to swear that it was the gentleman who owed him the money.[15] This took the heat off them for the moment; but Sharington still knew he was a man living on borrowed time.

Money matters were also becoming a concern for Elizabeth in her new environment. At Hatfield, for the first time in her life, she was mistress of her own household, numbering around 120 to 140 people, all there to serve her.[16] She was well aware of her status as a king's daughter and ensured that she lived like royalty. When she dined, she was served in a "prince-like" way, with a respectful hush over the room as she ate in the company of her ladies and the gentlemen of her household.[17] Roger Ascham, for one, considered that she rivaled her continental counterparts, her household being so "honourably handled." Such display was not achieved cheaply. After only a few weeks of independence, her accounts were in a mess thanks largely to her comptroller, who, it was discovered, "had little understanding to execute his office."[18] Her outgoings far exceeded her generous income and she was soon looking to make even small savings from her wage bill.

The household was also far from harmonious, with Roger Ascham failing to prove as popular as William Grindal had been. He continued to work daily with Elizabeth at her studies and was friendly with both the princess and Kate Ashley.[19] However, he would later complain that even before the move to Hatfield, he had suffered a "bitter injury" in the household, "out of a relationship from which I should fairly have expected the sweet fruit from my labours."* For him, it was to be a long two years with Elizabeth before he could finally be "released."[20]

In her own household, Elizabeth was beginning to show her promise as an adult princess, showing "beauty, stature, prudence, and industry."[21] She was dignified among her servants and gentle toward them too, as well as continuing to engage with her study of the reformed religion. However, Ascham, increasingly disaffected, suggested that she was not always scrupulously fair, telling his friend the theologian Martin Bucer that "I am fortified, my dear Bucer, by my own conscience, as regards all I said or did when I was at her court, and, if shame did not restrain me, I would tell you what advantages my illustrious mistress got from me." He could only hope that "the current of my illustrious mistress's favour again sets in towards me." Eventually it did—she later made him her private secretary, though this was nearly a decade after he left her household under a cloud in 1550.[22] Despite their difficulties, the two would eventually build up a lasting friendship and rapport, which would extend until Ascham's death.[23]

For the most part, Elizabeth confided in Kate, who remained her closest attendant. In 1548, the princess was second in line to the throne, after Mary who, it seemed, would probably remain unmarried. Edward, though, was young and healthy, his marriage already being considered by his Council. Elizabeth's most likely future was not as a monarch but as a great lady, married either to a foreign husband, for reasons of international diplomacy, or to a great nobleman at home. But the idea of marrying a man that she had never seen always filled her with horror. And why should she not please herself? Elizabeth liked attractive men, and she liked Thomas Seymour—and could see that she was becoming part of his plans.

---

* A letter from Ascham to Lady Jane Grey (18 January 1551) makes clear that Jane knew of the troubles in the household, implying that they began at Hanworth early in 1548, when Jane and Elizabeth were both staying with Catherine.

All indications suggest that she was considering tying the "knot that cannot be untied" with him.[24] Besides, as the king's uncle, he seemed a very suitable match for Edward's half-sister.

Kate Ashley certainly thought so. Toward the end of October, with the household newly established at Hatfield, she begged leave to go to London.[25] Surprised by the request, the princess demanded to know what her business was, and Kate replied that it was to speak with Thomas. On hearing this, Elizabeth shook her head: Kate should not go, since "it would be said that she did send her." Mistress Ashley, however, insisted, pointing out that she also wanted to speak to the gatekeeper at Durham Place, a house that had been granted to Elizabeth as her London residence but of which, as yet, she had not secured control.

Kate must have indeed made the trip, because while in the capital she was called to court, to answer to the Duke and Duchess of Somerset personally for Seymour and Elizabeth's relationship, which had begun to be talked about in London. The duchess took it upon herself to berate Kate, telling her that "another should have her place, fearing that she bare too much affection to My Lord Admiral."[26] It was an astute observation, for it was indeed Kate who provided much of the momentum for Elizabeth's contact with Seymour. The duchess had also heard that when Elizabeth had been at Seymour Place earlier in the year, she had been seen, at night, going in a barge on the Thames as well as in "other light parts." Since a Christian princess was supposed to avoid any such acts of levity and stay home, unless chaperoned, this was shocking.[27] Even dancing was meant to be avoided by a virtuous young maiden, as it was held to be "uncontrolled, audacious, arousing the passions, full of unchaste touches and kisses"—at least, in the eyes of the author of *The Education of a Christian Woman*.[28] The Duchess of Somerset told Kate that she "found great faults with her" and her conduct toward her charge,[29] regarding Kate as unworthy of the governance of a king's daughter. She was largely correct in her criticism of the dangerously lax Kate Ashley; but her tirade had little effect other than to further propel Elizabeth's lady mistress toward Seymour.

When she returned home defiant, Kate pulled Thomas Parry aside to tell him what had happened before loudly praising the admiral.

The princess still looked upon Thomas to fulfill something of a parental role, writing to him in November to ask him to show favor to her chaplain—a moderate evangelical named Edmund Allen.[30] At the end of the letter, Elizabeth asked him to "credit her trusty servant, her cofferer [Thomas Parry], in all other things." She would later insist that she had only meant by this that they were to discuss how she should go about claiming Durham Place from the Protector, but the phrase could be interpreted as having a much wider meaning. Parry himself wrote the letter, although Elizabeth saw it, and he set out to deliver it personally to Thomas in London. He needed to go to London anyway, for he had found the time to secure his election to Parliament as representative for Wallingford, and his presence was now required in the Commons[31]—as Seymour's was needed in the House of Lords.

When Seymour arrived in London in November 1548 to attend Parliament, the Marquess of Northampton came to visit him, the pair walking in the gallery at Seymour Place. Thomas was certain of his disenchanted brother-in-law's loyalty and gloated of his recent success. "There would be much ado for My Lady Jane, the Lord Marquess Dorset's daughter," he said, since the Somersets were already doing all they could to obtain her for their son.[32] Seymour was bullish, though, declaring that "they should not prevail therein" because Dorset "had given her wholly to him, upon certain covenants that were between them two." Northampton—a divorcé—knew enough of the complications of matrimony to sound a note of caution. "What he would do," he asked, "if My Lord Protector handling My Lord Marquess Dorset gently, should obtain his good will, and so the matter to lie wholly in his own neck?" Seymour merely said that "he would never consent thereunto." He was adamant that his consent was needed.

Not long afterward, Seymour casually mentioned to Northampton that "he had heard of a wonderful thing." He told Catherine's brother that he had been credibly informed that the Protector had said that he would "clap him in the Tower, if he went to My Lady Elizabeth." Northampton told him he thought it only a vain rumor, but in case it was not he urged Seymour to speak plainly to Somerset "and to break the matter in such sort to him, as he might put all suspicion out of My Lord Protector's head, if any there were, touching My Lady Elizabeth and him."[33] Seymour—lying—swore that "there was no woman living, that he went about to marry." Nonetheless, he told the marquess that he intended to ride shortly for Sudeley, but beforehand he would ask Somerset whether there was anything he wished to say or bring to Elizabeth, since he intended to visit her at Hatfield on his way. That way, he told Northampton, he would get a feel for Somerset's feelings toward him. Clearly, Elizabeth was much on his mind that November.

Northampton was but one of Thomas's visitors at Seymour Place that November, as the Lords and Commons began to converge on the capital in their droves for the long-delayed resumption of Parliament. Conscious that it was his duty to do so, the Earl of Rutland called on Seymour, walking with him in the wintry gardens at Seymour Place. He, too, found the Lord Admiral in confident mood, discussing with him a patent that Lord Abergavenny had promised him. Such levity surprised the astute young earl, who was well aware of the talk surrounding Seymour. Ignoring his empty chatter, Rutland cut him short, warning him "to beware whom he trusted." Thomas promised that "he would do so, as no man alive should accuse him."[34] But Rutland's warning fell on deaf ears.

On the day Parliament opened, William Sharington set out to take his seat, too, in the Commons.[35] While walking, he met a man of his acquaintance named William Smethwick, who seemingly appeared out of nowhere. In a "friendly" manner, Smethwick—also heading to Parliament—told Sharington not to come to Princess Elizabeth, although there is no hint that he had plans to visit Hatfield. To the master of the Bristol mint's surprise, Smethwick then hurried away, leaving him alone in the street once more. Sharington suspected that Thomas Seymour, who knew Smethwick, had sent the message, but he could not understand why.[36] He therefore decided to speak to him about this, but with the clamor of Parliamentary business he forgot for a week, until he happened to see Thomas passing his house one morning on the way to his barge.

Sharington hurried out to Thomas, and the pair walked together in Sharington's garden for a few moments. Seymour was in a hurry, but he returned later that day, as promised, once his business on the Thames was done. They talked in the barren, winter-stripped grounds until supper, where Sharington informed him of Smethwick's warning. Seemingly hurt, he told Seymour that he took it as a warning not to meddle in the matter of Elizabeth, declaring that he would indeed leave it alone. Seymour made light of it, declaring "that he had nothing to do there." He asked: "Why should not the king's daughter be married within the realm?" Seymour did not explain why the coiner had been warned off. Perhaps even Thomas was growing anxious of Sharington's visibility and his barely hidden criminality. Sharington would have done well to follow the advice of Smethwick, a man who was very good at keeping away from the unwelcome glare of the Protector's suspicion.*

Finally, on 24 November, everyone was ready for the second Parliamentary session of Edward's reign to assemble. The bishops, led by the bishops of London and Bath and Wells, and the peers, headed by Lord Chancellor Sir Richard Rich, arrived in the Upper House.[37] Although Somerset did not attend on this first day, his younger brother was there. The business was dull; proxies for the absent peers were considered and decided upon, but then everyone returned home for two days of rest. Seymour probably wanted to be

* William Smethwick was, as Sharington's account shows, associated with Seymour, yet he was able to avoid having his name further mentioned in the inquiries into Seymour's conduct early in 1549. He also—unlike Sharington—escaped arrest. The worst that seems to have happened to him is that he failed to secure reelection to Parliament during Edward VI's reign (*History of Parliament*, for William Smethwick).

there to ensure that his nomination as one of the proxies to Lord De La Warr was passed, allowing him to cast an additional vote on the peer's behalf.

The second session truly got under way on 27 November, when most of the peers were in attendance, including the Lord Protector himself. On 29 November, Seymour, who attended all that week, was appointed as Lord Zouche's proxy alongside Lord Russell. He sat resolutely in his seat the next week, hearing such humdrum matters as the jointure for the marriage of Lady Margaret Long, and provision for the sale of cattle in Calais. The two Seymour brothers were rarely in the same room if they could help it, so when that happened it must have made for a tense assembly, the pair eyeing each other warily from either side of the hall. Thomas did nothing, however, as his brother's further religious changes, with which he was largely sympathetic, were pushed through. New Acts of Parliament allowed clerics to marry and introduced a mandatory Book of Common Prayer, in English, to be used across the kingdom. These measures were by no means universally popular—as time would tell.

During the days of 14–18 December, the Lords were dominated by "a notable disputation of the sacrament," which caught even the boy-king's attention.[38] This great debate, in which the bishops considered the truth of the transubstantiation in the Eucharist, was a triumph for Somerset who presided, king-like, from his seat.* He was one of only three laymen to intervene, magisterially commanding the bishops to come to some agreement as he opened the debate.[39] His comments during the course of the often-heated exchanges also made it clear exactly where his own beliefs lay. At one point the Protector dismissively interceded, saying "he took bread, &c. Take, eat, this is my body. Who can take this otherwise but there is bread still?" The Earl of Warwick, who also spoke, was more forceful, heckling one bishop with whom he disagreed, asking

* The debate being whether the bread and wine of the communion ceremony were literally transformed into the body and blood of Christ or rather, as the (Protestant) reformers held, were merely symbolic.

"Where is your Scripture now, My Lord of Worcester?" when the bishop had failed to prove his point. Thomas was present, but he sat in silence, as did many of the other peers—who slowly began to melt away in the final fortnight before Christmas. With absences beginning to increase, on 20 December Thomas also lost patience and declined to attend, along with the Marquess of Northampton. The following day, only six peers and two bishops arrived to adjourn the Parliament until January 1549.

The short Parliamentary sessions each day had allowed Seymour considerable free time, and he continued to work to build support, directing his interest squarely toward Elizabeth. It meant he also had time to receive Thomas Parry, the emissary carrying a letter from the princess, who eventually—around 11 December—gathered his nerves and made his way to Seymour Place.

Chapter Fifteen

LONDON NEWS

Thomas Parry, a man in his mid-thirties, was a thick-set, large-nosed Welshman from the glorious slopes of Breconshire, where the hilltops stretched up high into the clouds. With a broad, friendly face,[1] he gave off a straight-forward, rural air; but Elizabeth's cofferer preferred rich clothes and finery to country simplicity, even if they sat uneasily with his florid features.

His family home was the stunning, but isolated, Tretower Court, a fortified manor house with its own ruined castle in the grounds.[2] In former times, the castle's thick stone walls had kept back invaders or raiders, intent on doing the family harm; but now sheep squeezed idly through gaps in the ruined masonry. Like Blanche Parry—who was no relation—he was really by name an "ap Harry," in his case hailing from an illegitimate branch of the prominent and wealthy Vaughans. He had first arrived at court to serve Henry VIII's great minister Thomas Cromwell, before drifting through various posts after his master's execution in 1540. Parry was a relatively new addition to Elizabeth's household in 1548; he was also keen to serve her well. She, in turn, liked and trusted him, as did Kate Ashley, whose passion for gossip and domestic intrigue he shared.

The idea of visiting the high and mighty Lord Admiral at Seymour Place daunted Parry. But he had to deliver Elizabeth's letter. And so he finally plucked up the courage to make the short walk from Westminster over to Seymour Place on 11 December 1548.*

Parry's resolution finally to convey Elizabeth's words may have been encouraged by Kate herself, who arrived again in London around three or four weeks before Christmas.[3] The princess had barely allowed Kate to make her previous London trip, and Kate knew that she would not get license again without a good excuse. She therefore concocted a lie, telling Elizabeth that she was troubled by a sore arm and that she needed to be bled for it. The princess, concerned for Kate, readily gave her her sympathetic blessing. Riding southward with a servant, Mistress Ashley could reflect that her arm did indeed ache, though she could not in truth say that it was sore, even with the jolting of her horse along the well-worn road. It certainly required no treatment; but Kate had her own personal reasons for needing to visit the capital.

Kate's husband, Sir John Astley, had also left Hatfield, to take up his seat in the House of Commons. He had had words for his wife, causing a "jar," or quarrel, between them. Neither husband nor wife told anyone what it was about, but, given Sir John's alarm

* Wightman suggested, in his confession (No. 2, in S. Haynes, p. 68) that Parry's first visit was three weeks before Christmas, but Parry was more specific, giving 11 December as the date ("Parry's Communication with the Lord Admiral," in ibid., p. 98). Since the visit was a more significant one for Parry, his date seems more likely.

at Seymour's conduct in Catherine's household, coupled with his growing suspicion of the admiral's motives after the queen's death, it might well have concerned Seymour. Kate later insisted on absolute secrecy with regard to her dealings with Seymour, lest her husband should hear of them. Sir John, packing up to ride south to London in November, could see clearly the danger his wife was in and was furious with her. When Kate wrote to him from Hatfield, he was so irate that he did not reply. Fearing for her marriage and knowing that "she could not be merry till she had spoken with him," Kate concocted her story of the sore arm to get to London. She had already made arrangements to stay in the village of Hampstead, in the home of William Slanning, a West Country friend of her family.[4]

Kate did not intend to be in London long, though, and had little luggage to unpack, instead immediately sending a servant with a message to her husband. He was surprised, but rode at once to her, whereupon the pair reconciled and spent the night together. The next morning, Thomas Parry arrived in time for breakfast, and the three talked quietly together, before the men left for the Commons. They doubtless discussed Elizabeth's message to Seymour, as yet undelivered.

Kate and Mistress Slanning also had plans for the morning. Taking horse, they rode to Fleet Street, to the house of Lady Berkeley, where Kate's sister Lady Denny joined them. Probably deliberately, Kate had not packed clothes other than those she was wearing and a russet nightgown—which meant that she could not go to court to present Elizabeth's token to the fearsome Duchess of Somerset. Instead, she conversed with the ladies before leaving for Hatfield at noon, only twenty-four hours after she had first arrived at the Slannings' house.

Kate later insisted, defensively, that she had not spoken with either Seymour or any of his men during her visit. Yet Fleet Street was conveniently close to Seymour Place, and messages could have been sent. She had also received more visitors than just her husband during her afternoon at the Slannings' house, including members of the West Country Carew family. Among them was Peter Carew, one of Thomas's vice admirals—who would have been able to take a message from Kate to Seymour, as indeed would Thomas Parry. Kate evidently managed to persuade her husband that she would have no more to do with Elizabeth's marriage—and he regularly warned his wife "that he feared that suitors of My Lord Admiral would sure come to anguish or to an evil end" and forbade her from meddling; but she could not help herself.[5] The advice of her brother-in-law Sir Anthony Denny was also to warn her of Seymour's obvious interest in the princess, and of Elizabeth's in him.[6] The danger seemed clear to everyone, except Kate and Parry, and Elizabeth and Thomas.

Although he carried Elizabeth's letter, on 11 December Parry had no appointment and was not expected at Seymour's London residence.[7] Looking around for a familiar face as he entered, he approached William Wightman, to ask his assistance in obtaining an interview with the Lord Admiral. Wightman, who had little desire to involve himself in his master's matrimonial schemes, showed scant interest, merely glancing up at his visitor as he sat at his writing desk. He was busy composing a letter, and after Parry was told to wait in another chamber he promptly forgot all about him.

Dismayed to find himself ignored, Parry finally located another servant, asking him to inform Seymour he had arrived. On hearing that Parry was there, Thomas immediately called him into his chamber. He was anxious to know what message the cofferer carried and, without waiting for his visitor to sit, ushered him into his long gallery, where they could talk entirely in private. Seymour greeted Parry jovially, turning all his charm on the princess's suggestible messenger. The cofferer was flattered and immediately handed over Elizabeth's letter. Seymour paused in his pacing to read it, considering briefly the question of the girl's chaplain, Allen, who was ostensibly the reason for Parry's visit. Once that was dealt with, Parry relayed a verbal message from his mistress, asking for Seymour's assistance in securing Durham Place. This fine old house, which "standeth on the Thames very pleasantly," was chiefly notable for a hall with a high ceiling supported by marble pillars.[8] Although it had been promised to Elizabeth as a London residence, the Protector had been making difficulties. Could Thomas assist her, since she needed her own residence if she were to visit London?

Seymour only had bad news on this score. He was sorry, he said, but Elizabeth had no hope of the house. It had already been decided that it was to be used as a mint, regardless of her prior claim.[9] He did, however, agree that the princess needed somewhere to stay if she were to come to London. As he strolled up and down the gallery with Parry, he suggested that he lend her Seymour Place, with all his household possessions and furniture. He had rooms at court that he sometimes used, so it seemed a practical solution. Thomas was sure that she would agree to his offer. It would also, of course, place her under his obligation and back under his own roof once more.

Thomas walked with Parry in the gallery for more than an hour, speaking earnestly about the princess in his West Country brogue. He sent Parry away feeling content with how the interview had gone and invited him to return again as soon as he was able. Elizabeth's cofferer did indeed come back, three or four days later, and was once again invited to accompany Seymour in the gallery, conversing for just under an hour. As they walked, the pair spoke again about Elizabeth, with Thomas informing the cofferer that he would go to see her.[10] Parry deflected this, declaring that he had no commission to consider it and did not know how Elizabeth would feel about it. Seymour laughed: "Why it is no matter now: for there hath been a talk of late, they say now I shall marry My Lady Jane." When Parry looked askance, Seymour merely laughed again: "I tell you this but merrily, I tell you this but merrily." Was he hoping that Elizabeth would believe that she had a rival? Perhaps he was trying to establish an alibi. If all the world thought he would marry Jane Grey, then a visit to Elizabeth at Hatfield, acting as a break in his journey to Sudeley, must be harmless.

Parry was very taken with the admiral and his hospitality, and he immediately wrote both to his mistress and to Kate Ashley, setting out the offer of Seymour Place. He also wrote that Thomas wished "to see her [Elizabeth] especially." Even Parry could see that she was the chief object of his desire.

Reading the letter at Hatfield, the fifteen-year-old princess summoned her lady mistress to her side. Although guarded both in nature and by necessity, Elizabeth was prepared to open her heart to Kate. Recalling that Kate had only just returned from London, she asked her whether there was any news. Kate, still basking in her own marital reconciliation, answered merrily: "They say there that Your Grace shall have My Lord Admiral, and that he will come shortly to woo you." Elizabeth blushed to hear this, dismissing it by declaring that "it was but a London News" and thus a report of no worth.[11] She did, however, inform Kate of Seymour's intention to visit Hatfield shortly, something that the lady mistress already knew from Parry. The idea worried Elizabeth, given the talk in London. Kate should write in reply "as she thought best," but she must be sure to show her the letter before it was sent. The lady mistress agreed, taking the decision for the indecisive princess.

Kate hurriedly wrote, setting out "that she thought it not best, for fear of suspicion." To soften the blow, she set out her own goodwill toward the Lord Admiral, but insisted that he should in nowise come without the Council's consent. The princess herself, responding to Kate's teasing, told her that "though he himself would peradventure have me, yet I think the Council will not consent to it; for, I think, by that you said, that if he had had his own will, he would have had me, I thought there was no let, but only the Council, of his part."[12] Elizabeth's mind, already preoccupied in negotiating the loan of furniture, carpets, and tapestries from the royal stores to furnish her house, was yet also wandering to marriage.[13] She was certainly interested in Thomas's suit rather than keeping her thoughts "under control through work or holy thoughts and conversations" as contemporary writers thought proper for a young lady.[14]

In London, Parry showed Kate's letter to Thomas the next time he saw him. As he read it, Seymour let show a rare crack in his composure toward the cofferer. As always when he was emotional, his face colored, and in outrage he demanded to know why he might not come to Elizabeth as well as he did to Princess Mary, whom he was then cultivating for her opinion concerning Catherine's jewels. He soon calmed down and appeared genial again; but Thomas Seymour was not prepared to take no for an answer.

With Parry gone after an hour, Seymour resolved to further press his suit. Making his way to court, he called for Mary Cheke, the wife of the king's tutor. Mary had been a friend to Catherine and was also seduced by Thomas's charms, as her arrival at Chelsea to console him after the queen's death suggested. She was embroiled enough in Seymour's affairs that her husband later felt compelled to apologize for her "misbehaviour," although the extent of her involvement was fairly marginal.[15] While she was with Seymour, he told her that there was a rumor "that he did not use My Lady Elizabeth well, when she was in his house." Defensively, he asked the lady for her view of how he had used himself when she had been there. Mistress Cheke answered as she had seen: she had never noticed his behavior toward the princess to be improper.

In late 1548 Mary Cheke was pregnant, although this did not stop her making the short journey to Hatfield on around 18 December, seeking out Kate Ashley. She probably felt obliged to do so, since her husband was as good as on the admiral's payroll, thanks to the money he passed from Seymour to the king. On meeting with Kate in private, Mary Cheke mentioned that she had a message from Thomas, who had said that he wished to come to see Elizabeth but feared that people would say "that he came a wooing."[16] After Mary recounted her meeting with Seymour, Kate remained noncommittal, still refusing to give permission for the Lord Admiral to visit. When talk of him wooing Elizabeth was mentioned, all she would say was "why do they say so?" as she laughed.

Even before Mary Cheke headed for Hatfield, Parry was writing to Kate again, renewing Thomas's offer to visit. It was now that

Elizabeth decided to take a more forceful approach, instructing Kate to write that, although she knew there was nothing untoward in the visit, they must be careful of rumors. Elizabeth always resolutely stated that this was as far as Thomas's wooing went, and that she never consented to anything without the Council's consent.

This was not, however, all that Kate wrote. In a second letter, quickly dispatched to the capital, she declared that, on reflection, the princess accepted Thomas's gentle offers and that he would be welcome at Hatfield, although "if he came not, she prayed God speed his journey." She wanted to make it clear that Elizabeth was not looking for a visit—Seymour could come or not, as he pleased. One of the letters ended with words of caution: "no more hereof, until I see My Lord myself, for My Lady is not to seek of his gentleness or goodwill." Elizabeth professed herself furious when Kate told her how she had written, telling her that she "would not have her take upon her the knowledge of any such thing." The princess later protested that, for the sake of her reputation, she had begged Kate not to write this letter.

Yet Elizabeth went on to lie about other matters too, including denying that she had been privy to the correspondence between Kate and Parry when she had certainly seen some of it. She was no ignorant child, and when she learned of Seymour's proposed visit it placed her in a quandary. She knew that she should not have dealings with this suitor without the express authority of the Council; but she cared about him and desired to see him again. She wanted to let her heart rule her head—and Kate's second letter suggests that she did just that.

Kate would write only one further letter to Parry while he was in London.[17] While still at Hatfield, she received a visit from the Tyrwhitts, who had been watching Seymour's activities warily. Lady Tyrwhitt told Kate that "men did think that My Lord Admiral kept the queen's maidens together to wait upon the Lady Elizabeth, whom he intended to marry shortly"; Sir Robert told her that she must take heed, since the marriage would be to the undoing of everyone if it were done without the Council's consent.

In London, Thomas Parry took little heed of Kate's advice when she wrote expressing the Tyrwhitts' concerns. Elizabeth's cofferer was letting himself be won over by Seymour's charm. On 20 December 1548, the only day that Seymour failed to attend Parliament, Parry came to him again at Seymour Place, spending two hours alone with him in the gallery.[18] A few days later, before Christmas, Parry came yet again. This time he arrived so early that he beat the increasingly watchful Wightman to the house, even though Seymour's servant had only to make the short walk from his lodgings in Fleet Street.[19] Parry slipped in quietly from the icy street, almost unseen.

It was only as Parry grew more sure of the admiral—on his third or fourth visit—that he opened up enough to speak candidly of his mistress. The two spoke at length, with Seymour questioning his visitor on a number of topics, including Elizabeth's household and the number of her servants.[20] He also asked where her lands were, to which Parry responded diligently. Seymour continued: were they good lands or no? Most were let, his visitor shrugged, and therefore of poor quality. Yes, but were they only held for her lifetime, or were they hers outright? Thomas's questions were sounding like those of a suitor. Parry was unsure, since he had not seen a copy of Henry VIII's will. Seymour then asked if Elizabeth yet had title to the lands with letters patent, which Parry knew that she had not, but that this meant that she could potentially exchange them. Mulling this over, Seymour said: "I would wish she had her lands westward or in Wales" and named an estate in Gloucestershire that had belonged to Catherine and which he would be sorry to lose now that the queen's life interest had expired. Parry was now certain "that there was some matter betwixt them," and he was curious to know what it was. He resolved to ask when he returned home to Hatfield, once Parliament adjourned for Christmas.

While still in London, Parry wrote to Kate stressing the "great friendship" that he perceived Seymour to bear toward Elizabeth.[21] She avoided putting a reply into writing but, when Parry arrived back at Hatfield, she immediately sought him out, asking him insistently just what he had meant by his words. She wanted to speak to him before he saw Elizabeth, so the two found a quiet corner in the house, already dark from the December dullness outside. Glancing around to make sure that they were not overheard, Kate told the cofferer that what he had written "was dangerous, lest it should kindle affection in her." Kate knew better than anyone that Elizabeth's feelings for Seymour were hardly those of a stepdaughter toward her stepfather. As the pair talked quietly, Parry dismissed Kate's concerns, saying only that he thought that Seymour was Elizabeth's friend, to which Kate replied: "Think you, he goeth about marriage?" Parry shrugged his shoulders. He could not tell, although he thought that it would be a good match if the Council agreed. Elizabeth's governess concurred with this opinion but hastily told Parry that in the event that the Council did not agree, she would "rather he were hanged." Parry answered quietly that he thought so too. Kate, conflicted, ended by saying that she "would not be so glad that any man in the world should have her, as he; but without My Lord Protector's mind, let him never come here."

Naturally enough, Elizabeth summoned Parry to speak with her when she heard that he had returned. He had news concerning her suit on behalf of Edmund Allen, but reiterated that her hopes for Durham Place were impossible—it would certainly become a mint.[22] Elizabeth already knew this from Parry's letter, as she was also aware of Seymour's offer of his London residence. The cofferer watched his mistress closely as he spoke, since he had a question to ask and was not at all sure what the answer would be. To the Welsh gentleman, the princess seemed to take Seymour's offer "very gladly, and to accept it very joyfully and thankfully towards him."

Parry decided to be brave, and he suddenly pressed the princess, asking "whether that if the Council would consent that My Lord Admiral should have her, whether she would be content therewith, all or no." Elizabeth's and Parry's accounts of her response to this impertinent question later differed. The princess claimed that she was abashed by this questioning and refused to be drawn, declaring that "she would not tell what her mind was therein." Instead, she demanded what he meant or who had bidden him ask that question. Parry insisted that no one had asked him to speak of the matter, but it was something that he had gathered, through Seymour's questioning about her lands and household charges.[23] Elizabeth retorted sharply, with an acid tongue: "It was but his foolish gathering."[24]

Elizabeth's servant, though, recalled none of this. His mistress, he later claimed, merely answered: "When that comes to pass, I will do as God shall put in my mind." This encouraged him to probe deeper. He told her that Seymour considered that she should seek her letters patent to her lands, and Elizabeth asked "whether he was so desirous or no in deed." Parry nodded. The admiral had indeed been earnest in his desires, as well as seeking the exchange of some of her lands to better complement his. Intrigued, Elizabeth asked what Parry "thought he meant thereby." "I could not tell, unless he go about to have you also," said the cofferer. To Parry's surprise, Elizabeth suddenly appeared angry, declaring that she would do nothing of the sort. Later, though, she came to her cofferer again and asked him whether he had told Kate of Seymour's "gentleness and kind offers." He replied, untruthfully, that he had not. His mistress replied: "Well, in any wise, go tell it for I will know nothing but she shall know it." She was silent for a moment, before insisting that "in faith I cannot be quiet, until ye have told her of it."

Parry's account, which is the more detailed, seems to ring more true. The princess was known in the household for the easy manner with which she talked to servants, and she was fond of Parry.[25] By December 1548, Elizabeth was well aware of Seymour's interest and displayed every indication that she reciprocated it.

Elizabeth, Kate, and Parry always insisted, later, that they only desired the marriage in the event of the Council consenting to it. But no one can seriously have believed that Somerset would permit such a marriage. Seymour had taken a royal bride once before without official consent, so he might well take the same course again, by going over the Council's head. In December 1548, Thomas still had easy access to King Edward through John Fowler and John Cheke. To marry Elizabeth in secret, as he had done with Catherine, would have been a risk, but a calculated one since the boy-king loved his younger uncle and his "sweet sister temperance." Moreover, Edward had little love for the Protector.

Seymour agreed with the boy's sentiments. Before Christmas, Thomas invited the Marquess of Dorset to walk with him, again in his favored spot for intrigues in the gallery at Seymour Place. He was as loquacious as usual, telling his ally that "he in no wise liked the doings of My Lord Protector and Council."[26] He continued that "he loved not the Lord Protector, and would have the king have the honour of his own things, for of his years he is wise and well learned." Confidently, he asserted: "Let me alone; ye shall see I will bring it to pass within these three years." Dorset wondered just what he was planning.

He was not the only one. The authorities were also starting to look more closely at Thomas's doings. He had already begun to fortify Holt Castle, which stood at an important crossing point on the River Dee, giving it control of access to South Wales.[27] This was ominous in itself; but that Christmas, word also reached the Council that Seymour's deputy steward and other officers had been instructed to begin provisioning the castle with wheat, malt, beef, and "other such things as be necessary for the sustenance of a great number of men."[28] They might, though, have been mistaken.* The provisions might have been sent to Bewdley, in Worcestershire, where Thomas was intending to spend the summer of 1549 in princely splendor.[29] Although seventy miles from Holt, Bewdley was far to the northwest of London and strategically unimportant. But it was not a massive leap for the government to imagine that the provisions were actually

* Although the charge would later appear in the draft articles against Seymour, it was not in the final version.

meant for the fortress and that it was there that Thomas intended to keep his army. Perhaps they were right. Seymour was indeed planning to raise men to fight on his behalf.

By December 1548, Thomas had amassed a good sum of counterfeit coins with which to pay his men. He could also see that Sir William Sharington, who had returned to London in Christmas week from a visit to Canterbury, was deeply troubled.[30] Sharington went straight to Seymour to tell him that "I could not continue my doings in the mint," although he had—he thought—successfully covered his tracks in the record books there. But for Sharington, the omens were not good and fate did not seem to look favorably on counterfeiters that cold winter. He would have heard that on the evening of 21 November, part of the Tower of London had exploded when a light was dropped into a vessel of gunpowder. In the confusion of falling masonry one prisoner, a Frenchman, was killed when a slab of stone fell onto his bed as he slept.[31] He was a coiner, imprisoned for counterfeiting testoons.* Such stories made the already-nervous Sharington more anxious.

Sharington had become an unreliable ally, and his unease helped focus Thomas's mind toward action. Elizabeth, on the other hand, had been frightened into inaction. When she asked for Sir Anthony Denny's advice regarding Thomas's offer of Seymour Place, he warned her not to accept. She heeded his warning, taking to her sickbed once again at Hatfield over Christmas.[32] She did not even rouse herself enough to arrange a New Year's gift for the king, instead writing to apologize for the lapse on 2 January.

The atmosphere at Hatfield was tense that Christmas. On Twelfth Night, Parry came to Kate's chamber, and the pair sat companionably together in rooms warmed by fires and lit by candles. A few weeks before, Elizabeth had told Parry to inform Kate of all

* Fire was an unfortunately common occurrence in winter, where light and warmth both required naked flames. Only the Friday before, at eleven o'clock at night, St. Anne's church in nearby Aldersgate Street had also burned (Wriothesley, p. 6).

Seymour had said, and now he did so, telling his fellow servant that "it seemed to me, that there is good will between the Lord Admiral and Her Grace; I gather it both by him and Her Grace also." "Oh!" exclaimed Kate, "it is true, but I had such a charge in this, that I dare nothing say it, but I would wish her his wife of all men living." She continued, saying that she dared not speak of it further, "till I see him," before outlining the history between the princess and Seymour. Secrecy was vital, she said, as she asked Parry to pass on her goodwill to Seymour. He would, he said, before reassuring her that he would "rather be pulled with horses" than betray Elizabeth and her suitor.

Thomas Parry returned to London as soon as the days of Christmas were over, going straight to Seymour, whom he found staying at the court at Westminster. He was again there a week later, speaking privately with the Lord Admiral for a long time.[33] It was evening and black as pitch in the streets outside. Elizabeth's cofferer found his host tense and alert.[34] Thomas immediately asked Parry "how doth Her Grace," to which the cofferer answered "well." He then asked when Elizabeth would be in London, and Parry replied that the Protector had still not given her a date. Thomas nodded: "No, that shall be when I am gone to Boulogne," recognizing that his brother had no desire for the pair to meet.

To lighten the mood, Parry sent Mistress Ashley's commendations. "Oh," said Thomas, "I know she is my friend." Parry spoke a few more words, before adding bravely: "Sir, she would Her Grace were your wife of any man's living." Thomas shook his head. "Oh, it will not be. My brother will never agree unto it." He muttered—and Parry strained to hear—"I am kept back or under." Seymour seemed furious, but the cofferer did not really understand what he said. It was 13 January 1549, or possibly the following evening, and Parry was alarmed at the change in the admiral, who dismissed him abruptly, saying only: "I pray you let me know when she comes up, and come another time."

Leaving Seymour Place, Parry worried that Thomas Seymour was "in some heat, or very busy, or had some mistrust in me." He never saw him again.

Chapter Sixteen

LABORING FOR THE TOWER

On 6 January 1549, three of the Lord Protector's servants gathered together at Bristol Castle to compose a letter. They had arrived in the city some hours earlier, having first called at Lacock Abbey, home of Sir William Sharington.[1] There, in the presence of Lady Sharington, they had collected all the writings, money, plate, and jewels that they could find. Sharington's wife stood mute as the items were sealed into chests and placed in the custody of four servants who remained at the house to ensure that no word leaked back to London of what had happened.

The three agents—masters Chamberlain, Berwick, and Fisher—then rode hard for Bristol. They entered the mint, calling the officers there before them and examining them in turn. They were disappointed to learn that only the Wednesday before, James Paget, a teller at the mint, had arrived from London and hurried away with all of Sharington's papers, stopping at Lacock on his way home. To avoid suspicion, the men ordered that work should continue as usual at the mint, while they planned their pursuit of the elusive Paget, whom they believed "knoweth much" (and who was probably a relative of Lady Sharington).[2] The government was already reading Sharington's correspondence.[3] Within days, the coiner was taken in for examination.

Seymour had been oblivious to the events in Bristol. On the day the mint was searched, he was visiting the king's apartments at Westminster, where he helped himself both to bread and wine from the cupboard, while talking jovially to the king's attendants celebrating the New Year.[4] Thomas was again at court the night that Sharington was apprehended. He was disturbed by John Fowler bursting into his chamber in a state of alarm and crying: "Alas, what have Mr. Sharington done?"[5] Seymour calmly replied: "By my troth I hear no great matter as yet laid to his charge." It was nothing, he assured the agitated gentleman. "Marry, there is one accuses him for coining of testoons since the commandment given by the Council, but he denies it." Feigning innocence, Thomas added that "if Sharington be a false man, I will never trust man for his sake." According to the Lord Admiral, the arrest was an attack on him by the Council—nothing more.

Fowler, in the dusky light of the chamber, was not mollified. He had had some dealings with Sharington himself and was terrified. "My Lord," he said, "remember about a twelvemonth ago you willed me as I lacked any money for the King's Majesty I should send in your absence to Mr. Sharington?" Well, continued Fowler, he had done just that, writing to him for £20 when Thomas had been out of town. Cursing his foolishness for putting this in writing, he bemoaned the fact that "if that letter be found I am utterly undone." He felt he had to confess to the Protector, before his name was mentioned.

This roused Thomas somewhat, who sought to reassure his skittish companion. "Doubt you not, he would not keep your letter." Fowler had not thought of that, yet he was still deeply concerned and leaning toward a confession. "Well," said Seymour, he should say that the money was given to the king. "But, what is that to me?" retorted Fowler. Thomas shrugged: he would just have to devise some answer if he were questioned on it. By that point, the king's attendant was very nearly hysterical, begging the admiral: "I pray you devise to save me." Thomas nodded. He would protect him if the worst happened, promising, as his visitor left, that he would always use him gently.

Seymour also had some thinking to do. News of Sharington's incarceration can hardly have been unexpected, but it was nevertheless alarming. It would be impossible to keep his own name out of the inquiries into Sharington's behavior. Although his own schemes were still at an early stage, Thomas resolved to bring forward his plans. He now needed to act quickly.

It is likely that at this point Seymour decided to acquire the person of the king, marry Elizabeth—and bring down his brother.

Parliament had reconvened on 2 January, whereupon Thomas Seymour, along with other members of the Lords, diligently made their way to chilly Westminster. Already, the festivities of the day before were fading into memory.[6] Many of the Lords, still celebrating Christmas on their estates, were absent, including Seymour's allies Dorset, Northampton, and Rutland. Even Somerset failed to make the journey.

Two weeks before Christmas, Thomas had informed Sharington that "he was not contented that he was not placed in the Parliament House as one of the king's uncles," and matters had not changed with the New Year.[7] He sat as the leading baron in Parliament, but far beneath Somerset and other members of the Council.

Only a handful of peers attended on 3 January; even Thomas remained at home, at Seymour Place, where he missed very little of interest—discussions of how murders and other felonies should be tried, and thoughts about the true making of malt. Those peers who did attend struggled to keep warm, in their furs, in the drafty chamber. It is no surprise that attendance was sparse that week—the comforts of home must have been inviting. But after a day of rest on 4 January, considerably greater numbers attended the next day, including the Seymour brothers—in the same room as each other for the first time since Christmas. There is no record that the pair acknowledged each other during the session. Thomas attended every day the following week, until he was absent on 10 January.

It was around 10 January that Seymour began to invite the Marquess of Dorset and the Earl of Huntingdon to Seymour Place in the evenings. According to Dorset, the talk was mundane yet still infused with discontent. Once, Thomas idly said: "I hearsay that there shall be a subsidy granted to the king this Parliament."[8] This was hardly news, since Tudor parliaments were usually summoned in order to raise taxes. Nonetheless, Dorset asked: "What subsidy?" "Marry," said Seymour, "every man that hath sheep shall pay to His Grace 2d [pence] yearly for every sheep, and to that I will never grant unto it." "Why?" asked Dorset languidly, before pointing out that such a subsidy was better for both of them than one based on land ownership, given their substantial estates. "Well," responded Thomas, "do as you will, I will not," revealing that he was as discontented as he had been before the Christmas break.

On each evening these meetings broke up suddenly. After nine o'clock every night, the Lord Admiral left his friends in his house before setting out alone for the court at Westminster.[9] This surprised Wightman, a man who had little love for Seymour, though it was also welcome for him, for it allowed the servant to return to his own lodgings for an early night: he was told he need not wait up for his master.

At court, Thomas's behavior was suspicious. He would go quietly to the buttery, where alcohol for the court was kept.[10] Pouring himself a drink, he would wait alone among the bottles and barrels until John Fowler appeared. Close together, in a space lit only by torchlight, Seymour, with alcohol on his breath, would ask his companion "whether the king would say anything of him?" "Nay in good faith," Fowler typically replied. At once melancholy, Thomas wished aloud that Edward were still only five or six years old. Every visit was the same, and before Fowler departed Seymour would insist that he "bring him word when the king was rising." The servant nodded, ensuring that each morning he did as he was bid.

Parliament did not sit on 11 January, and the Protector took the opportunity afforded to summon his brother. He was intent on nipping any disloyalty in the bud. Thomas, however, refused to leave Seymour Place, telling Somerset that he would see him the next day at the Parliament House or at Westminster Palace the following afternoon.[11] He had no intention of speaking to him unless he had to, and seems to have successfully avoided Somerset on his visits to Parliament and the court. Seymour's nocturnal activities had no effect on his Parliamentary attendance: he diligently rode to Westminster every day between 12 January and 17 January. Each morning, after snatching only a few hours of sleep, he traveled to Somerset Place, taking to his horse in procession behind the Protector. Most days he rode with the ancient Lord Russell, who served as Lord Privy Seal—and long ago as Lord High Admiral—and who was one of the men on the Council that Seymour accounted his friend.

Russell, however, was worried about what he had been hearing. Turning to Seymour one day as they rode, he observed: "My Lord Admiral, there are certain rumours bruited of you which I am very sorry to hear."[12] What were they, demanded Thomas. Why, said Russell, that you "made means to marry either My Lady Mary, or else with My Lady Elizabeth."* As their horses stepped lightly over the cobbles, Russell warned his companion that if he did any such thing he would undo himself "and all those that shall come of you."

* This uncertainty over which princess Seymour was courting suggests that the information came from the Tyrwhitts, who were only privy to the general outline of his plan.

Seymour ignored this conclusion, instead insistently asking who had informed Russell of these rumors. Russell merely shrugged, replying that he had heard it from a number of the admiral's own friends, men who "wish you as well to do as I do myself." Thomas merely denied everything and the pair dismounted, still ostensibly on friendly terms.

Two or three days later, it was Thomas who pulled his horse in beside Russell. He was wondering why Russell seemed "very suspicious" of him, asking whether it was to do with the marriage they had discussed the other day. Russell merely responded that he would not tell him who had reported the rumors to him, but assured him that they were not malicious reports. He reiterated his warnings that marriage to one of the princesses would undo Seymour—it would be interpreted as a maneuver to obtain the throne for himself.

Thomas made no answer to this, merely saying that the husband of one of the princesses would have £3,000 a year. Russell shook his head. Their spouses would receive no land, only money, plate, and goods—and how could he "maintain his charge and estate" with that? Seymour refused to believe this, repeating that "they must have the £3,000 a year also." It was getting heated now. "By God but they may not," exclaimed Russell, spluttering through his thick white beard. "By God, none of you all dare say nay to it," grimaced Thomas. Russell answered: "By God, for my part I will say nay to it," and spurred his horse away from his companion. The message from the Lord Privy Seal was clear. If Thomas were to marry Elizabeth, she would not get her patent to her lands.

In spite of the increasing rancor between the two men, they continued to ride together to Parliament. On the third occasion, the talk turned to William Sharington. Thomas had been making inquiries into how his friend was held, and, turning to Russell, he commented that it seemed to him "that more extremity was shown to Sharington than his fault or offence did deserve." He pointed out that, with his records confiscated, the master of the Bristol mint could not possibly hope to clear his name. But it was a "most heinous" matter, Russell spluttered, since it touched the king's coin. They arrived at the Parliament House before they had finished speaking, but the next time they rode together Seymour once again spoke up for his friend. Pulling out a copy of Sharington's patent from the mint, the Lord Admiral declared that it seemed to him that the testoons had been lawfully made. With increasing frustration, Russell retorted: "My Lord, you shall not do well to take upon you to defend Sharington's causes." "It was a foul matter," the old peer muttered, and he should leave it at that. They rode in silence the rest of the way.

Thomas's strange behavior at court was beginning to be noted. One day that month, while walking in the garden at Westminster Palace with the Earl of Arundel, they found that the gate was shut. Arundel turned to Thomas and asked to be let through, insisting: "you have a double key. For so it is in the book."[13] At the time, Seymour professed ignorance of this duplicate key: "I cannot tell whether I have or not; but if I have any, it is in my casket, I think, at Bromham." Arundel must have wondered why Thomas would keep a key for Westminster Palace at his house in Wiltshire, but he made no further comment.

While talking to John Fowler one day, Seymour was informed about orders Sir Michael Stanhope had given to ensure that the king remained safely locked away at night. Thomas asked what was meant by this, but Fowler said he could not tell. Thomas concurred: "Nor I neither. What is he afraid that any man will take the king away from him? If he think that I will go about it, he shall watch a good while."[14] It was hardly a baseless concern, though, since Thomas was taking considerably more interest in measures for the king's security than he should.

Not long before, while the court was still at St. James's Palace, Seymour had arrived early in the morning and wandered into the gallery to find Fowler playing his lute.[15] The king's servant stopped strumming as the admiral entered and commented that "there is a slender company about the king." Glancing around, Seymour continued: "I came through the Chamber of Presence and passed not a man, nor in all the house as I came I found not a dozen persons." Fowler nodded: "Thanks be to God we are in a quiet realm and the King's Majesty is well beloved. If it were not so, a hundred men would make a foul work here." This response did not satisfy Seymour, who observed that "a man might steal away the king now, for there come more with me than is in all the house besides." Perhaps he was tempted at that moment to do just that. If so, he silenced the urge, instead going in to speak to Edward for a time. Such a course, if successful, would, *de facto*, give Seymour the coveted governorship of the king's person. The boy might even have been desiring it—perhaps even, during Thomas's frequent visits to his nephew in January 1549, Seymour raised an "abduction" with the king himself. He was certainly thinking of it.

The youthful Earl of Rutland, always an uncomfortable ally of Seymour, appeared noncommittal and nervous when Thomas attempted to involve him in his schemes. Finally, on the evening of 15 January, Rutland summoned his secretary, speaking at length with him on the subject of Thomas Seymour.[16] The men conferred for some time, while the secretary drafted a note, carelessly discarding parts that did not meet his employer's liking. When he was satisfied with the document, Rutland ordered its dispatch to John Dudley, Earl of Warwick. He then left the room, leaving his servant Pigot alone to tidy up.

Approaching the desk in the candlelight, Pigot found a scrap of paper containing four or five lines of text. It seemed to him to be the beginning of a Parliamentary bill making accusations against Seymour. Furtively, he hid the paper about his person before hurrying away. By the morning, he had made his way to his brother, who was coincidentally in Seymour's service. This second Pigot went immediately to his master and secured an audience with him for his brother. Thomas took the paper into his hands and saw at once "that something was intended against him." Stunned, as he later confessed, he began to suspect "by diverse conjectures" that the Council intended his arrest.

Thomas's mind was troubled on the morning of 16 January as he rode to Parliament beside Lord Russell. Breaking the silence, he asked: "What will you say, My Lord Privy Seal, if I go above you shortly?"[17] This was a surprising question, since the office of Lord Privy Seal was the fifth-highest ranking in the Council, including the offices held by Protector Somerset and the Archbishop of Canterbury.[18] Calmly, Russell replied that he would be very glad of Thomas's preferment, and that he did not care if he were to go above him providing "that he took nothing from me." It seemed that Thomas was imminently expecting to be appointed to one of the highest offices in the kingdom—that of governor of the king. Nothing more was said—although later that same morning, Lord Russell reported the conversation to the Lord Chancellor.

Thomas entered Parliament that day as usual, where he found Rutland in his accustomed place. For Seymour, the morning's Parliamentary affairs, which concerned fines in Chester and measures to be taken for soldiers who had returned from war, must have seemed interminable. Later in the day, he heard that the Council was meeting secretly in the garden at Westminster Palace, but was unable to learn what was being said.[19] Haunting the palace, and finding the way into the garden barred to him, he spotted Lord Russell and barreled over, asking what the matter was. Russell, however, would tell him nothing, leaving Seymour only to return home impotently. None of the other Council members would even acknowledge his presence, even though some of them he accounted his friends.

That evening, an alarmed Thomas sent a message to his brother-in-law, Northampton, requesting that he come to him.[20] Northampton found him in a state of high agitation, rehearsing the day's events out loud. He had had some time to think and now believed that he knew what the Council had discussed, telling Northampton that "he thought they went about to see if they could get out anything of Sharington against him." He then complained that Sharington "was the straighter handled for his sake, but for that he cared not, for he was able to answer to all things that should be laid to his charge." He added, boastfully, "that My Lord his brother was in fear of his own estate, and had him in a great jealousy, the which, if I did well mark, I might well perceive, for he went better furnished with men about him than he was wont." Thomas had noticed that Somerset had begun to go everywhere with a substantial bodyguard, while the Earl of Warwick had moved to stay in the Protector's house, reputedly "for fear of his brother the Admiral."[21] After sending Northampton away, Seymour took a desperate decision, sensing that time was running out.

Imperial Ambassador Van der Delft had begun to make his journey back to England in January 1549, after visiting relatives in Flanders.[22] He was keen to return, but found himself forced to wait for some days at Calais for a break in the stormy weather.[23] While still there, on 27 January, he fell into conversation with two English messengers, both trying to make their own way across the Channel. They told him quite a tale, which he duly set down in a report to his master, Emperor Charles V.

On the night of 16 January 1549, the quiet of Westminster Palace had been broken by frantic barking outside the king's chamber. On being awoken, Sir Michael Stanhope, who slept in the king's chamber, groped for a light before rushing to the door. There, he found the king's dog stone dead and immediately cried out, "Help! Murder!" as everyone in the vicinity came running. Whoever had killed the dog had fled in the commotion. Yet there were those at court who had seen Thomas Seymour lurking around that night, while the guards testified that he had scattered their watch by giving them various errands to run on his behalf. Further details also later emerged. With a key given to him by one of the king's chamberlains, Seymour had been able to open the door to the room adjoining the king's bedchamber, "which he entered in the dead of night," accompanied by unnamed accomplices.[24] There he disturbed the little dog, which usually slept in the king's bedroom and was his "most faithful guardian." The animal had been accidentally left outside the door that night, and on hearing Seymour had rushed at him, barking out, only for the admiral to run him through with his dagger. At once, a guard entered and challenged the intruder, who said, visibly trembling, "that he wished to know whether the prince was safely guarded" before fleeing.

The Council tried at once to hush up the event, but word leaked out. The story, quickly all over Calais, was that Seymour had "tried to take the king away secretly from the guardianship of the Protector."[25] Independently, the emperor in Brussels received word that Thomas had entered the king's chamber by night ("at an undue hour"), accompanied by a party of armed men.[26] Even the powerful Paget confirmed the story, later telling Van der Delft that the final straw for the Protector had come when his brother had been discovered in the palace late at night, with a large company of men, while the dog that kept watch at the king's door was found dead.[27]

This was the rash move of a man who knew his plotting was soon to be uncovered. His contemporaries were adamant that Seymour intended to take the king into his custody before murdering both the boy and Princess Mary and then claiming the throne as Elizabeth's husband. [28]

There was no evidence that Thomas meant to murder his nephew. Almost certainly, though, he tried to take the boy that night. Later, he would be accused of trying "to instil into His Grace's head" the idea that he should "take upon himself the government and managing of his own affairs."[29] In his evening visits to court the week before, did he meet with the king and plan an "abduction" with him? It would seem plausible that the bedchamber key had been given to him at Edward's command, since none of his attendants (including Fowler, the most likely suspect) was ever accused of this.[30] Only a few weeks later, Seymour, while at his lowest ebb, wrote the line of verse: "forgetting God to love a king hath been my rod, or else nothing."[31]

By 7 February, Thomas's vigorous protests of innocence were all based on the claim that he had had the king's confidence and approval in everything he had planned.[32] How could it be treason to do as the king asked? Thomas probably hoped to collect Elizabeth at Hatfield on the way out of London, before taking both the king and the princess to Holt Castle or Bewdley to weather the resulting storm.[33] Unfortunately for Seymour, by leaving his dog in the chamber outside his bedroom, the boy-king botched his own escape attempt.

At Westminster Palace on the night of 16 January, Protector Somerset got very little sleep. Very late that night he sent for the Earl of Rutland, before questioning him closely in the near darkness on what he knew about Thomas's doings.[34] The earl told everything.[35]

Thomas also spent a sleepless, nervous night. Early on 17 January, the Marquess of Northampton came to him again at Seymour Place. He found Thomas bullish, even though he told Seymour that he would be called that day before the Council to answer accusations made against him by the Earl of Rutland.[36] Thomas now seemed more agitated than before, ranting about the doings at court. Could he speak to Rutland before the other lords arrived? He wanted to know exactly what had been said. He was not prepared to come quietly, he assured his brother-in-law. He would speak to Lord Russell and Sir William Paget "unto whom he would declare his mind," and he asked the marquess to fetch them. He must remember to say, he said, that "he would answer at his own liberty, and not to be shut up first, where he should not come to his answer." With that, Northampton left.

Although still highly unsettled, Thomas set out for Parliament, taking his seat in the same chamber as his brother. It was to be his final day in Parliament, and a short one. Still shivering in the January cold, the peers hurriedly considered fines to be levied in Chester and the matter of the Bishop of Peterborough's proxy, before the Duke of Somerset adjourned proceedings to allow everyone to go for dinner.

Thomas Seymour left the chamber to ride with the Marquess of Dorset toward the Earl of Huntingdon's house, where they had been invited to dine.[37] Seymour seemed, to his companion, to be troubled, confiding as they rode that Rutland had accused him to the Council. It must have been a tense meal. Afterward Dorset, Huntingdon, Sir Nicholas Poyntz, and Dorset's brother Lord Thomas Grey traveled together to Seymour Place. They immediately went to the gallery. As they paced together, Thomas went through everything that he had said to Rutland, trying to work out just what was the nature of the complaint against him. He declared himself a "true man," entirely innocent of any wrongdoing. Yet when a servant entered carrying a summons to go to the Council, he suddenly appeared "much afraid." He was not going, he said, unless Paget came to him as a hostage. He must have an assurance "that he would return as free as he went forth."[38]

Once the messenger had gone, Seymour called for John Harington, securing his promise that he would take custody of Paget when he arrived. Even the devoted Harington, however, considered this to be a foolhardy idea, although he agreed to act as hostage-taker if so commanded.[39] Dorset and his brother must have been aghast as they watched events unfold. It was left to Lord Grey, who was Dorset's closest confidant, to put a stop to this mad scheme. Turning to Seymour, he said: "Knowing yourself a true man, why should you doubt to go to your brother, knowing him to be a man of much mercy?" He added: "Wherefore, if you will follow my advice, you shall go to him." Besides, he pointed out practically, "if he list to have you, it is not this house that can keep you, though you have ten times as many men as you have."

Grey had a point. Just how did Seymour think he could hold out in his palatial—but unfortified—townhouse? He had not actually managed to secure the army that he so often boasted about and had instead been hoping to rely on his yeomen friends from the counties rising in his support. There was nothing for it but to flee or submit. In the early evening of 17 January he agreed to go to the Council by boat, accompanied by Dorset's brother. On finding himself released from the awkward situation, Dorset himself hurriedly returned to his own home, where he took to his chamber.

Seymour, together with Grey, climbed into his barge after making their way through the already-dark gardens at Seymour Place. As they glided quickly down the Thames, Grey attempted to reassure him. "Sir, arm you with patience, for now I think it shall be assayed."[40] Thomas declared: "I think no. I am sure I can have no hurt, if they do me right; they cannot kill me, except they do me wrong: And if they do, I shall die but once; and if they take my life from me, I have a master that will once revenge it." Even in extremity, he was boastful. He had no cause to be.

During the hours of 17 January, Westminster Palace had been abuzz with talk of the admiral.[41] Sitting down together at last, the Protector and the entire Council had met "to consult and determine upon a certain order for the stay and repressing of the said admiral's attempts." Somerset recalled to them all how his brother had tried to lay his hands on the king and to manipulate the Parliament. They rehearsed everything that they knew about Seymour's previous dealings. They also spoke of his attempts to marry Elizabeth and, with "one whole mind, consent and agreement" ordered that he be sent to the Tower. The fallen Lord Admiral was already as good as a condemned man when he arrived at Westminster. After entering the palace, he was immediately dispatched to the Tower, arriving at eight o'clock that night.[42]

Thomas entered the ancient fortress in cold darkness. Even for the law-abiding, the building, which loomed up on the Thames, was awe-inspiring. For prisoners, it was terrifying. Already frightened, tense, and tired, Seymour kept his composure only with difficulty. There were two ways into the Tower, either by water through the notorious Traitor's Gate, or on horseback—tied to the horse to prevent escape—crossing the bridge over the moat. The land route, though avoiding Traitor's Gate, was almost more disconcerting, since visitors had to pass through the Lion Gate, which was named for its proximity to the royal menagerie.[43] For centuries those in the Tower had been unnerved by the roaring lions and growling bears in the royal collection, while the pungent smell of this private zoo assaulted them. Few escaped from the Tower of London, and the prisoners' lodgings were spartan. In the chill of winter, there was little comfort and not much sleep to be had there.

After Thomas's arrest, the Protector and the Council busied themselves in collecting evidence against him, including ordering a search of his residences.[44] On 18 January, members of the Council came to Seymour Place and ordered Seymour's secretary to surrender his signets of office.[45] At the same time, they also began to interrogate members of his household. William Wightman, who so disapproved of his master's dealings, was interviewed either on that day or the next. He told what he knew of Seymour's activities regarding Catherine's jewels. John Harington quickly became a particular focus of the inquiry. He freely admitted to his own part in Seymour's doings, letting slip so much that Sir William Petre, making a note of his answers, recorded drily that "he labors to have been in the Tower with the Lord Admiral."[46] Harington got his wish later that day.[47]

Parliament did not sit on 18 January, although the peers reassembled the following day. It must have been a strange assembly, with both Seymour and his brother absent from their seats. Business continued as usual, considering trade, fines, and customs, but it was Lord Chancellor Lord Rich who adjourned proceedings. Somerset was still occupied in gathering evidence against his brother. Later that day William Sharington was moved to the Tower as prisoner. The hapless John Fowler joined the others there too.[48]

Although he had been held under investigation for some time, the slippery Sharington had maintained some contact with the outside world. When men came to take him to the Tower, he was searched and found carrying a letter from Thomas Dowrishe, his deputy at the Bristol mint, setting out details of the mass of coins and silver they had ready.[49] In the face of such evidence, there was little defense to be mounted. Despite this, he was subjected to particularly intense interrogation in the Tower. At first, the focus was on his own misdoings, his interrogators demanding to know how many testoons he had made and who had funded the operation.[50] When asked: "What money hath comen through his hands within these six months, to be delivered to any nobleman; to whom, when, and how much?" he answered that he had delivered money only to the Lord Admiral, giving him the £900 that was paid to Dorset and a further £600 to buy wool.

Once he had given his answers, the examiners came back to him with another list of questions.[51] Sharington kept his answers brief, unwilling to incriminate himself or his confederates further if he could help it. To the question "When you began the melting down, and how long you continued the same?" he answered only: "I can say nothing without my books by the which I am bound." He was highly anxious. When asked what money he had given to his wife, he replied that "I am not able to say, if my wits were a hundred more; she knoweth much better I think."

In the face of such probing, and in terror of his life, Sharington finally decided to abandon Seymour. From his prison, he wrote to the Protector offering his complete testimony in return for clemency.[52] His approach was accepted. It was not Sharington that Somerset wanted to catch, but his brother.

Ignoring the biblical day of rest, the Council met again on Sunday 20 January. They received worrying news from Sir Thomas Cawarden, who had been sent to Sussex to make an inventory of the admiral's property there. While he found the manors neglected, Cawarden discovered that Thomas had used his expertise as Master of the Ordnance to set up furnaces deep within the Forest of Worth to cast guns and shot.[53] There was an alarmingly large quantity of such hidden military supplies, with £66 of shot alone squirreled away at the manor of Sheffield, in Sussex, at Thomas's command. The illicit production was immediately halted on Thomas's arrest. On his arrival, Cawarden was asked plaintively by the skilled gunfounders whether "they shall cast any more ordnance and shot or no and of what kind?"[54] No accounts of the furnaces and mills at Sheffield had been made since 1546. The clerk there, John Sherief, had agonized over this discrepancy, but Thomas had not wanted to open his endeavors to scrutiny. He had probably hoped to transfer the munitions to his army—when it was raised.

The Council was busy that Sunday, as witnesses clamored to exonerate themselves. Keeping his hands as clean as he could, Somerset appointed Lord Russell, William Petre, and the former Lord Chancellor, Wriothesley, to hear the investigation.[55] Carrying out a thorough job was almost certainly the price of the conservative Wriothesley's rehabilitation: he threw himself into the task.[56] It was all rather neat, since he had only again taken up a seat on the Council that month.[57]

The Marquess of Dorset immediately became talkative in a bid to clear himself, supplying a number of depositions against Thomas. The Protector left no stone unturned, even seeking a version of events from Edward, signed by the young king himself.[58] The boy had no compunction in telling his Council of all Seymour's dealings, including his behavior at the opening of his first Parliament and Seymour's attempts to enlist Fowler to his support. He probably hoped to absolve himself of any collusion with his younger uncle. In spite of his youth, he was calm, signing "Edward" neatly at the foot of the page.[59]

On the same day that Russell, Wriothesley, and Petre were appointed, they summoned William Wightman to inquire if he could recall anything more of the Lord Admiral's dealings. He could, he said, telling them of Parry's visits to Seymour Place. Explosively, he added that he had seen Elizabeth's cofferer speak with Seymour only "three or four days before his apprehension."[60]

Suspicion now fell squarely on the princess who was living at Hatfield.

Chapter Seventeen

VANITY OF VANITIES

The house at Hatfield was quiet on the morning of 21 January 1549. Although still deep winter, the days were slowly beginning to draw out, with the sun rising earlier each day to reveal the morning frost. The day began with the usual hustle and bustle of life in a great noble household. No messengers were expected, but the sound of approaching hooves caused uproar.[1]

Someone, looking out of the window, recognized Lord St. John and Sir Anthony Denny. On hearing that these two members of the Council were at the gate, Thomas Parry turned pale and immediately ran to his own chamber, where he found his terrified wife. Tearing his chain of office from his neck and wrenching the rings from his fingers, he cried out: "I would I had never been born, for I am undone." In the commotion, his servant and other members of the household entered to see him pacing the floor in distraction, continually wringing his hands. Another servant recalled that he looked very pale and sorrowful, to their surprise. The news of Seymour's arrest had reached Hatfield some days earlier, and now it seemed to Parry as though the end had come for him too.

It was with difficulty that Parry's wife, Lady Fortescue, managed to calm her husband. She had been a widow before she married the cofferer, choosing the lower-ranking gentleman out of love rather than status.* Composing themselves, the couple left their chamber, going to greet the visitors with Kate Ashley before sitting down with them at the table to dine. Lord St. John, as Lord Great Master, was an important member of the Protector's government. The meal was tense and highly charged. To the surprise of Parry and other of Elizabeth's servants, the visitors left them alone for a time after eating, in order to begin their interrogation of the princess.[2]

Elizabeth, who already knew of the doings in London, kept her cool and revealed little. She, Kate, and Parry had already sat down together to agree their stories, saying—almost as a mantra—that nothing had been considered matrimonially without the Council's consent. She kept silent on whether or not she had agreed to marry the Lord Admiral—even though, given the tenor of the messages passed between her and Seymour, she most likely would have gone willingly as his fiancée had he arrived at Hatfield on the morning of 17 January with the king in his possession.

The princess was a good deal more composed than Parry's wife. Once the company had left the table, Lady Fortescue looked at her husband and now broke down into fits of weeping, declaring to Kate: "I am afraid lest they will send my husband to the Tower, or what they will do with him."[3] Elizabeth's lady mistress, who was calmer, stopped her, declaring: "Nay I warrant you there is no such

* Her first husband was a cousin of Elizabeth through the Boleyns, a connection that might have been enough to secure Parry a place in the princess's household (McIntosh, p. 92). It was a closer relationship than that between Elizabeth and John Astley, whom she referred to as her "kinsman."

cause." Everything Kate and Parry had said was in private conversations; she was sure they had committed no offense. The three separated, but later Lady Fortescue came to Kate with a message from her husband, saying that "he would be torn in pieces rather than he would open the matter." Kate again sent to Parry to insist that he keep his dealings with Seymour secret, lest her husband should hear of it.

Kate had still not grasped the seriousness of her involvement with Seymour, but she soon learned. Late that night, after the household had retired to bed, Kate and Parry were summoned once more.[4] The lady mistress, who appeared wearing her nightdress, was horrified to find that she and Parry were placed under arrest "for the matter of the Admiral," to be carried to the Tower that very night.[5] They were not even given time to dress.

Parry's wife had been roused along with her husband, and on learning of his arrest she immediately rode to London. Although she was not imprisoned herself, she was kept under government observation while it was decided whether she should be examined.[6] Sir John Astley, who was already in the capital, was also summoned to account for his actions. Entirely unfairly—since he had always counseled his wife to keep away from Seymour—he was locked in the Fleet Prison on 23 January.[7] He may have been thankful that he was not sent to the doleful Tower, but his new lodging was little better.[8] It had stood close to the River Fleet, in Farringdon, for nearly four hundred years and was a tattered, miserable place. As a gentleman, Astley might have been able to secure some comfort through payments to the jailers; but the experience must have been terrifying, and he would have been forgiven for cursing his wife for her meddling.

By contrast, the fifteen-year-old Elizabeth slept soundly on the night of 21–22 January, entirely unaware of the commotion in her household. But she was also "under grave suspicion."[9] Somerset and the Council strongly suspected that Seymour had intended to marry her without permission, before contriving to secure the consent of Edward, who would have been already in his custody, and they were determined to have the truth about the matter.

Either that night of 21–22 January, or perhaps early the next morning before he rode for Parliament, the Protector summoned Sir Robert Tyrwhitt. Sir Robert—a younger son—had spent a lifetime in service at court and was well versed in the politicking and plots that existed in the seat of government. He had been without official employment since Catherine Parr's death, and he now agreed readily to ride for Hatfield to conduct the investigation into Elizabeth's own conduct.

His wife, Elizabeth, went too, since without Kate the princess required an acting lady mistress.[10] Catherine's cousin by marriage, Elizabeth was as staunchly religious as the former queen, with distinctly puritan tastes.[11] On being interviewed by the Council at the same time as her husband, she appeared to them well qualified to straighten out the girl "to prosper in all virtue and honesty."[12] Privately, they instructed her "in such matters" in the way she was to handle Elizabeth, sanctioning the strict religious timetable by which she expected a household to live. The princess should confess her "grievous offences" committed "in thought, word and deed" each day before morning prayers.[13] Accepting her appointment, Lady Tyrwhitt must have regarded Elizabeth as a sinner into whom she could really get her teeth. And of course the Tyrwhitts had few warm feelings for Thomas Seymour.

The horses clattered over a well-trodden path, being admitted to Hatfield early in the morning of 22 January. The Tyrwhitts probably rode with Lady Browne, or met her on the way, since she also found her way to Hatfield.

Sir Robert set to work zealously from his arrival. As a former member of Catherine's household, he was as suspicious of her stepdaughter as he was of her husband, and held no affection for Elizabeth. His first act was an attempt to scare the princess into submission before he had even begun his interrogation. On arriving, he hurriedly forged a letter addressed to Blanche Parry, purporting to be from a friend of hers, which he had brought to deliver.[14] The spinster gentlewoman, who quietly adored Elizabeth, took it at once to her mistress after reading its contents with shock. It informed Blanche that both Kate and Parry, who had been spirited away to London, had been imprisoned in the Tower. This was devastating news for the princess, who was now barred from news of the outside world; she wept for a long time before sending for Lady Browne to ask whether the pair had confessed anything. This was suspicious, since it suggested collusion. Elizabeth was unaware that the pretty young widow was there to spy on her.

When Elizabeth heard that Lady Browne had gone to Sir Robert with her words, she sent for him herself. Perhaps he expected her to confess everything; he certainly found her red-eyed from weeping. Nonetheless, she was resolute. "She had forgotten," she said imperiously, "certain things to be opened to My Lord Great Master [St. John], and Master Denny."[15] She would tell him now, she added, "and all other things which she could call to her remembrance that she done." In spite of this, Elizabeth certainly did not intend to tell Tyrwhitt any more than she needed to. All she would say was that she had indeed written to Seymour, but in favor of her chaplain, Edmund Allen. She admitted, she said, that at the end of the letter she had asked Seymour to "credit her trusty servant, her cofferer, in all other things," but she assured Tyrwhitt that she had only meant with regard to the negotiations for Durham Place. Surely he could see nothing suspicious in that? Particularly since she assured her inquisitor that she had refused Seymour's offer to visit her on his way to Sudeley.

Elizabeth presented a picture of confused innocence; but Tyrwhitt was annoyed. He could see there was more to tell. Interrupting her, he advised the princess to consider her honor and the trouble that she might find herself in, and charged her on her loyalty to the king. He tried a new tack, lamenting "what a woman Mistress Ashley was." It would be a simple matter, he hinted, to lay the blame at the lady mistress's feet. Elizabeth ignored this move and would say nothing of "any practice" committed by Kate or Parry concerning Thomas Seymour. Tyrwhitt did not believe her. He wrote to the

Protector later that day to say that "I do see it in her face that she is guilty."[16] However, he could also see that she would abide many storms before she would accuse the woman that she loved most in the world. The interview was over for the day, and Elizabeth returned to the disapproving custody of her acting lady mistress. The pressure was intense. Day and night, Elizabeth was never free of the watchful Tyrwhitts.

Sir Robert summoned the princess early the following day, requiring her to "deliberate" on various matters.[17] Although attempts to persuade her to blame her servants had not been successful the previous day, he continued to employ "gentle persuasions" with her. As the day went on, he believed that he was growing "with her in credit," and it seemed as though victory was near. She told him of her meeting with Parry in December, when he asked whether she would marry the Lord Admiral were the Council to allow it. Where Tyrwhitt thought he was getting truth, however, she was almost certainly lying. Elizabeth's confession was considerably different from Parry's, which was drawn from him in the darkness of the Tower of London. Tyrwhitt ended the day hopefully, considering it to be "a good beginning," by which—as he wrote to Somerset—"I trust more will follow."[18]

Tyrwhitt had a trick of his own to play. As he ended this interrogation, he informed Elizabeth that Kate was actually not, as yet, taken to the Tower and that she remained imprisoned in "Petty Calais," an area of Westminster known for its wool dealers.[19] At this news, Elizabeth rejoiced; but it was a lie intended only to entice her to speak. Perhaps if she confessed, she might save Kate from the horrors of the Tower? Tyrwhitt thought he now had the measure of the princess, explaining to Somerset that "she hath a very good wit, and nothing is gotten off her, but by great policy."

Nevertheless, after two days of interrogating a fifteen-year-old girl, Sir Robert had actually achieved very little. Although still a minor, the princess was self-possessed in the extreme and highly conscious of her royal status. She had only recently taken possession of a throne, covered in cloth of gold and crimson velvet with a canopy above.[20] Sitting in her father's chair, she must have suddenly seemed a formidable opponent to her inquisitor.

On the following day, 24 January, Tyrwhitt received a letter from Somerset. This evidently repeated some of the rumors circulating about the princess, since (as Tyrwhitt claimed) he only showed it to her "with a great protestation" that he would not for £1,000 have the contents known. Both that day and the next, he tried to show her "great kindness" in the hope that she would unburden herself to him. He failed in his goal, and on the evening of 25 January he complained bitterly to his master that "I cannot frame her to all points, as I would wish it to be"; she was just too elusive. He had gotten nowhere with the princess, and so he asked Somerset to send Lady Browne to Hatfield again, since "for the experience that I have of her, there is nobody may do more good to cause her to confess the truth than she."

On receiving Tyrwhitt's letter, Somerset was growing impatient. Elizabeth's testimony was essential to his investigation. By 25 January, it had been over a week since Thomas had been committed to the Tower, and since then he had been largely ignored while the witness statements were gathered. He spent his time with his keeper, Christopher Ayer, but was cut off from the world outside. Finally, a deputation from the Council came to him on the twenty-fifth. Seymour, brought before them, had no interest in what they had to say; indeed, he appeared surly and unwilling to respond.[21] He had no desire to cooperate with the erstwhile colleagues who had imprisoned him. It was only with difficulty that he finally agreed to give a few brief answers.

When asked "whether he hath communed with any person or persons, touching an alteration of the order of the person of the King's Majesty, and of his Council," Seymour answered that, as he desired "to be saved," since the last Parliament he had spoken on such matters with no one save the Earl of Rutland, "upon occasion of talk of the King's Majesty's towardness, whom I said would be a man three years before any child living; and that I thought within two or three years, he would desire more liberty, and the honour of his own things." He had, he said, told Rutland that should the king command him to make a "motion" (i.e., raise the matter) to Somerset and the Council, then he would do so.

As he was speaking, Seymour had no idea just who had been interrogated and what the government knew at that point. Shrewdly, he kept his answers only to what he believed Rutland could have told them; as Elizabeth had done, he was determined to keep his silence. In spite of this, he was hopeful that he could make amends with his brother. Thomas therefore confessed that he had thought his brother should be merely chief of the Council rather than Lord Protector; yet, he insisted, "if I meant any hurt to My Lord's Grace my brother, more than I meant to my soul, then I desire neither life nor other favour at his hand." He asked the lords to bring a message to his brother to that effect, promising always to be at his commandment. It was a start, but far from what the Protector required to justify his proceedings against his brother. Certainly, there was nothing there that amounted to a confession of treason.

Somerset was haunted by the idea of just how close Thomas had come to marrying Elizabeth. The security of the princess's virginity became a prime concern. On 26 January, while he sat in the Lords, a bill was introduced to Parliament declaring that the marriage of the king's sisters without the Council's consent be considered treason. This was clearly aimed at Elizabeth; no one thought Princess Mary was in danger of eloping. On the same day, he wrote in frustration to Tyrwhitt, ordering him to continue to press the teenager to confess "by all means and policy."[22]

Somerset also found himself frustrated in Parliament. The bill was not as well received as he had hoped, and although it struggled through to a second reading on 28 January, it proceeded no further.*

---

* By convention, all bills were allowed to pass their first reading, even if their chances of success were slim (BL Harley MS 6807 f. 14v). The fact that this bill reached a second reading says nothing about its popularity in the House.

Bills required three readings and a vote in both Lords and Commons before royal assent was sought, and this bill was never going to pass. In addition, to his surprise, Somerset received a letter from his brother.

After his interrogation on 25 January, Thomas had spent a day alone in his room in the Tower. Although parts of the fortress included fine royal apartments and rich offices, for Thomas it was a prison, where conditions were basic. He must have feared that he would be confined there forgotten forever. With the hours dragging by, he finally resolved to write to his brother and was provided with writing materials. Signing himself "Your Grace's to command, and brother,"[23] he mentioned his previous deposition, in which he now assured "Your Grace, on my faith, I wrote all that came to my remembrance." However, he added that overnight he had recalled that he had once spoken to the king when he had walked with him in the gallery at Hampton Court. He commented that the boy "was grown to be a goodly gentleman, and trusted that within three or four years, he should be ruler of his own thing," to which Edward had only said: "Nay." They had then, Seymour said, discussed other matters, while Thomas confessed himself unsure of whether or not he had told this to John Fowler. He assured his brother that his failure to mention this had been innocent, before "requiring Your Grace to be my good lord, and to remit my oversight, as Your Grace hath done to a number of other. But if I meant either hurt or displeasure to Your Grace, in this or any other thing that I have done, then punish me to extremity."

Seymour had always been forgiven by his brother in the past, and it seemed possible—even likely—that the same would happen again now. He scrawled his letter over two sheets of parchment, the messy penmanship evidence of his unstable mental state.[24] Yet, for Somerset, Thomas's failure to confess all was infuriating. Elizabeth, too, was saying she had told all she could recall. In both cases, the Protector knew that they were lying.

While Somerset remained impotently furious at Elizabeth's defiance, Sir Robert Tyrwhitt was nonplussed. He replied to the Protector's letter of 26 January two days later on 28 January, after continuing daily interviews with the princess.[25] To Tyrwhitt's obvious frustration, Elizabeth continued steadfastly to deny that she knew anything more than she had already told him. She was growing angry—although she did appear "more pleasant" to her interrogator when he showed her Somerset's letter: she was wary of offending such a powerful man. Despite these pleasantries, Tyrwhitt did not believe a word that she told him. He had finally gotten the measure of her, telling Somerset plainly that "I do very believe that there hath been some secret promise, between My Lady, Mistress Ashley, and the cofferer, never to confess to death; and if it be so, it will never be gotten of her, but either by the King's Majesty, or else by Your Grace."

Tyrwhitt was admitting defeat in his battle with the self-possessed fifteen-year-old. He was forced to confine himself to the small triumph of noting some small household accounting irregularities, which he brought to the Protector's attention with relish. There was, though, a hint that while Elizabeth would support Kate Ashley in everything, she might be prepared to abandon Parry. In discussing her household expenses, Tyrwhitt told Somerset that "if any make suit to you to be her cofferer, that Your Grace will stay it, till she speak with you; for it is thought a meaner officer will serve that room, and save in her purse £100 a year." It seems Elizabeth could countenance Parry's replacement in order to save herself and Kate.

Later on 28 January, Elizabeth, sensing Tyrwhitt's failure, wrote herself to the Protector, in her fine italic hand. She was furious and wanted the pressure to end, but she wrote humbly, declaring: "My Lord, your great gentleness, and good will towards me, as well in this thing, as in other things, I do understand, for the which, even as I ought, so I do give you most humble thanks."[26] She acknowledged that the Protector "willeth and counselleth me, as an earnest friend" to declare everything she knew to Tyrwhitt, and also to write it herself, and promised that she would do so.

She set out everything she had told Tyrwhitt, speaking of the letter concerning Edmund Allen and her suit for Durham Place, as well as Thomas's offer of his own house. She mentioned some of Kate Ashley's speeches, saying that she had said the Lord Admiral would come a-wooing. She insisted, however, that "I never consented unto any such thing, without the Council's consent thereunto. And as for Kat. Ashley or the Cofferer, they never told me that they would practice it." She was the picture of innocence, insisting that this was all she knew, before calling on her conscience as her witness, "which I would not for all earthly things offend in anything; for I know I have a soul to save, as well as other folks have." She laid it on thick, promising that "if there be any more things which I can remember, I will either write it myself, or cause Master Tyrwhitt to write it."

As Elizabeth's defiance continued, Tyrwhitt now tried a harsher approach. He informed her of rumors that he had heard in London, which the princess admitted to Somerset "be greatly both against my honour, and honesty."[27] It was whispered, Tyrwhitt told her, that she was already in the Tower and, scandalously, "with child by My Lord Admiral." Seymour had not been seen in London for some days, and this tittle-tattle must have been spoken almost from the moment of Seymour's arrest, spreading like wildfire. Elizabeth was aghast and outraged at "these shameful slanders." She would come to court, she said, so "that I may show myself there as I am." Then people would see that she was not pregnant. But no invitation arrived from the Protector. She was almost as much a prisoner as Kate and Parry.

The interrogations at Hatfield continued without letup. On 31 January, Tyrwhitt informed Somerset that "I think nothing true" in what the girl was saying, since she insisted that "this Ashley" had not spoken to her seriously about marriage.[28] Elizabeth's loyalty to Kate had taken him by surprise. He had come to realize that "she will no more accuse Mistress Ashley than she will her own self." Indeed, if anyone criticized Kate or appeared to "disapprove her doings," the princess would defend her fiercely, but she would still confess nothing. As she started to demand to be allowed to see the king, Tyrwhitt became exasperated. It was not his fault, he pleaded to Somerset, since "If Your Grace did know all my persuasions with her all manner of ways weighing her honour and safety to the country, Your Grace will not a little marvel that she will no more cough out matters than she doth." He blamed Kate's "ill" influence, for "the love she hath to Ashley is to be marvelled at." In Tyrwhitt's opinion, they were looking in the wrong direction. If Kate would confess, then he was sure that he could make Elizabeth "cough out the full."

While Elizabeth suffered under the mental strain of her interrogation, her lady mistress's troubles were much more physical. Kate was kept in a dank chamber in the Tower, the floor covered in straw and the glassless window letting in the freezing January wind that gusted relentlessly.[29] She spent her nights hunched up and sleepless as she tried to keep warm: she was still wearing only the thin russet-colored nightdress in which she had left Hatfield. Even scrabbling around in the cold to stuff the window with straw did little to ease her suffering, instead plunging the room into murky blackness during the sparse winter hours of daylight; though the gloom was preferable to the winter chill. Within days she had become a hunched, shivering creature to be pitied. She begged that if only her conditions were to become more palatable, then her memory, "which is never good when I am in best quiet," might improve.

Thomas Parry, too, was suffering—and it was he, not Kate, who cracked first. On 2 February, Kate was hauled out of her cell and brought "face to face" with Parry, whom she had not seen for nearly two weeks.[30] The pitiable cofferer stood silently as his two handwritten confessions were read. He had broken his silence to speak of his meetings with Seymour and his conversations with the princess on his return to Hatfield.[31] Parry went far beyond what the three had agreed to reveal, even recounting Kate's tales of Elizabeth's relations with Thomas before the queen's death. As everything tumbled out, Kate turned to her fellow prisoner, almost daring him to deny the claims; but he "stood fast" to all that he had recounted. Kate, burning with anger, shrieked "false wretch" at him, furiously berating him for revealing what "he had promised he would never confess it to death."* Parry had acknowledged as much in his confession. The princess would later comment that it must have been "a great matter for him to promise such a promise and to break it."**

Kate's own resolve now faltered. She had held her tongue in the face of the cold and darkness in which she was kept, but she longed to be released. Later that day, she made her first declaration; others followed on 4 February.[32] She spoke of everything she could recall, going right back to within weeks of the old king's death. She unburdened herself about the morning romps at Chelsea, Hanworth, and Seymour Place, and she spoke of the incident in the gardens at Hanworth, when Elizabeth's dress was slashed. She spared few details, speaking of her own affection for Thomas and her desire that he should become the princess's husband. Always, however, she insisted—as did Parry—that no marriage had been intended without first obtaining the Council's consent. She hoped, unrealistically, that her depositions would see her released and reinstated with the princess. Although she would "look not" for it, if only she were to return to Elizabeth, then "never would I speak nor wis [know] of marriage—no, not to win all the world."[33]

* S. Haynes, p. 95. The cry of "false wretch" is often attributed to Elizabeth, but on a close reading of the source it appears more correctly to have been uttered by Kate when Parry was brought to her in the Tower.

** It was certainly Sir Robert Tyrwhitt's firm belief that there had been collusion among Elizabeth, Kate, and Parry—as is clear from their very similar accounts of what happened and the fury of Kate and Elizabeth when they realized Parry had confessed more than was agreed.

While Kate Ashley only wanted to be back at Hatfield, Elizabeth must have wished that she was almost anywhere else. On 4 February, Kate's and Parry's confessions were collected and hurried over to Elizabeth's residence, along with another letter from Somerset to the princess. Tyrwhitt read through the documents jubilantly. On the following day, he summoned the princess to him.[34] She was stunned when her interrogator produced the depositions. At a glance, the girl recognized the handwriting of both her servants. The horror struck her that "they have both confessed all they know."[35] She appeared "much abashed, and half breathless" as she read over the documents, struggling to get to the end of them. She had thought that her servants, who had taken an oath to serve her faithfully, would remain true.[36] Yet everything that she had tried to conceal was right there, inked in front of her. With her composure gone, Tyrwhitt allowed her to go. He promised his master, in a letter written the same day, that on the following day he would travail all he could "to frame her for her own surety, and to utter the truth." Elizabeth had some urgent thinking to do.

The following day Tyrwhitt came to a seemingly chastened Elizabeth. Without offering further proofs, he persuaded her "with good advice" to write to the Protector. She agreed, promising him that "she will call all things to her remembrance" in her letter. Returning to her chamber, and with the disagreeable Lady Tyrwhitt still in absolute control of her daily circumstances, she must have felt furious. It is just possible that she took this fury out on Seymour in one of the only hints that she was ever displeased with his actions. Taking a copy of Catherine Parr's *Psalms, or, Prayers* that had once belonged to her father, she turned to the words "certainly even from my beginning I have used myself proudly."[37] Beneath this, in her own hand and in Latin, the princess inscribed: "vanity of vanities, and the height of vanity. T. Seymour," before adding an insignia of a superimposed "T" and "R" for Thomas Rex. For the moment, beset by her own troubles, she saw her suitor for what he really was: a fortune hunter.

Despite the weight of testimony, Elizabeth's instinct remained, however, to fight. In the safety of her own chamber, she wrote a short note to the Protector. She was full of indignation at the continuing interrogations as "I would not (as I trust you have not) so evil a opinion of me that I would conceal anything that I knew, for it were to no purpose."[38] If she failed to admit anything, it was not her fault, she argued, since "surely forgetfulness may well cause me to hide things, but undoubtedly else I will declare all that I know."

Her tart letter badly misjudged the Protector's sympathies, and the princess received a stern rebuke in return for her discourtesy toward Tyrwhitt and—as Elizabeth summarized it—for seeming "to stand in mine own wit in being so well assured of mine own self."[39] Somerset took her letters in "evil part." He was furious that she did not seem more contrite. She needed to use herself more humbly.

Elizabeth must have felt entirely alone, but she still stood firm. On 7 February she silently passed a confession—written in her own hand—to Tyrwhitt.[40] It was a masterful document, accepting most of what had been revealed by her servants, but in no way incriminating herself. She began neatly, in her italic hand, before—writing more quickly—it became more of a scrawl.[41] She remained self-possessed throughout, however, signing "Elizabeth" with a looping flourish at the end of the document.

After reading it, Tyrwhitt was crestfallen. He wrote ruefully to Somerset that it was "not so full of matter as I would it were, nor yet so much as I did procure her to do." The most that she would admit to was that Kate had often counseled her on the marriage, but that it was dependent on achieving the Council's consent.[42] All Tyrwhitt could say, as he summed up the confession to Somerset, was that sadly "in no way, she will confess, that our Mistress Ashley, or Parry willed her to any practice with My Lord Admiral, either by message or writing." Their confessions were embarrassing to Elizabeth—with their talk of tickles in bed and of the size of her buttocks—but they did not amount to treason.

Elizabeth might well have feared that her servants had yet more to reveal. To neuter this, she ended her own deposition with a note of finality. She would offer nothing more, for "these are the articles which I do remember, that both she and the cofferer talked with me of; and if there be any more behind which I have not declared as yet, I shall heartily desire your lordship and the rest of the Council, not to think that I do willingly conceal them, but that I have indeed forgotten them." Finally, it was Elizabeth who prevailed—her secrets remained concealed from the world and unacknowledged.

If Elizabeth feared what more Kate or Thomas might say, she at least need not have worried about revelations from the man who would have been her husband. During the early part of February, he seemed to his jailer Ayer to be in reasonably good spirits. He was waiting for an answer to the letter to his brother. Several times he assured Ayer that he hoped to have his answer on Friday 13 February, since "on the Friday the Lords do not sit in the Parliament; and therefore then they will come, or send to me; if no, Saturday or Sunday; so that then I shall know somewhat of their minds towards me; if that day pass then I have no hope till Friday come again."[43]

No reply came. On the Friday, Seymour seemed to Ayer "very sad." The keeper, who kept his prisoner kindly enough, attempted to console him, saying that "he was very sorry to see his lordship so sad." Thomas replied that he "thought as that day to have heard somewhat from My Lord's Grace and the Council," but now he "seeth the contrary." Seymour was beginning to understand just how serious matters were. "I had thought before I came to this place that My Lord's Grace, with all the rest of the Council, had been my friends, and that I had had as many friends, as any man within the realm; but now I think they have forgotten me."

Pausing for a moment, Thomas mournfully asked Ayer the reason for his imprisonment. The jailer, incredulous that he should ask this, replied that he could not tell him, before asking him: "Do not you know, My Lord?" Seymour replied: "No by my troth, for

I cannot judge myself of an evil thought, never since last Parliament." He continued asserting his innocence: "I am sure of this, that as concerning the king, there was never poor knave truer to his prince than I am, and to all his succession, both My Lady Mary and My Lady Elizabeth. And as for My Lord my brother, I never meant evil thought to him. Marry, this, before the last Parliament, I thought that I might have the King's Majesty in my custody, with the consent of the Lords and Commons of the Parliament: and to say that ever I went about to take the king from My Lord my brother by force, I never meant nor thought." Thomas appeared genuinely baffled.

Seymour had taken the time to get to know his keeper during the weeks of his imprisonment, and he now declared to him that "if there be any man in all England to accuse me that I should be a false knave to the king or his succession, or to the realm, I will wish no life. For if I had, I thought the stones will rise against me."[44] He was still depressed two days later, refusing his breakfast. That day, however, he at last received the expected visit from the lords, who he was sure—as he informed Ayer—"went away pleased with my answer." Ayer told his prisoner: "I am glad My Lord to see you of better cheer and more merry," to which Seymour said he would not have eaten had the lords not come, "for I should have no stomach." But now, along with his appetite, he had some hope again.

For another of the Tower's prisoners, William Sharington, fate appeared to hang in the balance. On 14 February 1549, he was taken to the Guildhall, where he was indicted for treason.[45] The authorities had more than enough evidence to bring about his ruin but chose to charge him only with coining £2,000 worth of silver testoons the previous July. He confessed to this readily but before being returned to the Tower, he was sentenced to be hanged, drawn, and quartered. Yet even with sentence passed, Sharington remained the Crown's star witness against Seymour, recalling on 15 February that his former friend had spoken to him of his dislike of the Protector, as well as of his hopes of a marriage between the king and Jane Grey.[46] Ambassador Van der Delft, who had finally returned to London, considered that Sharington had been charged very leniently and, although sentenced to death, that he thought he would likely receive a pardon.[47] This was Sharington's reward for testifying against his friend.

By the second week of February, the Council felt that it had sufficient ammunition. Thirty-three charges had been drawn up against Thomas Seymour—and one of the most damning was the claim that he had practiced to marry Elizabeth without consent.

Chapter Eighteen

A MAN OF MUCH WIT

The month of February remained bitingly cold for those kept in the Tower. From within his chamber, Thomas Seymour could catch the sounds of life going on around him, but he was immured behind the gray stone walls. Parliament still sat almost daily, but there was one conspicuously empty place. From his cell, Seymour gave voice to his woes by composing poetry, complaining in verse that "God did call me in my pride lest I should fall and from him slide. For whom he loves he must correct, that they may be of his elect."[1] He ended on a loyal note, praying God that the king would have many years "in governing this realm in joy" before, too, finding bliss in Heaven. There was no word about the Protector. The brothers were entirely estranged.

Princess Elizabeth had continuing miseries of her own to contend with. Following her written deposition, the daily interrogations ceased; but Sir Robert Tyrwhitt was still firmly ensconced at Hatfield. She had a brief respite, though, from the supervision of Lady Tyrwhitt, who crept back to London for a visit in the second week of February. As far as the Council was concerned, this was a dereliction of duty, and they hauled her in on 17 February as soon as they heard "lately tell of her being here."[2] She had been instructed to stay at Hatfield, so in leaving she "hath not shewed herself so much attendant to her office in this part, as we looked for at her hands." The lords of the Council spoke to her "roundly in that behalf." Nonetheless, they still needed her and her services. She was packed off back to Elizabeth with a letter, informing the princess that since Katherine Ashley—"who heretofore hath had the special charge to see to the good education and government of your person"—had shown herself unfit for the office, Lady Tyrwhitt would be officially appointed in her place. Elizabeth was instructed to "accept her [Lady Tyrwhitt's] service thankfully, and also hear and follow her good advices from time to time, especially in such matters as we have at this time appointed her to move unto you."

No one can have expected Elizabeth to take the news well. Lady Tyrwhitt enlisted her husband to help break the news.[3] In reaction, the princess was outraged, declaring that "Mistress Ashley was her mistress, and that she had not so demeaned herself, that the Council should now need to put any more mistresses unto her." Privately, the dour Lady Tyrwhitt, having lived in Catherine's household and been the queen's confidante, probably had her own thoughts on this. She retained her composure, however, in the face of Elizabeth's fury, declaring tartly that "seeing she did allow Mistress Ashley to be her mistress, she need not to be ashamed to have any honest woman to be in that place." Elizabeth could never bear criticism of Kate. Powerless, she rushed to her chamber in tears, weeping loudly through the night, before mournfully moaning all the next day. The loss of the woman who had raised her was a terrible blow.

Elizabeth stopped her crying only late on 18 February 1549, when she received a letter from Somerset. Timidly, with a tear-stained face, she asked Tyrwhitt whether she was best to write to the Protector again. Her keeper replied that if she intended to accede to Somerset's demands, then he "thought it well done that she should write," but that if, as he perceived, she meant to disobey, then such a response was inadvisable. On the following day, Tyrwhitt himself wrote to the Protector, telling him that the princess was still indignant at Lady Tyrwhitt's appointment, fearing that "the world would note her to be a great offender, having so hastily a governor appointed to her." Neither Tyrwhitt nor Somerset, who both thought that she was indeed "a great offender," had any real sympathy for her. Sir Robert was certain that she still hoped "to recover her old mistress again." His own candid opinion ("if I should say my fantasy") was that she should have two lady mistresses, not just one. He evidently thought that the task of keeping Elizabeth's honor protected was a difficult one.

Tyrwhitt had become jaded in his dealings with the obdurate girl, offering advice on what she should write to the Protector but knowing that she would not heed it. Nonetheless, on 19 February he was able to report that "she beginneth now a little to droop." His wife had told him that this was because she had learned that Seymour's household had been broken up—a clear sign that he was expected to die. Lady Tyrwhitt informed her husband that even then Elizabeth could not bear to hear Seymour "discommended" in her presence. Any criticism of the Lord Admiral drew a vehement response from the teenager. This surprised Sir Robert, who had previously only seen her rise to such passion to defend Kate Ashley. Elizabeth was far from abandoning Thomas Seymour.

The breaking up of Thomas's household was ominous—and he may not even have known about it. While Elizabeth contended with domestic dramas at Hatfield, Seymour continued to languish in the Tower. On 18 February, he was interrogated again, once more showing himself uncooperative and refusing to answer all but two questions put to him.[4] To the first, he confirmed that he had learned of the Earl of Rutland's confession through his servant, Pigot—something that must already have been obvious to his examiners. He was then asked for the names of the men with whom he had spoken concerning removing the king from the Protector's custody. This drew an indignant response, since Seymour denied that this had been his purpose: he "did never determine, in all his life, to remove the king out of My Lord Protector's hands, but by consent of the whole realm." In refusing to give his answers, Seymour may have been hoping to gain time. More likely, he was waiting to see what evidence had been obtained against him. Sir Thomas Smith, the secretary of the Council, diligently wrote up Seymour's response, but he and his fellow questioners went away unsatisfied.

Elizabeth featured heavily in the questions put to Thomas. Had he talked to anyone of the marriages of the king's sisters, or received any tokens or letters from them?[5] He was asked, too, "whether he said at any time, that he knew My Lord Protector's Grace will commit him to the Tower, if he should marry My Lady Elizabeth?" and "whether he had heard any talk of the surrender of her title to the Crown, to the intent such marriage might be had between them?" He refused to answer all of these; but Elizabeth must have been in his thoughts as he remained locked away.

Elizabeth continued to struggle at Hatfield. But after her initial grief at losing Kate and acquiring Lady Tyrwhitt, she became calmer. She wrote to apologize to the Protector on 21 February. She had only complained—she insisted—about the change in her lady mistress because she "thought the people will say that I deserved through my lewd demeanour to have such a one." Even at Hatfield, she had heard rumors that horrified her. Although she knew that she could report them to the Council for punishment, "which thing, though I can easily do it, I would be loath to do it for because it is mine own cause, and again that should be but a breeding of an evil name of me that I am glad to punish them, and so get the evil will of the people, which thing I would be loath to have." The princess knew the value of public opinion. Would it instead be possible, she asked, for a proclamation to be issued, making it illegal to spread such scurrilous tales about the king's sisters? Somerset had already told her that the gossip was her own fault, since she gave "folks occasion to think in refusing the good to uphold the evil." Not so, she countered by letter, she was "not of so simple understanding." Elizabeth wrote in haste, anxious to clear herself with the Protector, but she was also defiant: how dare the son of Sir John Seymour of Wolf Hall criticize her, the daughter of a king?

When she wrote that day, Elizabeth was aware that—for her—the danger was over. She had suffered weeks of interrogation and had lost the services of her beloved Kate, but she was otherwise unscathed. Perhaps she hoped that Thomas would similarly clear his name, particularly since his brother had always forgiven him in the past. Indeed, Somerset would, some months later, go so far as to admit to Elizabeth that his brother would have been saved had he given him access—but that he had been so persuaded of his guilt he dared not.[6]

Thomas Seymour was undoubtedly guilty of much wrongdoing: the quantities of silver crowns and merchants' goods seized when Seymour Place was searched testified to this fact. Emperor Charles V was furious when he heard that much silver, "no small amount of which once belonged to our subjects," had been found in his house. As Lord Admiral, Seymour had indeed become England's "chief pirate" and very nearly caused a serious diplomatic incident. Limping back to London that February, attacked by gout, Van der Delft had immediately invited members of the Council to his house to discuss the restitutions to be made.[7] The Imperial ambassador was feeling vindicated, for ten months before he had informed Somerset that many of the goods seized by pirates would indeed be found in Seymour Place.* Paget nodded in agreement, saying of Seymour: "He has

* The stolen goods largely did not find their way back to their owners (Gruffydd, p. 60).

been a great rascal." Candidly, he considered that Thomas had "more greed than wit or judgment."

Paget came together with the rest of his colleagues in the Council chamber at Westminster on 22 February to consider the charges against the fallen admiral. The list of thirty-three articles that had been drawn up was based largely on the witness statements obtained over the previous few weeks.[8] They were highly detailed, covering Seymour's attempts to be appointed governor of the king, corruption of Edward's Privy Chamber, and his boasts of a "black Parliament" in 1547.[9] Three articles dealt with Thomas's attempts to take the king into his own hands, while his promise to marry Edward to Jane Grey was included too. Article 19 dealt with his attempts to marry Elizabeth before his wedding to Catherine, while Articles 20 and 21 concerned his scandalous marriage to the queen. Tellingly, Article 21, which set out the means by which Thomas had won the king's acceptance of his marriage to Catherine, concluded by saying that "it is to be feared, that at this present you did intend to use the same practice in the marriage of the Lady Elizabeth's Grace." Through such a marriage, the Council feared, he meant to murder the king and claim the crown himself.[10] His actions at the Bristol mint, together with his piracy, were added for good measure, giving a picture of a dangerous rogue. Nonetheless, there was a question mark hanging over whether it all amounted to treason, particularly since Seymour had made little headway in achieving his aims.

Once the information against Seymour had been gathered, it was handed to his fellow Privy Councillor Sir Edward Montagu, Lord Chief Justice of the Common Pleas.[11] This thin-lipped, stern-eyed lawyer had decades of experience in the judiciary to call upon. In sifting through the information, he was assisted by his fellow Privy Councillor Thomas Goodrick, Bishop of Ely, and John Gosnold, a lawyer. Both these men quickly came to the uncomfortable conclusion that Seymour's "fault was not treason, but misprision at the uttermost, if it could be proved that Sharington had done it was laid to his charge, and the Admiral should consent unto it."

The lesser charge of misprision—or failure to report treason—would not do at all. Montagu merely shook his head as the two lawyers stood before him. "Well," he said, "if you were fleshed as we be, you would not stick at this matter." Nonetheless, Goodrick answered: "If you take this matter to be treason, let him be indicted and tried by the order of the common law, the fault might hereafter, the king coming to his age, be imputed to us if it be done by Parliament we be discharged." In other words, at least if he were tried by his peers, the investigators could not be accused in years to come.

Sitting at the Council table at Westminster on 22 February, the Council was bullish, declaring that the charges against Thomas were "so manifestly proved against him by diverse ways that it appeared not able to be avoided but he should be guilty of them."[12] The councilors were not so confident, however, that they were prepared to commit him to trial without first obtaining a confession. It was therefore resolved that—as a body—they should go to the Tower the next day to interrogate their prisoner, "to the intent that he should, if he could, clear himself of them, or show some excuse or pretence, if he had any, whereby he could think to urge himself of them and avoid them."

On 23 February, the councilors made their way to the Tower of London, setting up their base in a chamber to the side of the king's gallery.[13] By then, Thomas had been a prisoner for more than a month. The contrast between his bare prison walls and the opulence of the royal apartments must have seemed gaping to him. To begin with, he was given no chance to speak. Instead, Lord Rich, the Lord Chancellor, methodically read out the thirty-three articles against him. It was the first opportunity that Thomas Seymour had had to learn exactly *what* he was charged with. It is probably only now that the thoroughness of the investigations carried out became clear to him. When Rich's monotone finally ended, the Lord Chancellor informed Seymour that this was his chance to clear himself—if he could.

Thomas Seymour shook his head. He "would answer to nothing laid to his charge, neither yea nor nay, except he had his accusers brought before him, and except he were brought in upon trial of arraignment, where he might say before all the world what he could say for his declaration." The lords looked around, agreeing as one that this was a "very strange" answer. Take "better advice," they told him sharply. Rich commanded him on his allegiance to the king to answer "yea" or "nay." Yet resolutely all he would say was that "if they would leave the articles with him he would thank them, but as for answering," he continued, "they should not look for it, for he would not do it otherwise than as he said before."

At that, he was sent from the chamber with his guard, while the councilors deliberated. They were not prepared to read the articles again or show them to him if he would not answer. Calling Seymour in again, they "desired, moved, exhorted, prayed and commanded him to hear and answer to the said articles," but Thomas "finally and obstinately," in their words, refused their pleading. Thwarted, they left, returning him to his prison room. It was a hollow victory for Seymour, although he must have realized that his chances of clearing his name in the face of the Council's certainty of his guilt were nonexistent.

The following day the Council conveyed to the Protector everything that had happened in the Tower.[14] Somerset, who had been diligently present at Council meetings, had so far kept his hands clean of the investigation. Nonetheless, he agreed to go with the Council after dinner to the king to report "both of such heinous and traitorous attempts and doings as the Lord Admiral had done and intended, and also of his obstinate refusal to answer to the same, or to excuse himself, if peradventure there might be any hope for him either to be proved guiltless or to receive pardon." Somerset was irritated, for his brother's confession would have saved the need for his own direct complicity in his fate. With the Council's urging, it was agreed that Lord Rich should ask Edward what his mind was and whether he would be content for them to proceed by Parliament.

As soon as the eleven-year-old king had eaten, his Council came to him and set out everything. With one voice, they agreed that

Seymour was guilty and should be attainted.* Somerset nodded, declaring only "how sorrowful a case this was unto him," but that "he did yet rather regard his bounden duty to the King's Majesty and the Crown of England than his own son or brother." He assured Edward that he "did weigh more his allegiance than his blood" and therefore could not resist the Council's request. He could not refuse justice, since he no longer considered his brother to be "worthy [of] life."**

After listening, the boy-king immediately said: "We do perceive that there is great things which be objected and laid to My Lord Admiral, mine uncle, and they tend to treason, and we perceive that you require but justice to be done. We think it reasonable, and we will well that you proceed according to your request." The speed of Edward's reply, and the fact that he required no prompting, surprised his Council. They rejoiced, giving him hearty praise and thanks. Thomas Seymour would have been horrified—he believed that his nephew loved him. He was wrong.

Later on 24 February, a second deputation from the Council arrived at the Tower to inform Thomas that he was to be attainted for treason in Parliament. The group numbered both members of the Lords and Commons: Lord Rich, together with the earls of Warwick, Shrewsbury, and Southampton, along with Sir John Baker, Sir Thomas Cheney, Sir Thomas Smith, and Sir Anthony

---

* A bill of attainder—used rarely, and for the most part in cases of treason—avoided a trial, instead requiring a vote in Parliament as to the person's guilt and then the sovereign's assent to the (almost inevitable) capital punishment. Catherine Parr's predecessor as queen, Catherine Howard, was attainted, although in her case the king evaded giving his formal assent to the subsequent beheading of his wife.

** Somerset, for all his show of reluctance, firmly drove the proceedings against Thomas. His wife may also have counseled him to this. The sixteenth-century Jesuit writer Nicholas Sander (though often unreliable) considered that "the Protector's wife gave her husband no rest, matters came at last to this: the Protector, who, though he ruled the king, was yet ruled by his wife, must put his brother to death" (Sander, p. 184). John Foxe also claimed that "the Duchess of Somerset had wrought his death" (Foxe, p. 283).

Denny.* After they assembled, at the chamber in the Tower that by now was almost becoming a courtroom,[15] Seymour was brought in once more. He was asked again that he provide a defense and promised that it would be heard in Parliament.

To begin with, the delegation was met only with the Lord Admiral's "stiff standing and refusal to answer." Yet, in the face of their persuasions and cajoling, Seymour's resolve finally broke. He agreed reluctantly to answer the articles.[16] Rich again began to read them out.

To the first article, Seymour admitted his discussions with Fowler regarding the ease with which someone could kidnap the king, as well as his hopes to be appointed the boy's governor. To the second article he confessed that he had given money to those about the king. He also mentioned that Edward himself had sent to him for money, a request he had obliged. To the third article, he agreed that he had drawn up a bill to appoint himself governor and had attempted to obtain the king's agreement. But then his compliance faltered. When it came to the fourth article, which dealt with his attempts to draw the Council to his party during the Parliament of 1547, he stopped short. It was no good, he told those assembled, "he would answer to no more before them"—and he refused all

---

* There is considerable dispute over the Earl of Warwick's involvement in Seymour's fall. Although he stirred up trouble between the two brothers in 1547, regarding the governorship of the king, he otherwise seems to have sat back and watched the admiral destroy himself. Seymour was not Warwick's main quarry since, politically, he was of little importance, and no contemporary records assign Warwick a leading role in the proceedings against Thomas. Where sources such as John Foxe state that "the subtle old serpent, always envying man's felicity, through slanderous tongues sought to sow matter, first of discord between them; then of suspicion; and last of all, extreme hatred" (p. 233), the people stirring up this trouble are not named. Warwick certainly helped to sow discord, but the rivalry between Seymour/Catherine and the Somersets largely did the damage. Seymour certainly did not view Warwick as an enemy (although they were far from friends). Not long before his arrest, Seymour told John Harington that he had recently met with Warwick, when one of them (Harington could not remember which) said that "the world said they were not friends," but the other answered that "the world should see the contrary, for the one of them would resort to the other's house" (S. Haynes, p. 83).

persuasions to answer anything else or even hear the remaining articles. He had made no mention of Elizabeth.

This might have been the point at which, with a firm hand, he carefully obliterated three pages of answers that he had previously begun to write out, heavily crossing through the words and rendering them illegible.[17] He even scribbled through his signature at the foot of the third page. This erasure must have taken him some time to achieve. The admiral's fury was evident with every stroke of the pen. He would not answer for himself; as far as he was concerned, there was no cause to do so.[18] He had committed no treason.

Seymour's interrogators thus returned from the Tower with his answers to the first three articles only, which had been written on a separate sheet. It was the last time Thomas would be so examined. Having refused to mount a defense, he rested his hopes entirely in the hands of Parliament. His insistence that "he had a right to a public hearing" went ignored.[19]

On the following day, 25 February, Lord Protector Somerset—for all his protestations of sorrow—led the Lords into the Parliament chamber. They crowded in, but, to the disappointment of those assembled, the attainder of Thomas Seymour was low down the agenda. They found themselves forced instead to sit through the reading of bills against unlawful hunting and for the regulation of merchants going to Iceland.

At last the moment was reached, as, against a hush, the bill of attainder against the Protector's own brother was read out. It did not disappoint, being drafted in the most lurid terms. There were claims that the admiral "not having God before his eyes" and "filled with the most dangerous, insatiable, and fearful vice of ambition and greediness of rule, authority and dominion" did intend to take the king into his possession "by violence, stealth or other undue means" and take on the role of Protector and governor of the boy-king.[20]

To prove the accusations, the witness depositions were then read out. Amid the clamor of voices, some of Thomas's accusers were brought in to be examined, standing bare-headed before the Lords.[21] Toward the end of the session, the judges and the Council declared "plain the case to be manifest treason."[22] That was enough for the day, and the Lords could go to their homes for dinner.

The next day, with Somerset again in attendance, the bill received its second reading, with its third on Wednesday 27 February. Now, it was time to vote, and the House was again packed to the rafters. With one voice, the Lords cried out, "Yea!" Only Somerset, "for natural pity's sake," abstained.[23] He would not add his own voice to the final condemnation of his brother—but, then, it was not required. He remained in his seat in the chamber.

With the passing of the bill in the Lords, it moved to the Commons. If Thomas had any hopes of a reprieve, it was in the Lower House of Parliament, filled with the gentlemen and yeomen he had done so much to charm and win to his side. Unusually, the Lords decided to send down a deputation with the bill, to declare "the manner after the which the Lords had proceeded in this matter."[24] They promised that they would send the noblemen who had given evidence against Seymour to declare "by mouth and presence, such matter as by their writing should in the mean time appear unto them." The Master of the Rolls, who carefully carried the bill before him, went over to the Lower House, walking with two companions from the Lords. They found the Commons—who outnumbered the Lords four to one—assembled in great number. Despite Parliament's prevailing absenteeism, on 28 February everyone had come to the Commons to hear the first reading of the bill against Thomas Seymour.[25]

As expected, it was a turbulent session. Why, asked some of the members, had the admiral received no trial?[26] Some spoke up on his behalf, demanding that he be allowed to defend himself personally, but such protests were ignored. The second reading, on the following day, was equally rumbustious, so much so that the Lords, listening to reports from their own chamber, doubted whether it would pass.

On 1 March, the same three gentlemen from the Lords, along with the king's solicitor, returned to the Commons to find out whether they intended to pass the bill.[27] They would consult once again, the Commons informed them, but hoped to send up their resolution with speed. In the Lords it appeared that the Lower House proceeded interminably slowly. Eventually, tired of waiting, the Lords went for their dinners, extracting only the promise that the Commons would inform Somerset of their decision before the Lords sat again on Monday 4 March.[28]

The Protector waited—but no decision arrived. That Monday, with still no word from the Commons, the Master of the Rolls and his fellows returned once again to the Commons, squeezing into the packed room. It was the "King's Majesty's pleasure," they declared, that Thomas was not—as the Commons had requested—to be permitted to appear in his own defense. Instead, if they were still uncertain, the Lords were prepared to come "to satisfy the House for the evidence against the Admiral." Even with this assurance, the Commons debated and argued. The lawyers among them, though, declared that the offenses were indeed "in the compass of high treason." The Speaker—who had visited Thomas in the Tower a few days before—demanded to know whether anyone could show that it was not treason; they could not. Out of a packed Commons chamber, "marvellous full" with four hundred people crammed into it, as they came to the vote only ten or twelve members ultimately dissented. The bill had passed, and the king's younger uncle was—in the eyes of the law—already dead.

Elizabeth's reaction to the news of Seymour's condemnation went unrecorded. But it can hardly have been a surprise. The attainder did serve to take some of the pressure off her, since the government was now no longer interested in collecting evidence against

Seymour from the princess. Emboldened, on 7 March Elizabeth dared to write to Somerset in favor of the still-imprisoned Kate Ashley.[29] She had not done so before, she said, for fear that the Protector and Council "will think that I favour her evildoing." It was a brave attempt. While she insisted that she did not "favour her in any evil (for that I would be sorry to do)," she was nonetheless duty-bound to speak for a woman "who hath been with me a long time and many years, and hath taken great labour and pain in bringing of me up in learning and honesty."

She also sought to excuse her former lady mistress, arguing that although she had indeed meddled in the projected marriage with Thomas, "she did it because, knowing him to be one of the Council, she thought he would not go about any such thing without he had the Council's consent thereunto. For I have heard her many times say that she would never have me marry in any place without Your Grace's and the Council's consent." Finally, she added for good measure that Kate's release was necessary for her own reputation. If she continued in the Tower, people would think Elizabeth was "not clear of the deed" herself. She could not bear to think of her beloved Kate "in such a place," where her own mother had died. She hoped that Somerset would take her words "no other ways that it is meant."

Elizabeth could not be sure of how the Protector—a man who had condemned his own brother—would react. While he had no interest in trying Kate Ashley, he also ignored Elizabeth's letter. His mind was on other things. On 10 March, while sitting in the Council chamber, it was noted that he appeared world-weary, with the case so "heavy and lamentable" to him.[30] It was no small matter to order his brother's execution, and the Protector quailed at it, both out of fraternal feeling and because of the damage that it would do to his reputation. The Council offered to organize the execution itself, "without further troubling or molesting in this heavy case either his Highness or the Lord Protector." Somerset did not, however, take them up on the offer, instead going with his fellows to the king after dinner. He sat down beside his nephew as the boy listened to Lord Rich confirm that the bill had passed. Edward did not hesitate to reply, saying: "he had well perceived their proceedings herein, and gave them his hearty thanks for their pains and travails." At that, the Council left.

Thomas remained in the Tower throughout the proceedings in Parliament. On 15 March the Bishop of Ely, who had doubted that he was guilty of treason, came to him. On greeting Thomas, the bishop informed him that he had come to help him prepare for death and "to instruct him of such things as might appertain to the wealth of his soul and to the patient taking of his worthy execution."[31] But it was a cursory visit, in truth designed more to salve the souls of those who had condemned him, and the bishop soon left. Two days later, the Council, meeting at Westminster,[32] called in the bishop, who informed them that he had been with Thomas to "instruct and comfort" him as they had asked. On hearing that this was done, the Council tersely agreed a "time most convenient for the execution of the said Lord Admiral." Between them, they settled on the next Wednesday—only three days away—and, as a body, they signed the warrant for Seymour's execution. Somerset, who had professed himself so unwilling to be involved in the condemnation of his brother, was the first to set his pen to paper.

With that, all that remained for Thomas Seymour was to prepare himself for death. The bishop was once again sent to him to inform him of the arrangements. Could the bishop also, the Council asked, "teach him the best he could to the quiet and patient suffering of justice, and to prepare himself to Almighty God"? They hoped he would die quietly.

The prelate found a more resigned prisoner. For once, Seymour was willing to speak. He told the bishop that he would like Hugh Latimer, the radical Bishop of Worcester who had been a favorite of Catherine Parr, to minister to him on the day of his death.[33] Suddenly hopeful, he then asked for a deferment of his execution; but the bishop could only shake his head. Resigned again, Thomas asked that some of his servants be permitted to attend his death, something that would ensure that he was decently buried. The bishop informed him that it was agreed that "his body and head" would be buried in the Tower chapel—a phrasing that can only have caused him to shudder. Thomas also thought of his baby daughter. Might she be sent to be raised with her mother's dearest friend, the Duchess of Suffolk, "to be brought up"? With that, Seymour's visitor left. The Lord Admiral spent his final two days in the Tower, alone apart from his jailer.

While Thomas's fortunes reached their lowest ebb, Elizabeth's began to rise again. On the day the death warrant was signed, the Council ordered that £300 19 shillings 7 pence be sent for her use from the value of the lands allotted to her.[34] There was no longer any danger that she would marry Thomas Seymour.

Somerset hurriedly left London on 19 March, anxious that he should not be in the capital when his brother died.[35] Hugh Latimer came to the Tower that day, but he found a prisoner unrepentant and defiant.[36] Latimer was a poor choice to comfort him in his final day, since secretly the bishop despised the Lord Admiral, considering him "a wicked man" of whom "the realm is well rid." Seymour, for his part, had little interest in religion; indeed, it was rumored that he had gone so far as to deny the immortality of the soul.[37] The uncompromising Latimer had no time for heretics. Thomas would only speak of the king, repeating "the king, the king" without elaborating further, to the bishop's annoyance. Was he hoping that his nephew, contrite in his own complicity in the offense, would send a last-minute reprieve? If so, nothing came.

On that evening, Thomas's last, he was alone in his chamber. Although denied a pen and paper, he was determined to write. Carefully, he pulled a small pointed aglet attached to the end of a lace in his hose.[38] Dipping it into a pot of improvised ink, he began to write, filling two small scraps of paper that he had found. One was addressed to Princess Mary and one to Elizabeth. In both, he begged the princesses to conspire against the Protector, before carefully sewing them into the sole of one of his velvet shoes. It was quite a feat, demonstrating the strength of his anger against his brother, as well as the fact that his thoughts turned again, near the end, toward Elizabeth. He carefully showed his servant where to find the notes, before spending his last night alive quietly in the Tower. At some point that evening, he swore before God that he had not "intended any harm to the king's body."[39]

The following morning—Wednesday 20 March—dawned all too soon. Slipping on his final outfit and his comfortable velvet shoes, Thomas stepped out of the Tower at some point between nine o'clock and twelve noon. He was separated from his servants as he walked to Tower Hill, close by the walls of the ancient fortress. A crowd had already gathered in anticipation. Seymour mounted the straw-strewn scaffold alone. Seeing the block for the first time, he turned suddenly to a servant of the Lieutenant of the Tower, who was standing nearby. "Bid my servant speed the thing that he wots of," he muttered.[40] It was customary for the condemned to make a short speech, admitting their guilt and the rightness of their punishment. Thomas Seymour, however, said only: "I have been brought here to suffer death, for as I was lawfully born into this world so I must lawfully leave it because there is some work to be accomplished which cannot be fulfilled unless I am put out of the way."[41] With this final act of defiance, he asked everyone assembled "to pray God of his mercy to receive" his soul, before falling to his knees and laying his head on the block.[42] He did not seek forgiveness—although, since it took two brutal strokes to sever his head from his body, Bishop Latimer tartly reflected: "Who can tell but that between two strokes he doth repent?"

It was a painful, bloody death. As Seymour's body and severed head were recovered from the scaffold's straw and laid in a wagon, his servant informed the authorities about the hidden letters. The head was placed alongside the body and buried quietly in the Chapel of St. Peter ad Vincula in the Tower. There, Thomas Seymour, Baron Sudeley, joined the equally headless bodies of

Elizabeth's mother and various others that he had known during his rise to power.

When word of Thomas's execution was brought to Elizabeth at Hatfield that afternoon, she said only that "this day died a man of much wit and very little judgment."* Yet in all her long life, it was he who came closest to being her husband.

* The source of this remark is the dubious Leti, and it is therefore suspect. However, it does echo very well Paget's own remark to Van der Delft, regarding Seymour's lack of judgment, and the sentiment rings true. It may be that Leti did see a document confirming the veracity of the words.

Epilogue

THE VIRGIN QUEEN?

As Christmas 1549 approached, Elizabeth's household was busy with packing. Kate Ashley helped to supervise, while the princess's cofferer, Thomas Parry, assisted with the arrangements for the journey. Less than a year after Thomas Seymour's execution, Elizabeth and her servants were being invited to court. They had weathered the storm.

Thomas Seymour's death shocked everybody. In choosing Hugh Latimer as his final confessor, Thomas had shown the bad judgment that plagued him throughout his lifetime. Just over a week after the beheading, the bishop—whom Seymour had accounted his friend—gleefully besmirched his memory in a sermon at Westminster. As the king and Protector sat by, he declared, his voice booming through the chapel, that the Lord

Admiral had died "very boldly": not a compliment. He doubted, he said, that he would even find his way to Heaven, since he had "heard much wickedness of this man." Thomas had been a man of action and had had little time for religion, but he had firmly believed himself to be one of God's elect—preordained to join him in eternal glory. Latimer considered this unlikely, summing him up as "a covetous man, an horrible covetous man; I would there were no more in England: he was an ambitious man; I would there were no more in England: he was a seditious man, a contemner of Commune Prayer, I would there were no more in England." His words caused murmuring, mostly of sympathy for the dead admiral.*

Catherine's cousin Nicholas Throckmorton had more mixed feelings. Although he had rather liked Seymour, he thought him unwise. Reflecting later on the death, he considered that Seymour had been "a beast" who "causeless laboured to defile his nest"[1] and "through malice, went to pot"—but nevertheless found him "guiltless" of treason. This was how most people saw it. While Thomas "deserved to drink as he did brew,"[2] and had thrown everything away that he had, nonetheless few believed that his foolishness really merited death. Even the Elizabethan Jesuit Nicholas Sander had grave doubts about the veracity of the charges, considering that "Thomas Seymour was innocent of everything for which he deserved to die, except heresy, and as the Protector, himself a heretic, could not lay that to his brother's charge, it was necessary to have recourse to falsehood."[3] Seymour was guilty of plotting against his brother, but the probable collusion of the king meant that it was not treason. He had tried to marry Elizabeth without the Council's consent, but, thanks to the failure of the Protector's bill to outlaw that possibility, this was also not treason. He was, rather, the casualty of his dispute with his brother.

---

* Starkey (2000, p. 76), referring to Latimer, notes that "kicking a man when he is down, still more when he is dead, is something that even the worst of us revolt from."

Protector Somerset had stayed out of the way at Syon when Thomas was executed. But every time he passed the nursery there, he was met with an uncomfortable reminder of his involvement in his brother's death. Mary Seymour, Thomas's "pretty" little daughter, had been moved to Syon following her father's arrest, accompanied by her nurse Mrs. Aglionby and at least eleven other servants.[4] She was seven months old in March 1549, and oblivious to both her father's death and to the financial ruin occasioned by his attainder. On taking her into their house, the Somersets ensured that her fine nursery furniture traveled with her. The baby could settle down for the night in her familiar cradle, furnished with a scarlet tester and curtains of crimson taffeta. Her nurse slept beside her, to care for her when she cried. There was a chair with cushions of cloth of gold, should anyone of importance visit her, and she could play in a room decorated with tapestries showing the twelve months of the year. She was a princess in all but birth, her simple weaning food served up to her on silver plates. To support her, Somerset also arranged for an allowance to be paid to her from the royal treasury. Yet she could hardly remain indefinitely with him given the circumstances of her orphaning.

Seymour had asked that Mary be sent to live with her mother's friend, the Duchess of Suffolk. Lady Suffolk did not readily agree to this, aware that the girl, as the daughter of a queen, was expected to live in an almost royal style. To help persuade her, the Duchess of Somerset promised that Mary's possessions, including her silver tableware, should be transported with her.[5] This settled the matter, and Mary moved to Grimsthorpe in Lincolnshire with her twelve servants in spring 1549.[6] Unfortunately, however, Lady Somerset's promise proved worthless, and Mary's valuables disappeared into the duchess's grasping possession. At the same time, Protector Somerset neglected to pay the infant's pension.

Mary Seymour was a burden that the Duchess of Suffolk had not looked for. By July 1549 she was furious that this penniless "queen's child" was still in her house.[7] She wrote countless letters to the Protector and his wife, before complaining to William Cecil that month that funding the baby's household "will not bring me out of debt this year." She had already spoken to the baby's uncle, the Marquess of Northampton ("to whom I ought to deliver her"), but, as the duchess found, "he hath as weak a back for such a burden as I have." She was writing to Cecil in the hope that the Protector could be prevailed upon to support his niece: but Somerset showed no such inclination.

Mary was finally restored to her father's lands and titles toward the end of 1549. On 13 March 1550, the Council granted money for household wages, servants' uniforms, and food[8]—and no more was heard of her. For centuries, her fate remained a mystery, although her disappearance from the records was taken to indicate that she had died in infancy. Recent research has all but confirmed this. A Latin epitaph in the first person, published by Catherine's chaplain John Parkhurst, refers to "I whom at the cost of her own life, my queenly mother bore with the pangs of labour," before lamenting the fact that a stone of marble is now "a memorial to my brief life."[9] Thomas and Catherine's "little knave" never did revenge her parents as they had hoped. She followed them, all too quickly, to the grave.

In spite of the wide net that Thomas cast in his intrigues, no one else died with him. The Marquess of Dorset successfully managed to extricate himself, to be created Duke of Suffolk in right of his wife in 1551. Both he and she continued in their ambitions for their daughter. But shortly before King Edward's own juvenile death in July 1553, the regime made a doomed attempt to forestall Catholic Princess Mary becoming queen by altering the succession in favor of the unfortunate Jane Grey. Following Mary's triumphal accession that year, Jane was beheaded the following February. She went to the scaffold carrying Catherine Parr's prayer book, perhaps as a memento of happier times. Her father and her uncle, Lord Thomas Grey, were also executed for good measure.

William Sharington did achieve his pardon, in November 1549; even his lands and property were returned the following year. His wife was unable to secure the return of her jewelry, though, which had passed into the Duchess of Somerset's coffers. Otherwise, the couple survived unscathed. Sharington was even trusted with money again, being appointed one of the commissioners to collect 200,000 crowns from the French in 1550 as part of the purchase price for Boulogne.[10] He died later that year, so fully rehabilitated that Bishop Latimer declared him to be "an honest gentleman and one that God loveth."[11]

John Fowler, too, fared well. After being released from the Tower he was allowed to retain his post in the king's Privy Chamber and continued to prosper in the succeeding reigns of both Mary and Elizabeth.[12] He died around 1575. Even the discontented Marquess of Northampton was brought back into the fold, taking up a seat on the Council in July 1549, following the finalization of his divorce.[13]

Although they remained in favor during the reign of Edward VI, the Tyrwhitts fared rather less well. Lady Tyrwhitt, whom her husband proudly considered to be "half a scripture woman," failed to build a relationship with Elizabeth during her period as the princess's lady mistress.[14] By late spring 1549, Kate Ashley and Thomas Parry had been released from the Tower and were able to return to their old posts with the princess.[15] Elizabeth bore a grudge against the Tyrwhitts. Soon after her accession to the throne in 1558, she confiscated Mortlake and other manors from them.[16] Sir Robert died in 1572. His wife, imitating her friend Catherine Parr, published her own prayer book in 1574, and died four years later.

Elizabeth's contemporaries believed that "if some slur has attached to a girl's reputation from men's opinion of her, it usually remains forever and is not erased except by clear proofs of her chastity and wisdom."[17] Faced with rumors of a pregnancy or a concealed baby, Elizabeth set about ensuring that her conduct was blameless for the rest of her brother's reign. Habitually wearing somber black, she presented herself as a model to other young Protestant maidens to follow.*

Elizabeth finally turned sixteen on 7 September 1549. She had reached her majority.** In March of the following year she received her long-desired patents to her lands, making her a considerable landowner in her own right.[18] She had become a figure of international importance, and on 24 September 1549 received ambassadors from Venice, whose duke was considering a matrimonial alliance with her.[19] Elizabeth was careful this time, immediately instructing Parry to write to Cecil to inform him of the duke's suit. She would not be accused of trying to arrange her own marriage again. As Parry noted, the talk did not seem to be of any great weight, but she needed advice on how to reply: "Her Grace will neither know nor do in matters that either may sound or seem to be of importance without doing of My Lord's Grace [Somerset] to understand thereof." As the cofferer assured the Protector's secretary, even Elizabeth's mind was open to scrutiny. Any thought "shall no sooner be in Her Grace's head than My Lord's Grace shall have intelligence thereof."

Elizabeth was invited to spend Christmas at court in 1549. She arrived there in the middle of December and was welcomed "with great pomp and triumph."[20] The king had missed her and they spent the season continually in each other's company. Elizabeth had grown into an assured young woman; there were now "great praises of her person and of her bringing up."[21] Her marriage continued to be raised. In August 1551, it was an Italian duke who sought her hand, while just under two years later she was courted by a German prince.[22] During what remained of her half-brother's

---

* Robinson (pp. 278–279). Elizabeth's co-religionist Jane Grey, when presented with some tinsel, cloth of gold and velvet as a gift from Princess Mary—who loved fine and showy clothes—had even declared that she would not wear it, since "that were a shame to follow My Lady Mary against God's word and leave My Lady Elizabeth which followeth God's word."

** In the sixteenth century, the age of majority was sixteen for women and twenty-one for men (McIntosh, p. 128).

reign, Elizabeth was considered "one of the darlings of fortune," and the pair shared genuine affection for each other.[23]

As Elizabeth began to regain her place in society, Protector Somerset was rapidly losing his. Both Seymour brothers had considered themselves "tossed upon the waves of fortune," and, although they could not know it, their fates were closely linked.[24] Contemporaries murmured that "the fall of one brother, would be the ruin of the other," while some suggested that it was God's judgment that the older brother should die in the same manner as the sibling he condemned.[25] In October 1549, it was Somerset's turn to fall.

During the summer of 1549, the kingdom had been troubled by rebellion and civil unrest at home, and by renewed threats from Scotland and France. In June, in the West Country, objectors to the imposition of the English Book of Common Prayer and the general Protestant direction of the country gathered forces in Cornwall. Soon they were besieging Exeter. In July, in Norfolk, Robert Kett led a popular uprising against the practice by landowners of enclosing common land, and took over Norwich. The revolts were put down by military force, led by Lord Russell and the Earl of Warwick respectively, but they contributed to a sense of an embattled regime.

By September 1549, Somerset and much of the Council, especially its more conservative members, were in dispute, with Warwick pragmatically backing Somerset's opponents in a bid to force him to "amend some of his disorders."[26] On 1 October matters reached a head, as Somerset issued a proclamation, ostensibly from the king, in which he commanded all his "loving subjects" to come armed to Hampton Court, "to defend his most royal person, and his most entirely beloved uncle, the Lord Protector, against whom certain hath attempted a most dangerous conspiracy."[27] In reality, just as with Thomas Seymour's own plots, the king was never in danger. It was the Protector who was the focus of the Council's coup. On 6 October Somerset ordered the armor to be brought out of the armory at Hampton Court as men began to gather. Late on the next evening, when the king was in bed, Edward was suddenly spirited away by his uncle to Windsor. Somerset effected the kidnap of the king that his late brother, at most, had attempted without success. This time, there was no question as to the boy's complicity or lack of it: he was furious.

As Warwick's troops gained support, Somerset remained holed up at Windsor. The king had caught a cold on the journey, and, being incensed at his treatment, complained loudly: "Methinks I am in prison; here be no galleries nor no gardens to walk in."[28] The memory of the Protector's fratricide was uppermost in many minds as Somerset clung on to power. Sir Thomas Smith, who had served as the Council's secretary during Seymour's incarceration, now took part in the action against the Protector. He rode to Windsor, and wrote to Sir William Petre on 8 October that he had been with the Protector that day. He had persuaded him, he said, to give up his office—and he hoped, therefore, that "no man seeks the blood of him who has been too easy of others."[29] The ghost of Thomas Seymour still haunted the Duke of Somerset. Three days later, Somerset was taken to the Tower.[30] Less than seven months after Seymour's death, his brother was finally divested of his offices of Protector and governor of the king.[31] The office of Lord Protector was abolished. Thomas Seymour had moved too soon.

For the moment, though, Somerset's fate was different from that of his brother. After admitting all the charges against him and throwing himself on the Council's mercy, he was released early in 1550.[32] He even managed to return to the Council that April, although his rehabilitation was short-lived. Under the aegis of the Earl of Warwick—who had now become the Duke of Northumberland—he was arrested again on 17 October 1551, charged with treason, and returned to the Tower, with his wife accompanying him the next day. This time there would be no reprieve. Tried before twenty-eight peers, he was acquitted of treason but found guilty of gathering armed men, a capital offense.

Somerset had once been popular. Despite his autocratic methods and self-aggrandizement, he was also lauded by many in England for his perceived sympathies with the poor, notably in trying to crack down on the practice of illegal enclosures, and for attempts to turn the country toward the reformed religion.[33] He was led out to Tower Hill at eight o'clock on the morning of 22 January 1552, to be faced by the greatest crowd that anyone could remember.[34] It was a tense assembly. The Council had taken the precaution of ordering a sizable armed guard to ensure that no rescue was attempted. Shortly before Somerset died, a great rumbling was heard, as if guns were shooting and horses thundering toward them; some of the skittish crowd fell down in fear.[35] No one tried to save him, however. Like his brother, Somerset refused to admit any guilt, declaring only that "I am brought hither to suffer death, albeit that I never offended against the king, neither by word nor deed, and have been always as faithful and true unto this realm, as any man hath been."[36] He had no regrets: "Neither I repent my doings, but rejoice therein." He died on the straw of the scaffold and was buried close to his brother. His wife, the domineering Anne Stanhope, was lucky to escape with her own life. She later remarried, living until 1587. Her half-brother Sir Michael Stanhope, whom Thomas Seymour had so deplored for his influence over the king's household, was less fortunate. He followed his brother-in-law to the block the following month.[37]

The Duke of Northumberland's triumph was brief, for the young king fell ill at Easter 1552, failing to recover and dying at the age of fifteen the following year. For Elizabeth, Edward's death changed everything. Her half-sister Mary was thirty-seven and unmarried when she overthrew Jane Grey (by then Northumberland's daughter-in-law) to take the throne—and begin the return of the kingdom to the religious embrace of Rome. Northumberland surrendered, was quickly tried for treason, and was executed on 22 August 1553.

During Mary's reign, Elizabeth's security was by no means guaranteed, and she fell under suspicion. In March 1554, after the defeat of a rebellion led by Sir Thomas Wyatt against Mary's imminent marriage to Philip II of Spain, the queen ordered her sister's imprisonment in the Tower, suspecting her of involvement (although Wyatt never implicated her). In the time of her greatest peril, Elizabeth's thoughts turned to Thomas Seymour. Hoping to delay her death, she wrote her famous "tide letter" to Mary. In it, she referred to the quarrel between Seymour and Somerset, blaming it on false reports being made to the Protector of his brother's conduct. She hoped that, unlike this case of brothers, "the like evil persuasions persuade not one sister against another."[38] If only Somerset had agreed to meet his brother. Elizabeth was released from the Tower in May 1554, initially moving to Woodstock, where she remained closely monitored.

Elizabeth was at Hatfield in November 1558 when she learned of Mary's death and her own accession to the throne. Falling to her knees, she cried out that "this is the work of the Lord, and it is wonderful in our sight."[39] In recognition of his long and loyal service, Thomas Parry was appointed to the important role of Comptroller of the Household, while his wife, Lady Fortescue, was also rewarded, becoming one of Elizabeth's senior ladies in 1558.[40] Kate Ashley was appointed chief gentlewoman of the Privy Chamber when Elizabeth became queen, becoming one of the most influential women in England at a stroke.[41] She remained in office until her death in 1565, when, finally, quiet Blanche Parry succeeded her as the queen's closest confidante.

In spite of Elizabeth's new status in 1558, Kate was far from done with matchmaking. It was obvious to all that Lord Robert Dudley, who resembled Thomas Seymour both in looks and character, had attracted the queen. Kate also favored him as her mistress's husband and set about trying to persuade her former charge as to his merits. Elizabeth, however, was older and wiser. "Dost thou think me so unlike myself, and so unmindful of my Royal Majesty, that I would prefer my servant, whom I myself have raised, before the greatest princes of Christendom, in my choosing of an husband?"[42] Kate said no more. Nonetheless, one of Elizabeth's last suitors, Sir Walter Raleigh, owed his arrival at court to the queen's former lady mistress—for he was Kate's great-nephew.[43]

John Astley remarried after Kate's death and produced a family. His young wife—who this time pronounced his last name correctly—was the daughter of Lord Thomas Grey, the man who had persuaded Seymour to hand himself in. Astley served Elizabeth as her Master of Jewels to die a wealthy and prominent individual in 1596.[44]

Elizabeth eventually ruled England for over forty years, surprising her contemporaries by failing to marry. She had learned well the lessons of her youth, seeming to have acquired "wisdom beyond her age" by the time of her accession.[45] As queen, she made no recorded mention of Thomas Seymour. He was nearly a decade dead by the time she gained the throne—but far from forgotten by all.

Not everyone fell away from Seymour at his fall. His faithful servant John Harington's loyalty ensured him ten months in the Tower, being eventually released in October 1549.[46] He remained in touch with Elizabeth, and during Mary's reign was imprisoned again for carrying a letter to Elizabeth when she was in disgrace.[47] During Elizabeth's rule, he kept out of trouble and lived to a ripe old age; but he never forgot his devotion to Thomas.

According to his son, also named "John,"* only a week before his death in 1582 John Harington senior carefully wrote out the names of all those who were still living "of the old Admiralty (so he called them that had been My Lord's men)."[48] Members of this exclusive club stuck together for over thirty years after the loss of their master. Thirty-three were still living in 1582, representing a diverse subset of society, since, as the younger Harington recalled, "many were knights and men of more revenue than himself [the elder John Harington], and some were but mean men, as armourers, artificers, keepers, and the farmers; and yet the memory of his service, was such a band among them all of kindness, as the best of them disdained not the poorest." Thomas Seymour had been the

* The younger Harington (1561–1612), who was born to his father's second wife, was a godson of Elizabeth I. He achieved fame, and some notoriety, for diverse achievements, including his translation of Ariosto's *Orlando Furioso* and his design for England's first flushing lavatory.

common bond for these men, and they continued to cherish him, long after his demise.

In 1567, John Harington even presented a portrait of Thomas to the queen, with two poems inscribed on either side of the former admiral's head.[49] Both poems praised Seymour, the second recording that he was "of person rare, strong limbs, and manly shape." Harington recalled him as "of friendship firm," both wise and brave. He was, Harington claimed, "a subject true to king, and servant great." "Yet against nature reason and just laws / His blood was spilt, guiltless without just cause." Elizabeth accepted the work—and presumably its sentiments—and hung it in the gallery of Somerset Place, the edifice that had been the Protector's monument to his own glory.[50]

Thomas Seymour once said that the memory of brave men lived forever and that "a good name is the embalming of the virtuous to an eternity of love and gratitude among posterity."[51] To future generations, his good name was lost; but those who had known him still remembered him fondly. He was a turbulent, troublesome individual, but also a likable one, and—at the start of 1549—the man who would come closest to marrying the future Queen Elizabeth. As far as is recorded, no other man ever climbed into bed with England's virgin queen, or trimmed her clothes and intimately appraised her body. As Elizabeth looked at Thomas's portrait in the gallery at Somerset Place, she would have been able to reflect upon the man who had so nearly seduced her.

He was the temptation of Elizabeth Tudor.

NOTES ON THE TEXT

Full details of the primary and secondary sources referred to in these notes may be found in the bibliography. In all quotations from these sources, the spelling has been modernized.

S. Haynes's *Collection of State Papers . . . Left by William Cecil* includes printed transcripts of many of the original manuscripts concerning the Seymour scandal held by the Marquess of Salisbury at Hatfield House. Following a comparison of these transcripts with the originals (microfilm versions BL M485/39), it is clear that, with one exception, discussed elsewhere, Haynes made accurate transcripts. For ease of reference, the documents' page numbers are, in most cases, given below in preference to their manuscript numbers.

The following abbreviations are used below for certain frequently appearing sources.

"A Journal"	Adams *et al.* (eds.), "A 'Journall' of matters of state . . .
APC	*Acts of the Privy Council*
"Certain Brief Notes"	Adams *et al.* (eds.), "Certayne Brife Notes . . .
CSP Domestic	*Calendar of State Papers, Domestic . . .*
CSP Domestic (Knighton)	*Calendar of State Papers, Domestic . . . 1547–1553*
CSP Foreign	*Calendar of State Papers, Foreign*
CSP Spanish	*Calendar of Letters . . . Between England and Spain*
HMC	Historic Manuscripts Commission
L&P	*Letters and Papers . . . of the Reign of Henry VIII*
ODNB	*Oxford Dictionary of National Biography*
VCH	*Victoria Country History* series

PROLOGUE: 6 FEBRUARY 1559

1. *Journal of the House of Commons*, 6 February 1559.
2. J. Hayward (1840), pp. 30–32.
3. Elizabeth's coronation portrait at the National Portrait Gallery (NPG 5175) shows the queen with a significant resemblance to Henry VIII.
4. *Journal of the House of Commons*, 4 February 1559.
5. Ibid., 23–30 January 1559.
6. Portrait of Sir Thomas Gargrave (NPG 1928).
7. *History of Parliament*, for Sir Thomas Gargrave.
8. Indeed, as Duncan (p. 35) notes, her half-sister Mary I had appeared similarly unwilling to Parliament when its members petitioned her to marry.
9. Mueller, Levin, and Shenk (p. 24) note that the first evidence that Elizabeth was averse to matrimony came in November 1556.
10. Ibid., p. 16: They also see this as a point of metamorphosis for Elizabeth, noting a marked change in her perception of selfhood in her letters during and after the Seymour scandal.

PART 1: THE SEEDS OF SCANDAL

CHAPTER 1: AFFECTION SHALL LEAD ME TO COURT . . .

1. Wriothesley.
2. Ibid., p. 64.
3. *CSP Spanish*, Vol. V, Part 2, p. 43.
4. Seymour (1972) gives considerable detail about Edward's early life.
5. Skelton.
6. Survey of Wolf Hall from Edward VI's reign (Locke, p. 5).
7. Locke (p. 29) and Ward (p. 264). The Seymours had always been country gentry, inheriting Wolf Hall from the Esturmy family. Details of the relationship are in BL Stowe MS 143 f. 29, f. 34, f. 35 and 40.
8. He is not, sadly, the Sir Thomas Seymour who in 1529 was an alderman of London and elected to Parliament for the capital (J. G. Nichols, 1859, p.

295). This was a distant cousin, Sir Thomas Seymour of Saffron Walden: see *History of Parliament*, Sir Thomas Seymour I, and also *The Aldermen of the City of London Temp. Henry III–1912* (London, 1908: pp. 168–195). This same Sir Thomas later served as mayor of the Staple of Westminster (*L&P*, Vol. V, 1040). It is most likely the elder Sir Thomas who was appointed to commissions for the peace for Essex and Hertfordshire in 1532 (*L&P*, 1694).

9. *ODNB*, for Sir Thomas Seymour. Also, in Bryan's letter to Henry of 20 April 1530 he records that his "cousin Seymour" had delivered the king's letter to him (*L&P*, Vol. V, 202).
10. HMC, *Bath*, 222 and 371.
11. BL Add. MS 46354.
12. BL Sloane MS 1523 f. 36v.
13. *L&P*, Vol. XIV, Part 2, Appendix 9.
14. Welsh poem composed by Lewys Morgannwg for Lady Troy (quoted in Richardson, p. 3).
15. TNA PROB 11/21/327.
16. Latimer made his will at York on 12 September 1542, suggesting that he was unwell.
17. Catherine Parr to Thomas Seymour, *c.* February 1547 (Parr, p. 131).
18. Sir Ralph Sadleir to Cromwell, 14 July 1538 (Maclean, p. 4).
19. Ibid.
20. *L&P*, Vol. XXI, Part II, 555.
21. Leti (paraphrased in Bernard, p. 212).
22. Although George Constantyne in the late 1540s referred to Henry and other old men as lusty and able to father children (Norton).
23. Verses written by Henry VIII in a volume containing a sermon by St. John Chrysostom, belonging to Catherine Parr, between February and July 1543 (Parr, p. 40).
24. Notarial Instrument witnessing the marriage of Henry VIII and Catherine Parr, 12 July 1543 (Parr, p. 44).
25. Catherine Parr to Thomas Seymour, *c.* February 1547 (Parr, p. 131).
26. Ibid.
27. Ibid., p. 48.
28. Notarial Instrument witnessing the marriage of Henry VIII and Catherine Parr, 12 July 1543 (Ibid., p. 45).
29. John Neville named his eldest daughter (b. 1545/6) "Catherine" after the queen. It was only his second daughter (b. 1548) who received the name of his mother, Dorothy. Margaret Neville's will contains strong evidence of her affection for Catherine (PROB 11/31/45).
30. Elizabeth to Catherine, 31 July 1544 (Perry, p. 15).
31. Resolution Taken by Henry and His Privy Council, 7 July 1544 (Parr, p. 50).
32. Edward VI, *Diary*, p. 15.

33. Resolution Taken by Henry and His Privy Council, 7 July 1544 (Parr, p. 50).
34. Inventory of Catherine Parr's personal effects (ibid., p. 625).
35. *CSP Spanish*, Vol. IX, p. 124. Princess Mary declared in 1547 that she had only met Thomas once, suggesting that he had not been a regular visitor to the queen. In a letter to his brother of 14 March 1544, however, Seymour did comment from Westminster that "our master and mistress, with My Lord Prince, are merry," indicating that he had seen Queen Catherine at court (*L&P*, Vol. XIX, Part I, 198).
36. Maclean, p. 8.
37. Thomas Seymour to Henry VIII, 4 July 1542 (ibid., p. 8).
38. Thomas Seymour to Henry VIII, 10 July 1542 (ibid., p. 9).
39. Thomas Seymour to Henry VIII, 8 August 1542 (ibid., p. 10).
40. *History of Parliament*, for Sir Thomas Seymour.
41. Thomas Seymour to Henry VIII, 16 May 1543 (Maclean, p. 19).
42. Maclean, p. 21
43. *L&P*, Vol. XII, Part I, 601.
44. Ibid., 602.
45. Loades, p. 9.
46. *L&P*, Vol. XIX, Part II, 501.
47. Ibid., 502.
48. Ibid., Vol. XII, Part I, 600.
49. Ibid., Vol. XIX, Part II, 502. Loades (p. 96) gives details of the weaponry aboard the ships. The similar sized *Mary Rose* carried ninety-six guns in 1540, for example, six of which were classed as heavy.
50. Thomas Seymour to the Council, 6 November 1544 (Maclean, p. 30).
51. Thomas Seymour to the Council, 12 November 1544 (ibid., p. 31).
52. Ibid.
53. Loades, p. 128.
54. See *L&P*, Vol. XX, Part I, 856, 872, 1144; *L&P*, Vol. XX, Part II, 389, 391, 513; *APC*, Vol. I, pp. 245, 253.

CHAPTER 2: . . . INTEREST KEEPS ME THERE

1. *CSP Spanish*, Vol. IX, p. 7.
2. Burtt.
3. Somerset to Mary, early in Edward's reign (Burnet, pp. 161–162), notes Princess Mary's doubts over the will. She also voiced these to Van der Delft in conversation.
4. *Testamenta Vetusta*, Vol. I, p. 38.
5. *CSP Spanish*, Vol. IX, p. 101.
6. *APC*, Vol. I, 2 January 1547.
7. Earl of Hertford to Sir William Paget, 29 January 1547 (Tytler, p. 16).
8. *APC*, Vol. I, 9 January 1547.
9. Ibid., 16 January 1547.

10. Edward wrote regularly in Latin to his stepmother, including on 12 May 1546, 24 May 1546, 10 June 1546, 12 August 1546, 20 September 1546, 7 November 1546, and 10 January 1547 (Parr, pp. 116–125).
11. A silver-gilt inkwell is mentioned in an inventory of Catherine's possessions taken after her death (ibid., p. 636)
12. *CSP Spanish*, Vol. IX, p. 2.
13. Hayward and Ward, f. 515r.
14. *CSP Spanish*, Vol. IX, p. 2; Hume, p. 147.
15. BL Sloane MS 1523 f. 29v.
16. Hume, p. 147.
17. *CSP Spanish*, Vol. IX, p. 2.
18. Hume, p. 147.
19. The inventory of items taken after Henry VIII's death includes two silver and gilt watering cans from the gallery at Westminster (Starkey 1998, f. 83v).
20. Alford, p. 67.
21. *CSP Spanish*, Vol. IX, p. 7.
22. Surrey History Centre, LM 1331/1.
23. *CSP Spanish*, Vol. IX, p. 31.
24. Ibid., p. 19
25. Hayward and Ward, f. 510r–510v.
26. Description taken from the Longleat portrait of Hertford, which names him as Earl of Hertford (dating it to 1537–47).
27. TNA E101/424/12 f. 135.
28. Ibid., f. 76.
29. Ibid., f. 74 and f. 76.
30. The fact that Catherine briefly visited Westminster in January can be demonstrated from her accounts for that month, which include a record of milk and cream purchased for her at Westminster (ibid., f. 80). In January, Thomas Beck was paid for arranging the boat "for going of the queen's highness from Greenwich and Westminster going and coming" (ibid., f. 78).
31. Ibid., f. 69.
32. *CSP Spanish*, Vol. IX, p. 341.
33. Certain Brief Notes (BL Add. MS 48126, f. 6–16, and in Adams *et al.*).
34. *APC*, Vol. I, 23 January 1547.
35. Ibid., 26 January 1547.
36. *History of Parliament*, for Sir John Harington II.
37. Hughey (p. 22) and Harington II (*Orlando Furioso*, p. xvi).
38. John Harington's Examination (S. Haynes, p. 83).
39. BL Sloane MS 1523 f. 34v.
40. Tytler, p. 14.
41. *CSP Spanish*, Vol. IX, p. 4.
42. Colvin, Vol. III, Part I, p. 254.
43. Endorsement to Hertford's letter to Paget, 29 January 1547 (Tytler, p. 16).

44. Earl of Hertford to Sir William Paget, 29 January 1547 (ibid.).
45. Naunton, p. 172.
46. Perry, p. 24.
47. Colvin, Vol. III, Part I, p. 87.
48. J. Hayward (1840), p. 7.
49. Naunton, p. 172.
50. Colvin, Vol. III, Part I, p. 87.
51. J. Hayward (1630), pp. 4–5.
52. Henry VIII's personal entreaty to one of his daughters at Elton Hall (Parr, p. 626).
53. William Wightman to Cecil, 10 May 1549 (SP 10/7/33).
54. BL Sloane MS 1523 f. 38v.
55. *CSP Spanish*, Vol. IX, p. 7.
56. Locke, p. 48.

CHAPTER 3: ADORATION UNTIL DEATH

1. Leti.
2. Dent, p. 316, and Nash, p. 2.
3. Leti (from Bernard, p. 213). Leti is a disputable source, since many of the letters that he published have not been found to exist in any archive. However, his very specific detail for the relationship between Seymour and Catherine, and for Seymour's interest in Elizabeth, does accord with other sources, suggesting it is accurate.
4. Leti.
5. HMC, *Salisbury*, Vol. I, p. 220.
6. Tantalizingly, in a file of heavily damaged letters relating to Catherine Parr (TNA E101/426/3), two letters are signed in this way, including that on f. 23, which is just a fragment of letter with no surviving date. Most of the letters in the file date to the reign of Edward VI, so it is tempting to assign these two to that period. However, Catherine had, of course, served as regent—and signed in this way—in 1545, and some of the letters, such as that on f. 22, date to Henry VIII's reign.
7. Duke of Somerset's Commission to Be Protector (Burnet, Vol. 2, Part II, p. 137).
8. For details of some of Seymour's lands, see TNA SC/6/EDWVI/188, TNA SC6/EDWVI/187 and TNA SC6/EDWVI/630.
9. Loades, p. 77.
10. Ibid., p. 88.
11. *CSP Spanish*, Vol. IX, p. 19.
12. Surrey History Centre, LM 1865.
13. *Spanish*, Vol. IX, p. 31.
14. Ibid.
15. Ibid, p. 341.

16. Ibid.
17. "A Journal" (BL Add. MS 48023 f.380-369v), p. 54, and "Certain Brief Notes," p. 124.
18. "Certain Brief Notes," p. 124.
19. "A Journal," p. 55, and "Certain Brief Notes," p. 124: both give the same account.
20. "A Journal," p. 55.
21. "Certain Brief Notes," p. 124.
22. Ibid., p. 123.
23. John Harington's Confession (in S. Haynes, p. 83).
24. *CSP Spanish*, Vol. IX, p. 89.
25. Ibid., p. 99.
26. Ibid., p. 341.
27. Duke of Somerset to Princess Mary (Burnet, Vol. 2, Part II, pp. 161–162).
28. *CSP Spanish*, Vol. IX, p. 101.
29. Ibid., p. 47
30. Maclean, p. 43.
31. Elizabeth's Dedication to Henry VIII, 30 December 1545 (Perry, p. 20).
32. Articles Against Thomas Seymour (Cobbett *et al.*).
33. Leti.
34. Ibid.
35. Thomas Seymour to Catherine Parr, 17 May 1547 (Parr, p. 138). The letter ends: "from him whom ye have bound to honour, love, and such in all lawful things obey."
36. Articles Against Thomas Seymour (Cobbett *et al.*).
37. Strype (1822), Vol. II, Part I, p. 197.
38. *CSP Foreign*, p. 22
39. *CSP Spanish*, Vol. IX, p. 49.
40. Gardiner, Bishop of Winchester, to Sir William Paget, 5 February 1547 (Tytler, p. 21).
41. *CSP Spanish*, Vol. IX, p. 52.
42. Ibid., p. 7.
43. Surrey History Centre, LM 1865.
44. *CSP Spanish*, Vol. IX, p. 19.
45. Ibid., p. 48.
46. TNA E15/340 f. 21.
47. SP 46/124 f. 24.
48. SP 46/1 f. 16.
49. *CSP Spanish*, Vol. IX, p. 85.
50. Ibid., p. 52.
51. Two entries in Catherine's accounts make this move to St. James's clear (TNA E15/340 f. 22v). Also, milk and cream were purchased for her use at St. James's in March (TNA E101/424/12 f. 80).

52. Deposition of Katherine Ashley, 4 February 1549 (SP 10/6/57).
53. TNA E15/340 f. 22v.
54. Catherine Parr to Thomas Seymour (Parr, p. 130).
55. Catherine Parr to Thomas Seymour (ibid., p. 135).

CHAPTER 4: WHAT WE CANNOT REMEDY

1. Catherine Parr to Thomas Seymour, *c.* mid-February 1547 (Parr, p. 130).
2. Thomas Seymour to Catherine Parr, March 1547 (ibid., p. 133).
3. Ibid.
4. Hume.
5. Thomas Seymour to Catherine Parr, March 1547 (Parr, p. 132).
6. TNA E15/340 f. 23v.
7. Ibid.
8. Thomas Seymour to Catherine Parr, March 1547 (Parr, p.133).
9. Catherine Parr to Thomas Seymour, *c.* April 1547 (ibid., p. 134).
10. Thomas Seymour to Catherine Parr, March 1547 (ibid., p. 133).
11. *CSP Spanish*, Vol. IX, p. 83.
12. SP 10/1 f. 120.
13. Raleigh, p. 307.
14. Raleigh's report notes that the changes had happened in the previous forty years (Raleigh, p. 309).
15. *CSP Spanish*, Vol. IX, p. 57.
16. Ibid., p. 72.
17. Ibid., p. 88.
18. Ibid., p. 85.
19. Catherine Parr to Thomas Seymour, *c.* April 1547 (Parr, p. 134).
20. TNA E101/424/12 f. 12, f. 26.
21. Roger Ascham to Anne Parr Herbert, 1545 (Ascham, *Letters*, p. 75).
22. Thomas Seymour to Catherine Parr, 17 May 1547 (Parr, p. 137).
23. Ibid.
24. Catherine Parr to Thomas Seymour, late May 1547 (ibid., p. 139).
25. Thomas Seymour to Catherine Parr, late May 1547 (ibid., p. 143).
26. The draft articles against Thomas (Article 19c) first stated that Seymour "procured the L. Protector to labour for the queen," before amending it to "speak to the queen" (BL Harley MS 249).
27. Edward VI to Catherine Parr, 7 February 1547 (Parr, pp. 128–129).
28. Somerset kept Catherine politically at arm's length, for example see Catherine Parr to Thomas Seymour, *c.* April 1547 (Parr, p. 135).
29. TNA E15/340 f. 23v.
30. Edward VI to Catherine Parr, 30 May 1547 (Parr, pp. 144–145).
31. Catherine Parr to Thomas Seymour, late May 1547 (ibid., p. 139).
32. Catherine Parr to Thomas Seymour, late May 1547 (ibid., p. 140). There is no record of a visit to court in Catherine's accounts for May, but she did travel to

St. James's Palace in June (TNA E15/340 f. 24v, f. 25). The letter most likely dates to early that month.

33. Edward VI to Catherine Parr, 30 May 1547 (Parr, p. 144) notes that the pair had still not met and, giving up hope, Edward had decided to write to his stepmother.
34. E15/340 f. 24v, f. 25.
35. See *CSP Spanish*, Vol. IX, p. 101 for her loneliness, and p. 220 for her depression.
36. Ibid., p. 89.
37. Princess Mary to Thomas Seymour, 4 June 1547 (Parr, p. 146).
38. *History of Parliament*, for John Fowler.
39. Deposition of John Fowler (SP 10/6/24).
40. Articles Against Thomas Seymour (Cobbett *et al.*).
41. Deposition of John Fowler (SP 10/6/24).
42. Edward VI to Catherine Parr, 25 June 1547 (Parr, pp. 147–148).
43. *CSP Spanish*, Vol. IX, p. 123.
44. Articles Against Thomas Seymour (Cobbett *et al.*), and Edward VI (*Diary*), p. 21.
45. *CSP Spanish*, Vol. IX, p. 101.
46. SP 68/14 f. 71.
47. The similarity of the two men's signatures is particularly noticeable in SP 68/1 f. 159, for example: in this document, from December 1547, the signatures are of comparable size and larger than those of the other councilors.
48. *CSP Spanish*, Vol. IX, p. 123.
49. Leti (in Bernard, p. 213).
50. Elizabeth to Mary, 1547. Leti, translated in M. A. E. Wood (ed.), *Letters of Royal and Illustrious Ladies*, Vol. 3 (London, 1846), p. 93, sets out that this was what Mary said to Elizabeth in her earlier letter, which does not survive.
51. Surrey History Centre, LM 1865.
52. *CSP Spanish*, Vol. IX, p. 429. James (p. 272) considers that there was truth in the rumors of the duchess's influence over Somerset.
53. HMC, *Salisbury*, Vol. I, p. 256.
54. Princess Mary to My Lady of Somerset, 24 April 1547 (Tytler, p. 52).
55. Princess Mary's and Queen Katherine's Joint Letter to Anne Seymour, Countess of Hertford, 3 June 1544 (Parr, p. 78).
56. Later Apprehension and Examination of Anne Askew (*Writings of Edward VI . . .*, pp. 27–28).
57. SP 10/1 f. 120. In this letter of 20 April 1547, Thomas asked to be commended to "My Lady's Grace my sister" when he wrote to his brother.
58. *CSP Spanish*, Vol. IX, p. 123.
59. Vives, p. 228.
60. Inventory of Catherine Parr's Personal Effects (Parr, 635).
61. SP 10/6/72.

62. James, p. 271.
63. Inventory of Catherine Parr's Personal Effects (Parr, p. 628).
64. Deposition of John Fowler (SP 10/6/24).
65. Hume.
66. "A Journal," p. 55.
67. A note in *Vincent's Baronage* in the College of Arms states that Catherine was *"repudiata quia pater ejus post nuplias, eam cognovit,"* which suggests that her lover was also her father-in-law. The seventeenth-century writer Peter Heylin (Locke, p. 31) also alludes to this rumor.
68. Somerset's mother, Margery, stood as godmother to the second of the two elder sons (PROB 11/33/458).
69. BL Egerton MS 2815, which contains the accounts of Somerset's cofferer of the household between April 1548 and October 1551, includes annuities of £20 each to Lord Edward Seymour and John Seymour Gentleman. John Seymour's will (PROB 1/29) also includes his brother, Edward, as his sole executor, indicating that there was no estrangement between the brothers. The fact that John Seymour, unlike his younger full brother Edward, does not appear to have been styled "Lord" after his father became a duke is, perhaps, telling as to Somerset's thoughts on his paternity. John Seymour was, however, employed in Somerset's household and his name appears regularly in the accounts of Somerset's cofferer. John is particularly likely to be the illegitimate son, since the reference to Catherine Filiol's affair with her father-in-law states that they had sexual relations immediately after the wedding—so his paternity may well have been unclear. This is also suggested by the private Act of Parliament that Somerset obtained in April 1540, in which his lands were entailed first on his male heirs by his second wife, then his male heirs by any subsequent wife, then on Edward Seymour (his son by Catherine Filiol), then on his brothers Henry and Thomas in turn, and finally on his daughters, "with remainder to the right heirs of the said Edward Seymour." John Seymour's exclusion from this exhaustive list almost conclusively demonstrates that his father thought him illegitimate (*L&P*, Vol. XV, Acts of Parliament, c78).

PART 2: THE SCANDAL DEEPENS

1. Confession of Katherine Ashley (S. Haynes, p. 99).
2. M. Hayward, p. 169.

CHAPTER 5: THE YOUNG DAMSELS

1. Strangford, p. 30.
2. Ibid.
3. *L&P*, Vol. X, 1187 (list 1).
4. Strangford, p. 31.
5. In Strangford, the laundress is Elizabeth Ballard (p. 11).

6. *L&P*, Vol. X, 1187 (list 2).
7. Richardson (2007), p. 4.
8. Blanche's tomb depicts Elizabeth as something of a religious icon, for example (Richardson, 2009, p. 13).
9. Garrett, p. 73.
10. Ascham to Princess Elizabeth, 1545 (Ascham, *Letters*, p. 77).
11. Ascham to John Cheke, *c.*13 September 1544 (Ascham, *Whole Works*, Vol. I, Part 1, letter XXIII).
12. Strype (1821) suggests that the pair were related.
13. Ascham to John Cheke, *c.*13 September 1544 (Ascham, *Whole Works*, Vol. I, Part 1, letter XXIII).
14. Payment to Johannes Spithovius, in Strangford (p. 39).
15. Strangford notes that she received a book from her tutor, Johannes Spithovius.
16. Adams and Gehring.
17. Ascham to Princess Elizabeth, 1545 (*Letters*, p. 77).
18. Ascham to John Astley, 1545 (ibid., pp. 77–79).
19. Ascham to Princess Elizabeth, 1545 (ibid, p. 77).
20. Ascham to John Astley, 1545 (ibid., pp. 77–79).
21. Richardson (2007), p. 45.
22. Strangford, p. 40.
23. TNA PROB 11/21/327.
24. Richardson (2007), p. 55.
25. New Year's gifts to Elizabeth, 1562.
26. Sir Robert Tyrwhitt to Somerset, 31 January 1549 (SP 10/6/16).
27. Parr, p. 29.
28. Perry, p. 17.
29. Elizabeth, "A Godly Medytacyon. . . ."
30. Deposition of John Fowler (SP 10/6/24).
31. *See* letters from Edward VI written from there, including 24 August 1547 (Edward VI, *Literary Remains*).
32. *CSP Spanish*, Vol. IX, p. 141.
33. Depositions of Sir William Sharington, January 1549 (SP 10/6/35).
34. *CSP Foreign*, p. 64.
35. Knighton and Loades, p. 6.
36. Instructions to Lord Clinton, 1 August 1547 (ibid., p. 22).
37. Depositions of Sir William Sharington, January 1549 (SP 10/6/35).
38. Edward VI's Confession (Edward VI, *Literary Remains*, p. 59).
39. Surrey History Centre, LM 1865.
40. *CSP Spanish*, Vol. IX, p. 50.
41. Edward VI's Confession (Edward VI, *Literary Remains*, p. 59).
42. Ibid.
43. "A Journal," p. 54.
44. Vertot, Vol. I, pp. 129–131.

45. TNA E15/340 f. 28v.
46. Ibid., f. 29.
47. Nicholas Udall's Letter to Catherine Parr, prefacing the first volume of English translations of Erasmus's *Paraphrases upon the New Testament*, 31 January 1548 (Parr, p. 160).
48. TNA E15/340 f. 24.
49. Ibid., f. 26v, f. 28.
50. The Answer of Katherine Ashley, 2 February 1549 (Elizabeth, *Collected Works*, p. 25).
51. Ibid.
52. John, Earl of Warwick to Somerset, 30 September 1547 (SP 50/1/128).
53. Instructions to Lord Clinton, 1 August 1547 (Knighton and Loades, p. 22).
54. Strangford, p. 10.
55. Sir Robert Tyrwhitt to Somerset, 31 January 1549 (SP 10/6/16).

CHAPTER 6: GO AWAY, FOR SHAME

1. *L&P*, Vol. XXI, Part I, 321; and Vol. XIX, Part II, 400.
2. Lambert, pp. 462–463.
3. "North View of Arundel House 1646 (BM 1880, 1113.2930). Seymour Place and Arundel House are the same building.
4. "The Ground Plot of Arundel House and Gardens," 1792 (BM Q, 6.86).
5. After the death of Adrian Stokes, Frances's second husband, he was found to possess a portrait of Catherine Parr. This almost certainly came from his wife and implies a fond relationship with Catherine.
6. Frances Brandon to Thomas Seymour (S. Haynes, p. 78).
7. John Ascham to Lady Jane Grey, 18 January 1551 (Ascham, *Whole Works*, Vol., Part II, p. 240).
8. Strype (1821), pp. 195–196.
9. Clifford, p. 86.
10. Cole, p. 5.
11. Clifford.
12. Merton (p. 64) notes that Elizabeth would usually rise before nine o'clock.
13. The Confession of Katherine Ashley (S. Haynes, p. 99.).
14. Vives, p. 144.
15. TNA E15/340 f. 29v, f. 30, f. 30v.
16. Colvin Vol. IV, Part II, pp. 64–65.
17. TNA E15/340 f. 42 concerns payments for lodgings for servants at Hanworth and also close to Seymour Place when the household moved to London. Folio 21 notes that some of Catherine's yeomen and grooms left her service in May 1547.
18. Ibid., f. 42v, f. 49v, f. 50.
19. James, p. 278.
20. TNA E15/340 f. 24, f. 25v, f. 28v, f. 29, f. 29v.

21. Ibid., f. 30.
22. A clear example of Catherine's passionate nature can be seen in her letter to Thomas of late May 1547, when she referred to wanting to bite the Protector when he angered her in an argument (Parr, p. 140).
23. TNA E15/340 f. 29, f. 38.
24. Ibid., f. 39v.
25. Colvin, Vol. IV, Part II, p. 65.
26. Elizabeth to the Lord Protector, 7 March 1547 (Elizabeth, *Collected Works*, p. 34).
27. Ibid.
28. Catherine dated letters from Hanworth that month, including TNA E101/426/3 f. 3, f. 1 and f. 25. She was still there in September (f. 21). She had previously been based at Chelsea, into the summer, as letters dated May and June show (f. 5 and f. 17).
29. Lysons and *VCH Middlesex*, Vol. II, pp. 391–396.
30. TNA E15/340 f. 28.
31. Dugdale.
32. TNA E15/340 f. 21v, f. 25, f. 26.
33. TNA E101/424/12 f. 11, f. 14.
34. Thomas Seymour gives these details of Catherine's household in his letter to the Marquess of Dorset, 17 September 1548 (S. Haynes, pp. 77–78).
35. Evans, p. 37.
36. BL Harley MS 6807 f. 11.
37. *Statutes of the Realm*, Vol. 3 (London, 1817)—"Chapter XXIII: The Assurance of the Titles of the King's Manor of Hanworth," pp. 143–144.
38. Ibid.
39. Camden (1789), Vol. II, p. 2.
40. Thomas Seymour to Elizabeth, early 1547.
41. Confession of Sir Thomas Parry (S. Haynes, p. 96).
42. Ibid.
43. Confession of Katherine Ashley (ibid., p. 99).
44. Further Confession of John Harington Concerning the Lord Admiral, 2 February 1549 (*Calendar of the Cecil Papers*, Vol. 1, p. 281).
45. Vives, p. 155.
46. Confession of the Lady Elizabeth (S. Haynes, p. 102).
47. TNA E101/426/3 is a letter of Catherine's dated 29 July 1547, from Sheen, when she was otherwise staying at Hanworth.
48. TNA E101/426/3 f. 21.
49. Katherine Ashley's First Handwritten Deposition, late February 1549 (Elizabeth, *Collected Works*, p. 28).

CHAPTER 7: A DRESS SO TRIMMED

1. See letters by Edward VI, including that of 18 September 1547 to Somerset and 19 September 1547 to Catherine Parr (Edward VI, *Literary Remains*, p. 510).

2. TNA E15/340 f. 41v. Catherine's accounts record a payment in this month to Dr. Huicke, her personal physician, for "diverse charges."
3. Ibid., f. 28.
4. Ibid., f. 28v, f. 29.
5. Alford, p. 39.
6. Articles Against Thomas Seymour, No. 8 (Cobbett *et al.*).
7. Edward VI to Catherine Parr, 19 September 1547 (Parr, p. 148).
8. Loach, p. 4.
9. Colvin, Vol. IV, Part II, p. 147, and Lysons, p. 93.
10. Further Deposition of Katherine Ashley, 4 February 1549 (SP 10/6/55).
11. This deposition was originally printed, erroneously, with the claim that Elizabeth was wearing a black dress. In fact, the color is not given in the original deposition.
12. Confession of Katherine Ashley (S. Haynes, p. 99).
13. Vives, p. 145.
14. TNA E15/340 f. 42.
15. Ibid., f. 30v and f. 32.
16. Edward VI's Deposition (Edward VI, *Literary Remains*, pp. 57–58).
17. Deposition of Sir John Cheke (Tytler, p. 155).
18. Ibid.
19. Articles Against Thomas Seymour, No. 3 (Cobbett *et al.*).
20. Amended Draft Articles Against Thomas Seymour, No. 3 (BL Harley MS 249).
21. *History of Parliament*, for Sir George Blagge.
22. Deposition of George Blagge (Tytler, p. 147).
23. Ibid.
24. Ibid.
25. Deposition of the Earl of Warwick (SP 10/6/47).
26. Draft Articles Against Thomas Seymour (BL Harley MS 249).
27. SP 10/6/7.
28. Depositions of Sir William Sharington, January 1549 (SP 10/6/35).
29. Loach, p. 43.
30. *Journal of the House of Lords*, Vol. 1, 4 November 1547.
31. BL Harley MS 6807 f. 73.
32. Sharington's Confession (S. Haynes, p. 91) and Sharington's Answers (S. Haynes, p. 93).
33. *CSP Spanish*, Vol. IX, p. 221.
34. Dorset's Second Examination (S. Haynes, p. 76).
35. Draft Articles Against Thomas Seymour (BL Harley MS 249).
36. "A Journal," p. 55.
37. Ibid.
38. SP 68/1/159.
39. *Journal of the House of Lords*, 14 December 1547.
40. Articles Against Thomas Seymour (Cobbett *et al.*)

41. Ibid.
42. Throckmorton, p. 19.

CHAPTER 8: IN A MAIDEN'S CHAMBER

1. "Polar Ice . . . p. 26.
2. *CSP Spanish*, Vol. IX, p. 16.
3. Ibid., p. 245.
4. Examination of the Marquess of Dorset, No. 1 (S. Haynes, p. 75).
5. Edward VI's Confession (Edward VI, *Literary Remains*, pp. 57–58).
6. Amended Draft Articles Against Thomas Seymour, No. 10 (BL Harley MS 249).
7. Ascham to Sturm, 4 April 1550 (Ascham, *Whole Works*, Vol. I, Part 1, p. lxiv).
8. Shrewsbury, p. 183, and Kohn, p. 104.
9. Ascham to William Cecil, 5 January 1548 (Ascham, *Whole Works*, Vol. I, Part 3, p. 6).
10. Ascham to Princess Elizabeth, 22 January 1548 (ibid., p. lvi).
11. Ascham to the Master of St. John's College, January 1548 (ibid., p. liii).
12. Francis Goldsmith's Latin Letter to Catherine Parr, Early January 1544 (Parr, pp. 77–78).
13. Ascham, *Whole Works*, Vol. I, Part 3, p. xi.
14. Letter XXIV (Ascham, *Whole Works*, Vol. I, Part 3, p. xliv).
15. Letter II (ibid., p. xviii).
16. Roger Ascham to his wife, *c.* November 1568 (ibid., Vol. II, p. 170).
17. Ascham to John Cheke, 14 January 1551, complains of his neglected talents (ibid., Vol. I, Part 2, p. 235); and Ascham to Mr. Edward Raven, 20 January 1551 (ibid., p. 244) refers to the pelican.
18. Letter XXI (ibid., Vol. I, Part 3, p. xxix).
19. Ascham to Mrs. Astley (ibid., Vol. I, Part 1, p. 87).
20. Ascham to Princess Elizabeth (ibid., p. 87).
21. Ascham to John Cheke, 12 February 1548 (ibid., Vol. I, Part 3, p. lvii).
22. *CSP Spanish*, Vol. IX, p. 250.
23. Wotton to Sir William Petre, Paris, 7 March 1548 (Tytler, p. 78).
24. Wotton to the Protector and Council, Paris, 7 March 1548 (ibid., p. 80).
25. *CSP Foreign*, p. 77.
26. Ibid., p. 84.
27. Ibid., p. 109.
28. SP 10/4/13.
29. Draft Articles Against Thomas Seymour, No. 23 (BL Harley MS 249).
30. Ibid., No. 28.
31. Ibid., No. 25.
32. Ibid., No. 24.
33. Articles Against Thomas Seymour, No. 23 (Cobbett *et al.*).
34. Draft Articles Against Thomas Seymour, No. 26 (BL Harley MS 249).

35. Gruffydd, p. 59.
36. *L&P*, Vol. XVIII, Part I, 47.
37. Van der Delft to the Emperor, 23 February 1548 (*CSP Spanish*, Vol. IX, pp. 250–254).
38. Deposition of William Parr, Marquess of Northampton (SP 10/6/39).
39. Ascham to Sturm, 4 April 1550 (Ascham, *Whole Works*, Vol. I, Part 3, p. lxiv).
40. Perry, p. 28.
41. Ibid., p. 28.
42. BL STC 17320.
43. Confession of Katherine Ashley (S. Haynes, p. 99).

CHAPTER 9: THE QUEEN'S DISPLEASURE

1. Biblical Verses Inscribed by Queen Katherine in Her Volume Containing a Sermon of St. John Chrysostom (Parr, p. 48).
2. Thomas Seymour to Catherine Parr, 9 June 1548 (Parr, p. 167).
3. Catherine Parr to Lady Wriothesley (*Writings of Edward VIII . . .*, p. 14).
4. Elizabeth to Catherine, July 1548.
5. Catherine to Thomas, probably 9 June 1548 (Parr, p. 170). The letter answers Seymour's letter of 9 June. Since he returned to Hanworth early on 11 June, Catherine's reply must date to either 9 or 10 June.
6. Ibid., p. 167.
7. Thomas to Catherine, 9 June 1548 (ibid., p. 167).
8. Catherine to Thomas, probably 9 June 1548 (Parr, p. 168).
9. "The Countess of Lincoln's Nurserie at Oxford printed 1622 (Harleian Miscellany, Vol. IV, p. 27).
10. Answers of the Lord Admiral to Articles Objected Against Him (*CSP Domestic*, 24 February 1549).
11. J. Hayward (1630) p. 81.
12. *History of Parliament*, for William Wightman.
13. Wightman's Confession (S. Haynes, p. 71).
14. Sharington's Confession (ibid., p. 91).
15. John Harington's First Examination (ibid., p. 84).
16. SP 10/4/13.
17. SP 10/4/28.
18. Thomas to Catherine, 9 June 1548 (Parr, p. 168).
19. Colvin, Vol. IV, Part II, p. 253.
20. BL Egerton MS 2815.
21. Deposition of John Fowler (SP 10/6/24).
22. *CSP Spanish*, Vol. IX, p. 278.
23. The Inventory of Catherine Parr's Personal Effects (Parr, pp. 627–632).
24. Catherine Parr to Thomas Seymour (S. Haynes, p. 62).
25. Gruffydd, p. 59.
26. Deposition of John Fowler (SP 10/6/24).

27. Ibid.
28. Ascham, *The Schoolmaster.*
29. Ascham to Sturm, 14 December 1550 (Ascham, *Whole Works*, Vol. I, Part 1, p. lxxi).
30. Ascham to Lady Jane Grey, 18 January 1551 (Ascham, *Letters*, p. 147).
31. Confession of Thomas Parry (S. Haynes, p. 96).
32. Elizabeth's inscription on Catherine's letter to Thomas of 9 June 1548 (S. Haynes, p. 17). The analysis comes from this work.
33. Confession of Thomas Parry (S. Haynes, p. 96).
34. Ibid.
35. Ibid.
36. Perry, p. 32.
37. Will of Sir Edmund Denny, 1519 (*Testamenta Vetusta*, Vol. II, p. 559).
38. For example, in his will Sir Edmund gave his daughter four marks each for their marriages. Sir Anthony gave his daughters 1,100 marks each.
39. Will of Dame Joan Denny (PROB 11/36/157) is that of a conventional wealthy widow.
40. Garrett, pp. 141–144.
41. Elizabeth to Catherine (Parr, 171).
42. Elizabeth to Catherine (ibid., 172).
43. Confession of Thomas Parry (S. Haynes, p. 96).
44. Confession of Katherine Ashley (S. Haynes, p. 101).
45. *VCH Hertford*, Vol. 3.
46. *Ambulator*, p. 59.
47. Will of Thomas Denny, 1527 (*Testamenta Vetusta*, Vol. II, pp. 628–629).
48. Ascham to Sir Anthony Denny, 1545 (Ascham, *Whole Works*, Vol. I, Part 1, p. 82).
49. Ascham to William Ireland, 8 July 1549 (Ascham, *Whole Works*, Vol. I, Part 1, pp. lvii–lix).

CHAPTER 10: A CHILD BORN AND MISERABLY DESTROYED

1. Furdell, p. 67.
2. Ibid.
3. Clifford, p. 87.
4. Ibid. The cuckold mentioned can be no other than Somerset in this context. The only other possibility would be Catherine Parr, who was dead by 1550.
5. Long, No. 2, p. 213.
6. Aubrey, p. 253.
7. Rede.
8. Stansfield, pp. 61–62.
9. "Barnes" is a common name in the Great Shefford parish registers, which survive from 1571; others from that decade include Katherine Barnes (christened 2 April 1572), Agnes Barnes (christened 14 February 1574), and Anna Barnes (christened 14 December 1576).

10. Long, No. 3.
11. Quoted in Rice, p. 87.
12. There were two successive Sir Henry Knyvetts at Charlton. The elder Sir Henry had died in May 1547. His youngest child, Alice, was born around that time. His eldest son, the second Sir Henry, did not marry until the early 1560s. This detail almost certainly means that Mother Barnes's story does not relate to Elizabeth, although it is just possible that Mother Barnes was always engaged by Mrs. Knyvett for her confinements and had received no specific instructions in 1548, but knew a further birth was possible. She could have been unaware of the elder Sir Henry's death the year before, given the distance from her home to Charlton.
13. Rice, p. 89.
14. Ibid., p. 90.
15. Long, No. 4.
16. Ibid, p. 219.
17. Rice, p. 92.
18. Long, No. 2.
19. Ibid., p. 204.
20. Ibid.
21. Rice, p. 84.
22. Clifford, p. 55.
23. Ibid.
24. Ibid., p. 56.
25. Long, No. 3, p. 396.
26. A Credulous Archaeologist, p. 48.
27. Ward.
28. A Credulous Archaeologist, pp. 45–51.
29. De Luna, p. 49. In this work it is convincingly and authoritatively asserted that Avisa can be considered to represent Elizabeth I, and that the nobleman can be identified as Thomas Seymour.
30. Ibid., p. 137.
31. Princess Elizabeth to Somerset, September 1548 (SP 10/5/8a).
32. Furdell, p. 69.
33. Munk, p. 35.

CHAPTER 11: THE LITTLE KNAVE

1. Catherine to Thomas, 9 June 1548 (Parr, p. 170).
2. Bingham, p. 68.
3. John Leland (quoted in J. Nichols, 1823, Vol. III, p. 217).
4. Willyams, p. 11.
5. Holbein's drawing of Sir William Sharington (Royal Collection, Windsor Castle).
6. Clark-Maxwell.

7. Howarth, p. 21.
8. Ibid., p. 22
9. Clark-Maxwell, p. 177.
10. Lady Jane Grey to Thomas Seymour, 1 October 1548 (Tytler, p. 133).
11. For example, in November 1547 Catherine had sent a messenger with letters to Newhall, in Essex, which belonged to Mary (TNA E15./340 f. 42).
12. Princess Mary to Catherine Parr, 9 August 1548 (Parr, p. 175).
13. Elizabeth to Catherine, *c.* June 1548 (ibid., pp. 171–172).
14. Elizabeth to Thomas Seymour, *c.* July 1548 (Elizabeth, Letters, p. 8).
15. Elizabeth to Catherine, 31 July 1548 (Perry, p. 35).
16. Edward VI's Confession (Edward VI, *Literary Remains*, p. 58).
17. John Fowler to Thomas Seymour, 19 July 1548 (SP 10/4/61).
18. SP 10/4/62.
19. SP 10/4/63.
20. TNA E101/424/12 has many documents signed by Tyrwhitt in his capacity as a household officer, including f. 1, which was an allowance paid to a servant going on the queen's business from Chelsea to London in July 1547.
21. Sir Robert Tyrwhitt's Confession (S. Haynes, p. 104).
22. Cheselworth Inventory (Ellis, p. 125).
23. Sheffield Inventory (ibid., p. 128).
24. Turner.
25. Grinsell, p. 13.
26. Sharington's Answers (S. Haynes, p. 92).
27. Ibid.
28. Examination of Sir William Sharington, 11 February 1549 (S. Haynes, p. 104).
29. Mr. Weston to the Lord Admiral, 18 July 1548 (S. Haynes, p. 73).

CHAPTER 12: LET ME BE NO MORE

1. *CSP Spanish*, Vol. IX, p. 279.
2. Ibid., p. 277.
3. Ibid., p. 279.
4. Thomas Seymour to James Walsh, 19 July 1548 (SP 61/1/105).
5. Thomas Seymour to James Walsh, Mayor of Waterford, 23 July 1548 (SP 61/1/106).
6. Receipt dated 19 June 1548 (SP 46/124/35).
7. Lord Russell to Lord Seymour, 13 August 1548 (SP 10/4/87).
8. Thomas Seymour to unknown, 16 July 1548 (SP 46/124/42).
9. Thomas Seymour to William Cecil, 18 June 1548 (SP 10/4/42).
10. Somerset to Thomas Seymour, 6 August 1548, was written from Hampton Court, while his letter of 13 August was dated at Oatlands and his letter of 16 August at Sheen (SP 10/4/72).
11. Seymour to Somerset, 10 August 1548 (SP 10/4/83).
12. Somerset to Seymour, 6 August 1548 (SP 10/4/72).

13. Ibid.
14. John Greenfield to Thomas Seymour, 7 September 1548 (SP 10/5/4). Greenfield was Thomas's vice admiral for Cornwall and one of the recipients of his orders of 9 August to move against the French.
15. Thomas Seymour to Sir Peter Carew and others, 9 August 1548 (SP 10/4/77).
16. John Greenfield to Thomas Seymour, 7 September 1548 (SP 10/5/4).
17. Somerset to Seymour, 16 August 1548 (SP 10/4/90).
18. Seymour to Somerset, 19 August 1548 (SP 10/4/92).
19. Somerset to Seymour, 13 August 1548 (SP 10/4/84).
20. Seymour to Somerset, 23 August 1548 (SP 10/4/94).
21. Somerset to Seymour, 1 September 1548 (SP 10/5/1).
22. Elizabeth to Catherine, 31 July 1548 (Perry, p. 35).
23. Strangford, p. 34.
24. Munk, p. 33.
25. Elizabeth Tyrwhitt's Confession (Parr, p. 178).
26. Porter (2010), p. 319.
27. Somerset to Seymour, 1 September 1548 (SP 10/5/1).
28. John Fowler to Seymour (18 July 1548) refers to the Duchess of Somerset's son.
29. Somerset to Seymour, 1 September 1548 (SP 10/5/1).
30. Elizabeth Tyrwhitt's Account of Catherine Parr's State of Mind and Behaviour, 3 September 1548 (Parr, p. 177).
31. Somerset to Seymour, 1 September 1548 (SP 10/5/1).
32. William Wightman to Mr. Cecil, 10 May 1549 (Tytler, p. 169).
33. TNA PROB 11/32/283.
34. James suggested this in her biography of Catherine. It is also raised in Parr, p. 178.
35. Catherine Parr to Thomas Seymour (S. Haynes, p. 62).
36. Catherine's prayer book (Parr, p. 619).

PART 3: THE SCANDAL UNVEILED

CHAPTER 13: HE THAT HATH FRIENDS

1. Seymour to Dorset, 17 September 1548 (S. Haynes, p. 77).
2. Dent (p. 174) contains a contemporary account of the funeral.
3. Confession of the Lady Elizabeth (S. Haynes, p. 102).
4. Answers of Katherine Ashley, 2 February 1549 (Elizabeth, *Complete Works*, p. 25).
5. Confession of William Wightman, No. 2 (S. Haynes, p. 68).
6. Depositions of Sir William Sharington, January 1549 (SP 10/6/35).
7. BL Sloane MS 1523 f. 32. Sir William Fitzwilliam was able to make such a boast. On his ships, "there was not a serviceable man belonging to him but he knew by name."
8. Confession of William Wightman (S. Haynes, pp. 68–70).

9. Ibid.
10. Throckmorton.
11. Seymour to Dorset, 17 September 1548 (S. Haynes, p. 77).
12. HMC *Salisbury*, Vol. I, p. 221.
13. Frances Dorset to the Lord Admiral, 19 September 1548 (S. Haynes, p. 79).
14. Dorset's Confession, No. 5 (ibid., p. 77).
15. Seymour to Dorset, 17 September 1548 (ibid., p. 78).
16. Confession of William Wightman (ibid., p. 72).
17. Deposition of William Parr, Marquess of Northampton (SP 10/6/39).
18. Ibid.
19. Ibid.
20. Sir Robert Tyrwhitt's Confession (S. Haynes, p. 104). Seymour told Sir Robert that he had said this to Somerset at dinner shortly afterward.
21. Confession of the Earl of Rutland (ibid., p. 82).
22. Deposition of Richard Cotton (SP 10/6/23). Cotton's evidence came from his maid, who was a sister of Pigot, one of the Lord Admiral's servants. This Pigot had a number of well-connected siblings and seems to have been something of a gossip.
23. William Wightman's Confession (S. Haynes, p. 72).
24. Sir Robert Tyrwhitt's Confession (ibid., p. 104).
25. Ibid.
26. Dorset's Examination (Tytler, p. 140).
27. Ascham, *The Schoolmaster*, pp. 35–36.
28. Dorset's Confession, No. 4 (S. Haynes, p. 76).
29. Harington to the Lords of the Council, 3 February 1549 (ibid., p. 93).
30. Examination of Harington (ibid., p. 94).
31. Lady Jane Grey to Thomas Seymour, 1 October 1548 (Tytler, p. 133).
32. Lady Frances Dorset to Thomas Seymour, 2 October 1548 (ibid., p. 134).
33. The Marquess of Dorset's Examination (ibid., p. 179).
34. Depositions of Sir William Sharington (SP 10/6/35).
35. Dorset's Confession, No. 5 (S. Haynes, p. 77).
36. Enis, p. 68.
37. Depositions of Sir William Sharington (SP 10/6/35).
38. Examination of Sir William Sharington, 11 February 1549 (Haynes, p. 105).

CHAPTER 14: BEWARE WHOM YOU TRUST

1. Deposition of Richard Cotton (SP 10/6/23).
2. Wightman's Confession (S. Haynes, p. 72).
3. Wriothesley, Vol. II, p. 5.
4. Ibid.
5. Ibid.
6. Ibid.
7. Colvin, Vol. II, p. 149.

8. Bramley, p. 163.
9. Rowe and Williamson.
10. Katherine Ashley's Confession (S. Haynes, p. 100).
11. Sharington's Answers (ibid., p. 64).
12. Sharington's Confession (ibid., p. 90).
13. Sharington's Answers (ibid, p. 64).
14. Ibid., p. 65.
15. Draft Articles Against Thomas Seymour, No. 22 (BL Harley MS 249).
16. Parry's Communication with the Lord Admiral (S. Haynes, p. 97).
17. Ascham to Edward Raven, 20 January 1551 (Ascham, *Whole Works*, Vol. I, Part 2, p. 244).
18. Sir Robert Tyrwhitt to the Protector, 28 January 1549 (S. Haynes, p. 89).
19. Ascham to Lady Jane Grey, 18 January 1551 (Ascham, *Letters*, p. 147).
20. Ascham to Sturm, 4 April 1550 (Ascham, *Whole Works*, Vol. I, Part 1, p. lxlv).
21. Ibid.
22. Ibid.
23. Ascham to Sir John Cheke, 11 November 1550 (Ascham, *Whole Works*, Vol. I, Part 2, p. 216) and Ascham to Cecil, 8 June 1567 (ibid., Vol. II, pp. 149–151).
24. Vives, p. 157.
25. Katherine Ashley's Answers, 2 February 1549 (Elizabeth, *Collected Works*, p. 26).
26. Katherine Ashley's Confession (S. Haynes, p. 100).
27. Vives, p. 126.
28. Ibid., p.140.
29. Confession of Thomas Parry (S. Haynes, p. 96).
30. Sir Robert Tyrwhitt to the Lord Protector, 22 January 1549 (ibid., p. 70).
31. *History of Parliament*, for Thomas Parry.
32. Deposition of William Parr, Marquess of Northampton (SP 10/6/39).
33. Ibid.
34. Confession of the Earl of Rutland (S. Haynes, p. 82).
35. Depositions of Sir William Sharington (SP 10/6/35).
36. *History of Parliament*, for William Smethwick.
37. *Journal of the House of Lords*, Vol. I, 24 November 1548.
38. Edward VI (*Diary*), p. 28. For a discussion of the debate, see Pollard, pp. 98–100. A transcript can be found in Appendix V of Gasquet and Bishop.
39. Gasquet and Bishop, p. 397.

CHAPTER 15: LONDON NEWS

1. Drawing of Parry by Hans Holbein (Royal Collection).
2. *History of Parliament*, for Thomas Parry.
3. Further Depositions of Katharine Ashley, 4 February 1549 (SP 10/6/53).
4. Drake, p. 76.
5. Further Depositions of Katharine Ashley, 4 February 1549 (SP10/6/53).
6. Ibid.

7. Confession of William Wightman, No. 2 (S. Haynes, p. 68).
8. Norden's Description of Westminster (in J. Nichols, 1823, Vol. 5, p. 133).
9. Confession of Thomas Parry (S. Haynes, p. 95).
10. Parry's Communication with the Lord Admiral (ibid., p. 98).
11. Confession of the Lady Elizabeth (ibid., p. 102).
12. Ibid.
13. McIntosh, p. 52.
14. Vives, p. 92. Starkey (*Elizabeth*, p. 72) notes Elizabeth's obvious interest in Seymour.
15. Warnicke, p. 93.
16. Katherine Ashley's Confession (S. Haynes, p. 100).
17. Ibid., p. 101.
18. Confession of William Wightman, No. 2 (ibid., p. 68).
19. Ibid.
20. Parry's Communication with the Lord Admiral (ibid., p. 97).
21. Katherine Ashley's Confession (ibid., p. 100).
22. Sir Robert Tyrwhitt to the Lord Protector, 23 January 1549 (ibid., p. 71).
23. Ibid.
24. Confession of the Lady Elizabeth (ibid., p. 103).
25. Throckmorton, p. 19.
26. Dorset's Examination (Tytler, p. 140).
27. *ODNB*, for Sir Thomas Seymour, p. 898.
28. Draft Articles Against Thomas Seymour, No. 30 (BL Harley MS 249).
29. Bernard, p. 226.
30. Depositions of Sir William Sharington, January 1549 (SP 10/6/35).
31. Wriothesley, p. 7
32. Perry, p. 37.
33. Confession of William Wightman, No. 2 (S. Haynes, p. 68).
34. Parry's Communication with the Lord Admiral (ibid., p. 98).

CHAPTER 16: LABORING FOR THE TOWER

1. HMC, *Hatfield*, Vol. I, p. 58 (No. 252).
2. *History of Parliament*, for Sir William Sharington.
3. HMC, *Hatfield*, Vol. I, p. 60 (No. 255): in this letter, Thomas Dowrishe complains of Sharington's accusation, in a letter of 5 January, that he had disclosed the contents of an earlier letter. Dowrishe completely denies doing so. It seems likely that the letter in question was intercepted, and that Sharington's correspondence was being monitored.
4. Deposition of John Fowler (SP 10/6/24).
5. Ibid.
6. *House of Lords Journal*, Vol. 1.
7. Depositions of Sir William Sharington, January 1549 (SP 10/6/35).
8. Dorset's Examination 3 (S. Haynes, p. 76).

9. Confession of William Wightman, No. 2 (S. Haynes, p. 68).
10. Deposition of John Fowler (SP 10/6/24).
11. *CSP Domestic*, Vol. 1.
12. Depositions of Lord Russell (SP 10/6/43).
13. Examination of the Lord Admiral, 18 February 1549 (S. Haynes, p. 108).
14. Ibid.
15. Deposition of John Fowler (SP 10/6/24).
16. Examination of the Lord Admiral, 18 February 1549 (S. Haynes, p. 107).
17. Depositions of Lord Russell (SP 10/6/43).
18. Hoak, p. 49.
19. Deposition of William Parr, Marquess of Northampton (SP 10/6/39).
20. Ibid.
21. "A Journal," p. 60.
22. *CSP Spanish*, Vol. X, 10 January 1549.
23. Ibid., 27 January 1549.
24. John Burcher to Henry Bullinger, 15 February 1549 (Robinson, pp. 647–648).
25. Gruffydd, p. 60.
26. *CSP Spanish*, Vol. IX, 30 January 1549.
27. Ibid., 8 February 1549.
28. Ibid., 5 February 1549 and 31 January 1549.
29. Articles Against Thomas Seymour, No. 8 (Cobbett *et al.*).
30. Indeed, Robinson (p. 648) suggested Fowler in his notes to Burcher's letter.
31. Harington II, *Nugae Antiquae*, Vol. II, pp. 328–329.
32. *CSP Spanish*, Vol. X, 8 February 1549.
33. Skidmore (p. 102) speculates that Seymour intended to use Holt Castle as a base during any resulting civil war.
34. Deposition of William Parr, Marquess of Northampton (SP 10/6/39).
35. Confession of the Earl of Rutland (S. Haynes, pp. 81–82).
36. Deposition of William Parr, Marquess of Northampton (SP 10/6/39).
37. Examinations of the Marquess of Dorset (Tytler, p. 141).
38. *CSP Spanish*, Vol. X, 8 February 1549.
39. Touching Harington (S. Haynes, p. 84).
40. John Harington's Examination, No.1 (ibid., p. 84).
41. *APC*, Vol. II, p. 236.
42. *CSP Spanish*, Vol. X, 8 February 1549.
43. Hahn, p. 33; also Bennett, and Henry.
44. *CSP Domestic*, Vol. VI, p. 2.
45. *APC*, Vol. II, p. 239.
46. Touching Harington (S. Haynes, p. 85).
47. *APC*, Vol. II, p. 239.
48. Ibid.
49. HMC, *Hatfield*, Vol. I, p. 58 (No. 255).
50. Interrogatories to Sharington (S. Haynes, p. 62).

51. Ibid., pp. 65–67.
52. Sir William Sharington to Somerset (S. Haynes, p. 67).
53. Ellis, p. 129.
54. Ibid.
55. *APC*, Vol. II, p. 239.
56. Gibbons 1999, p. 233; Hoak, p. 50. Wriothesley also provided his own deposition, concerning his dealings with Thomas (SP 10/6/15).
57. Hoak, p. 49.
58. Confession of King Edward VI (S. Haynes, pp. 74–75).
59. To see the signature, it is necessary to view the original. A microfilm version is BL M485/39 f. 51.
60. Confession of Wightman no. 2 (S. Haynes, p. 68).

CHAPTER 17: VANITY OF VANITIES

1. Tyrwhitt to Somerset, 22 January 1549 (S. Haynes, p. 70–71).
2. Ibid. (p. 70).
3. Further Depositions of Katharine Ashley, 4 February 1549 (SP 10/6/53).
4. Kate refers to wearing her russet nightgown in the Tower in her deposition of 4 February.
5. *APC*, Vol. II, p. 240.
6. Tyrwhitt to Somerset, 22 January 1549 (S. Haynes, p. 70).
7. *APC*, Vol. II, p. 240.
8. "A Brief Account of the Ancient Prison Called "The Fleet" . . .
9. Van der Delft to Charles V, 27 January 1549 (*CSP Spanish*, Vol. IX, p. 332).
10. The Council to Elizabeth, 17 February 1549 (S. Haynes, p. 107).
11. Tyrwhitt, p. 74.
12. The Council to Elizabeth, 17 February 1549 (S. Haynes, p. 107).
13. Tyrwhitt, p. 74.
14. Tyrwhitt to Somerset 22 January 1549 (S. Haynes, p. 70).
15. Ibid.
16. Tyrwhitt to Somerset, 22 January 1549 (S. Haynes, p. 70).
17. Tyrwhitt to Somerset, 23 January 1549 (ibid., p. 71).
18. Starkey (2000, p. 73) also considers that Tyrwhitt misjudged Elizabeth.
19. Wheatley, p. 79.
20. McIntosh, p. 55.
21. Examination of the Lord Admiral, 25 January 1549 (S. Haynes, p. 87).
22. Tyrwhitt to Somerset, 28 January 1549 (ibid., p. 88).
23. Seymour to Somerset, 27 January 1549 (ibid., pp. 87–88).
24. M485/39 f. 65.
25. Tyrwhitt to Somerset, 28 January 1549 (S. Haynes, p. 88).
26. Elizabeth to Somerset, 28 January 1549 (ibid., pp. 89–90).
27. Ibid.
28. Tyrwhitt to the Protector, 31 January 1549 (SP 10/6/16).

29. Katherine Ashley's Final Deposition, 4 February 1549 (SP 10/6/57).
30. Tyrwhitt to Somerset, 5 February 1549 (S. Haynes, pp. 94–95).
31. Confession of Thomas Parry (ibid, p. 95).
32. As contained in SP 10/6/51, SP 10/6/55 and SP 10/6/53.
33. Katherine Ashley's Final Deposition, 4 February 1549 (SP 10/6/57).
34. Tyrwhitt to Somerset, 5 February 1549 (S. Haynes, p. 94).
35. Ibid.
36. McIntosh, p. 67
37. Parr, p. 624.
38. Elizabeth to Somerset, 6 February 1549 (Elizabeth, *Collected Works*, p. 31).
39. Elizabeth to Somerset, 21 February 1549 (ibid., p. 32).
40. Tyrwhitt to Somerset, 7 February 1549 (S. Haynes, p. 102).
41. BL M485/39 f. 89.
42. Confession of the Lady Elizabeth's Grace (S. Haynes, p. 102).
43. The Sayings of Christopher Ayer, 16 February 1549 (S. Haynes, p. 106).
44. Ibid.
45. Wriothesley, p. 7.
46. William Sharington's Confession, 15 February 1549 (S. Haynes, p. 106)
47. *CSP Spanish*, Vol. X, 20 February 1549.

CHAPTER 18: A MAN OF MUCH WIT

1. Harington II, *Nugae Antiquae*, Vol. II, pp. 328–329.
2. Council to Elizabeth, 17 February 1549 (S. Haynes, p. 107).
3. Tyrwhitt to Somerset, 19 February 1549 (ibid., p. 108).
4. Examination of the Lord Admiral, 18 February 1549 (ibid., p. 107).
5. Interrogatories for the Lord Admiral (ibid., p. 86).
6. Elizabeth's Tide Letter to Mary I, 1554 (Perry, p. 65).
7. *CSP Spanish*, Vol. X, 8 February 1549. The stolen goods largely did not find their way back to their owners, however (Gruffydd, p. 60).
8. The draft articles against Seymour, with amendments and additions, are BL Harley MS 249 f. 34 to f. 39. The final articles are in Cobbett *et al.*
9. Articles Against Thomas Seymour, No. 7 (Cobbett *et al.*).
10. Ibid., No. 22.
11. BL Add. MS 48023.
12. *APC*, Vol. II, p. 246.
13. Ibid., p. 247.
14. Ibid., p. 257.
15. Ibid. p., 258.
16. Answers of the Lord Admiral, 24 February 1549 (SP 10/6/69).
17. BL M485/39 f. 67.
18. Throckmorton, p. 20.
19. *CSP Spanish*, Vol. X, 19 March 1549.
20. Articles Against Thomas Seymour (Cobbett *et al.*).

21. BL Harley MS 6807 f. 14v.
22. *APC*, Vol. II, p. 260.
23. Ibid.
24. *House of Lords Journal*, Vol. I.
25. *House of Commons Journal*, Vol. I.
26. *CSP Spanish*, Vol. X, 19 March 1549.
27. *House of Lords Journal*, Vol. I, and *House of Commons Journal*, Vol. I.
28. *House of Lords Journal*, Vol. I.
29. Elizabeth to Somerset, 7 March 1549 (Elizabeth, *Collected Works*, pp. 33–34).
30. *APC*, Vol. II, p. 261.
31. Ibid., p. 262.
32. Ibid.
33. Strype (1822), Vol. II, Part I, p. 207.
34. *APC*, Vol. II, p. 266.
35. *CSP Spanish*, Vol. X, 19 March 1549.
36. Latimer, p. 161.
37. Strype (1822), Vol. II, Part I, p. 197.
38. Latimer, p. 161
39. Gruffydd, p. 60.
40. Latimer, p. 162, and BL Add. MS 48023.
41. Gruffydd, p. 60.
42. Ibid.

EPILOGUE: THE VIRGIN QUEEN?

1. Throckmorton, p. 20.
2. Ibid.
3. Sander, p. 184.
4. Strype (1822), Vol. II, Part I, p. 200.
5. Ibid., p. 201.
6. Duchess of Suffolk to Cecil, 24 July 1549 (SP 10/8/61).
7. Ibid.
8. *APC*, Vol. II, 13 March 1550.
9. Porter (2011).
10. *History of Parliament*, for Sir William Sharington.
11. Latimer, Vol. I, p. 263.
12. *History of Parliament*, for John Fowler.
13. Hoak, p. 50.
14. Sir Robert Tyrwhitt's Confession (S. Haynes, p. 104).
15. Tyrwhitt, p. 12.
16. Ibid., p. 14.
17. Vives.
18. McIntosh, p. 127.
19. Parry to Cecil, 25 September 1549 (Tytler, pp. 201–202).

20. *CSP Spanish*, Vol. X, p. 489.
21. *CSP Foreign*, p. 316.
22. Ibid., pp. 433, 620.
23. Naunton, p. 172.
24. BL Sloane MS 1523 f. 37.
25. Foxe, p. 283.
26. Edward VI, *Diary*, p. 36.
27. Proclamation of 1 October 1549 (Tytler, p. 205).
28. Cranmer, Paget and Wingfield to the Council, 11 October 1549 (ibid., p. 242).
29. *CSP Domestic (Knighton)*, p. 396.
30. Cranmer, Paget, and Wingfield to the Council, 11 October 1549 (Tytler, p. 242).
31. Alford, p. 137.
32. Article 28 (Cobbett *et al.*).
33. Pollard, p. 98.
34. Machyn, p. 14.
35. Ibid.
36. Cobbett *et al.*, p. 318.
37. Machyn, p. 15.
38. Perry, p. 65.
39. Naunton, p. 172.
40. Merton, p. 33.
41. Somerset, p. 61.
42. Camden (1688), p. 227.
43. Wilson, p. 148.
44. TNA PROB 11/88/89.
45. Camden (1688), p. 12.
46. Hughey.
47. Harington II, *Orlando Furioso*, p. xvi.
48. Hughey, p. 258.
49. Ibid., p. 52.
50. Ibid., p. 258.
51. BL Sloane MS 1523 f. 37.

BIBLIOGRAPHY

Abbreviations used in the Notes in the Text are given in square brackets.

MANUSCRIPT SOURCES

The manuscript series used are the following (more specific references are provided in the Notes on the Text):

The British Library, London: Add(itional) MSS; Egerton MSS; Harley MSS; Sloane MSS; Stowe MSS.

Hatfield House, Hatfield, Hertfordshire: M485/39 (microfilm held at The British Library).

The National Archives, Kew: E 15; E 36; E 101; E 163; SC 6/EDWVI; SP 10; SP 46; SP 50; SP 61; SP 68; PROB 1; PROB 11.

Surrey History Centre, Woking: Loseley MSS 1331; Loseley MSS 1865.

PRIMARY SOURCES

Acts of the Privy Council of England, edited by J. R. Dasent *et al.*, 36 vols. (1890–1964) [*APC*].

Adams, S. and D.S. Gehring, "Elizabeth I's Former Tutor Reports on the Parliament of 1559: Johannes Spithovius to the Chancellor of Denmark, 27 February 1559 in *English Historical Review*, 128 (2013): pp. 35–51.

Adams, S., I.W. Archer and G.W. Bernard (eds.), "A 'Journall' of matters of state happened from time to time as well within and without the realme from and before the death of King Edward the 6th until the yere 1562 (BL Add MS 48023 f.380–369v)" in I. W. Archer *et al.* (eds.), *Religion, Politics, and Society in Sixteenth Century England,* Camden Fifth Series, Vol. 22 (2003) [A Journal].

——, "Certayne Brife Notes of the Controversy Betwene the Dukes of Somerset and Duke of Northumberland (BL Add MS 48126, f.6–16)" in ibid. [Certain Brief Notes].

Ascham, R., *Letters of Roger Ascham,* edited and translated by M. Hatch and A. Vos (New York, 1989).

——, *The Schoolmaster,* edited by L.V. Ryan (Ithaca, NY, 1967).

——, *The Whole Works of Roger Ascham,* 2 vols. in 3 parts, edited by Dr. J. A. Giles (London, 1864).

Aubrey, J., *Brief Lives,* edited by J. Barber (Woodbridge, Suffolk, 1975).

Burtt, J. (ed.), "Inventories of Certain Valuable Effects of King Henry the Eighth, in the Palace at Westminster, AD 1543," in *Archaeological Journal,* Vol. 18 (1861): pp. 134–145.

Calendar of the Cecil Papers in Hatfield House, Vol. I, *1306–1571* (London, 1883).

Calendar of Letters, Despatches, and State Papers Relating to the Negotiations Between England and Spain, Preserved in the Archives at Vienna, Simancas and Elsewhere, Vols. IX and X, edited by R. Tyler (London, 1912) [*CSP Spanish*].

Calendar of State Papers, Domestic Series, of the Reign of Edward VI, Mary, Elizabeth, Vol. I, 1547–1580, edited by R. Lemon (London, 1856) [*CSP Domestic*].

Calendar of State Papers, Domestic Series, of the Reign of Edward VI, 1547–1553, edited by C. S. Knighton (London, 1992) [*CSP Domestic (Knighton)*].

Calendar of State Papers, Foreign Series, of the Reign of Edward VI, 1547–1552, edited by W. B. Turnbull (London, 1861) [*CSP Foreign*].

Camden, W., *Britannia,* Vol. II, edited by R. Gough (n.p., 1789).

——, *The History of the Most Renowned and Victorious Princess Elizabeth, Late Queen of England* (London, 1688).

Clifford, H., *The Life of Jane Dormer Duchess of Feria,* edited by E. E. Estcourt and J. Stevenson (London, 1887).

Cobbett, W. *et al., Cobbett's Complete Collection of State Trials and Proceedings,* Vol. 1, edited by T. B. Howell (London, 1816).

De Luna, B. N. (ed.), *The Queen Declined: An Interpretation of "Willobie His Avisa" with the Text of the Original Edition* (Oxford, 1970).

Edward VI, *England's Boy King: The Diary of Edward VI, 1547–1553,* edited by J. North (Welwyn Garden City, Herts, 2005) [*Diary*].

——, *Literary Remains of King Edward VI,* edited by J. G. Nichols (London, 1857).

Elizabeth I, *A godly medytacyon of the Christen sowle, concerning a loue towards God and hys Christe, comyled in Frenche by Lady Margarete Quene of Naverre, and aptely translated into Englysh by the right vertuouse Lady Elyzabeth Doughter to our late soverayne kynge Henri the VIII, 1548* (BL STC 17320).

——, *Elizabeth I: Collected Works*, edited by L. S. Marcus, J. Mueller, and M. B. Rose (Chicago, 2002).

——, *The Letters of Queen Elizabeth*, edited by G. B. Harrison (London, 1935).

Ellis, H. (ed.), "Inventories of Goods, &c, in the Manor of Cheselworth, Sedgwick, and other parks, the Manor Place of Sheffield, and in the Forest of Worth, with the Iron-Works Belonging to the Lord Admiral Seymour, at the time of his Attainder, taken 1549," in *Sussex Archaeological Collections*, Vol. XIII (1861): pp. 118–131.

Foxe, J., *The Acts and Monuments of John Foxe* [= Foxe's Book of Martyrs], Vol. VI, edited by G. Townsend (London, 1870).

Goddard, J., "A Discourse Setting Forth the Unhappy Condition of the Practice of Physick in London, and Offering Some Means to Put it into a Better; For the Interests of Patients, No Less, or Rather Much More, than of Physicians," in *Harleian Miscellany*, Vol. VII (1810; originally printed 1670).

Gruffydd, E., "Boulogne and Calais from 1545 to 1550," edited by M. B. Davies, in *Bulletin of the Faculty of Arts, Fouad I University*, Vol. XII (1950).

Harington (II), J., *Nugae Antiquae, being a miscellaneous collection of original papers, in prose and verse; written during the reigns of Henry VIII, Edward VI, Queen Mary, Elizabeth, and King James; selected from authentic remains by the late Henry Harington, and newly arranged, with illustrative notes*, Vol. II (London, 1804).

—— (trans.), *Ludovico Ariosto's "Orlando Furioso,"* edited by R. McNulty (Oxford, 1972).

Harleian Miscellany, vols. I–VII (1808–1810).

Haynes, S. (ed.), *Collection of State Papers Relating to Affairs in the Reigns of King Henry VIII, King Edward VI, Queen Mary and Queen Elizabeth from the Year 1542 to 1570, Transcribed from the Original Letters and Other Authentick Memorials left by William Cecil* (London, 1740).

Hayward, J., *Annals of the First Four Years of the Reign of Queen Elizabeth* (London, 1840).

——, *The Life and Raigne of King Edward the Sixth* (London, 1630).

Hayward, M. (ed.), *Dress at the Court of King Henry VIII* (Leeds, 2007).

Hayward, M. and P. Ward (eds.), *The Inventory of Henry VIII*, Vol. II, *Textiles and Dress* (New York, 2012).

Henry, D., *An Historical Description of the Tower of London and Its Curiosities* (n.p., 1753).

Historical Manuscripts Commission, *Calendar of the Manuscripts of the Marquis of Bath Preserved at Longleat, Witlshire*, Vol IV, *Seymour Papers 1532–1686* (n.p., 1968) [HMC, *Bath*].

——, *Calendar of the Manuscripts of the Marquis of Salisbury, Preserved at Hatfield House*, Part I (London, 1883) [HMC, *Salisbury*].

History of Parliament (London and Cambridge; online project).

Hume, M. A. S. (ed.), *Chronicle of King Henry VIII of England* (London, 1889).

Journal of the House of Commons, Vol. I, *1547–1629* (London, 1802).
Journal of the House of Lords, Vol. I, *1509–1577* (London, 1767).
Knighton, C. S. and D. Loades (eds.), *The Navy of Edward VI and Mary I* (Farnham, Surrey, 2011).
Latimer, H., *Sermons by Hugh Latimer*, edited by G. E. Corrie, 2 vols. (Cambridge, 1844–1845).
Leti, G., *Historia overo vita de Elisabetta, Regina d'Inghilterra* (Amsterdam, 1693).
Letters and Papers, Foreign and Domestic, of the Reign of Henry VIII, 1509–1547, 23 vols., edited by J. S. Brewer, J. Gardiner, and R. H. Brodie (London, 1862–1932) [*L&P*].
Machyn, H., *The Diary of Henry Machyn: Citizen and Merchant-Taylor of London*, edited by J. G. Nichols (1848).
Merriman, R. B. (ed.), *Life and Letters of Thomas Cromwell*, Vol. II (London, 1902).
Naunton, R., "Fragmenta Regalia, or, Observations on the Late Queen Elizabeth, Her Times and Favourites," in *A Selection from the Harleian Miscellany of Tracts, Which Principally Regard the English History* (London, 1793).
Nichols, J. (ed.), *The Progresses and Public Processions of Queen Elizabeth*, Vol. I (London, 1788; 1823).
Nichols, J. G. (ed.), *Narratives of the Days of the Reformation* (London, 1859).
Norton, E., *The Anne Boleyn Papers* (Stroud, Gloucestershire, 2013).
Parr, Catherine, *Katherine Parr: Complete Works and Correspondence*, edited by J. Mueller (Chicago, 2011).
Perry, M., *The Word of a Prince* (Woodbridge, Suffolk, 1995).
Raleigh, W., "A Discourse of Sea Ports; Principally of the Port and Haven of Dover: Written by Sir Walter Raleigh, Addressed to Queen Elizabeth," edited by T. Park, in *Harleian Miscellany*, Vol. IV (London, 1809).
Robinson, H. (ed. and trans.), *Original Letters Relative to the Reformation*, Vol. II (Cambridge, 1847).
Rutland Papers: Original Documents Illustrative of the Courts and Times of Henry VII and Henry VIII, Selected from the Private Archives of His Grace the Duke of Rutland, edited by W. Jerdan (1842).
Sander, N., *Rise and Growth of the Anglican Schism*, edited by D. Lewis (London, 1877).
Skelton, J., *The Book of the Laurel*, edited by F. W. Brownlow (Newark, DE, 1991).
Starkey, D. (ed.), *The Inventory of King Henry VIII*, Vol. I (New York, 1998).
Statutes of the Realm, Vol. 3 (London, 1817).
Strangford, Viscount (ed.), *Household Expenses of the Princess Elizabeth During Her Residence at Hatfield, October 1, 1551 to September 30, 1552* (London, 1853).
Strype, J., *Ecclesiastical Memorials, Relating Chiefly to Religion, and the Reformation . . . under Henry VIII, King Edward VI and Queen Mary I*, 3 vols. (London, 1822).
——, *The History of the Life and Acts of the Most Reverend Father in God, Edmund Grindal* (Oxford, 1821).

Testamenta vetusta, being illustrations from wills, of manners, customs, &c. as well as of the descents and possessions of many distinguished families. From the reign of Henry the Second to the accession of Queen Elizabeth, 2 vols., edited by N. H. Nicolas (London, 1826).

Throckmorton, N., *The Legend of Sir Nicholas Throckmorton*, edited by J. G. Nichols (London, 1874; digital edition, 2009).

Tyrwhit, E., *Elizabeth Tyrwhit's Morning and Evening Prayers*, edited by S. M. Felch (Aldershot, 2008): p. 74.

Tytler, P. F. (ed.), *England under the Reigns of Edward VI and Mary*, Vol. I (1839).

Vertot, Abbé de, *Ambassades de Messieurs de Noailles en Angleterre*, Vol. I (1763).

Vives, J.L., *The Education of a Christian Woman*, edited and translated by C. Fantazzi (Chicago, 2000).

Writings of Edward the Sixth, William Hugh, Queen Catherine Parr, Anne Askew, Lady Jane Grey, Hamilton, and Balnaves (London, 1831).

Wriothesley, C., *A Chronicle of England During the Reigns of the Tudors from 1485 to 1559, by Charles Wriothesley, Windsor Herald*, Vol. 2, edited by W. D. Hamilton (1877).

SECONDARY SOURCES

A Brief Account of the Ancient Prison Called "The Fleet," in the City of London (London, 1843).

A Credulous Archaeologist, "The Littlecote Legend: Remarks on Mr. Long's Papers," in *Wiltshire Magazine*, VII (1862): pp. 45–51.

Alford, S., *Kingship and Politics in the Reign of Edward VI* (Cambridge, 2002).

Ambulator, or, Pocket Companion in a Tour Round London (London, 1800).

Bennett, E. T., *The Tower Menagerie: Comprising the Natural History of the Animals Contained in that Establishment* (1829).

Bernard, G. W., *The Tudor Nobility* (Manchester, 1992).

Bindoff, S. (ed.), *The History of Parliament: The House of Commons 1509–1558* (London, 1982).

Bingham, J., *The Cotswolds: A Cultural History* (Oxford, 2009).

Bramley, P., *Henry VIII and His Six Wives: A Guide to Historic Tudor Sites* (Stroud, Gloucestershire, 2014).

Burnet, G., *The History of the Reformation of the Church of England*, Vol. 2, Part II (London, 1820).

Carley, J. P., *The Books of King Henry VIII and His Wives* (London, 2004).

Clark-Maxwell, W.G., "Sir William Sharington's Work at Lacock, Sudeley and Dudley," in *Archaeological Journal*, Vol. 70 (1913).

Cole, M. H., "Maternal Memory: Elizabeth Tudor's Anne Boleyn" in Stump *et al.*, op. cit.: pp. 1–14.

Colvin, H. M., *The History of the King's Works*, Vol. III, Part I and Vol. IV, Part II (London, 1975–1982).

Dent, E., *Annals of Winchcombe and Sudeley* (London, 1877).

Drake, H. H., "Original Notes," in *Western Antiquary*, Vol. 11 (1888): p. 76.
Dugdale, J., *The New British Traveller, or, Modern Panorama of England and Wales*, Vol. 3 (London, 1819).
Duncan, S. L., "The Two Virgin Queens," in Stump *et al.*, op. cit.: pp. 29–52.
Emery, A., *Greater Medieval Houses of England and Wales*, Vol. III, *Southern England* (Cambridge, 2006).
Enis, E. E., "The Warwickshire Gentry and the Dudley Ascendancy, 1547 to 1590," unpublished Ph.D. thesis (University of Reading, 2011).
Evans, V. S., *Ladies-in-Waiting: Women Who Served at the Tudor Court* (n.p., 2014).
Furdell, E. L., *The Royal Doctors, 1485–1714: Medical Personnel at the Tudor and Stuart Courts* (Rochester, NY, 2001).
Garrett, C. H., *The Marian Exiles: A Study of the Origins of Elizabethan Puritanism* (Cambridge, 1938).
Gasquet, F. A. and E. Bishop, *Edward VI and the Book of Common Prayer* (London, 1891).
Gibbons, G. N., "The Political Career of Thomas Wriothesley, First Earl of Southampton, 1505–1550," unpublished Ph.D. thesis (University of Warwick, 1999).
Grinsell, L. V., *The Bristol Mint* (Bristol, 1972).
Hahn, D., *The Tower Menagerie: The Amazing True Story of the Royal Collection of Wild Beasts* (London, 2003).
Haynes, A., *Sex in Elizabethan England* (Stroud, Gloucestershire, 1999).
Hoak, D. E., *The King's Council in the Reign of Edward VI* (Cambridge, 1976).
Howarth, D., *Images of Rule: Art and Politics in the English Renaissance, 1485–1649* (Berkeley, CA, 1997).
Hughey, R., *John Harington of Stepney, Tudor Gentleman: His Life and Works* (Columbus, OH, 1971).
James, S., *Catherine Parr: Henry VIII's Last Love* (Stroud, Gloucestershire, 2008).
Kohn, G. C. (ed.), *Encyclopaedia of Plague and Pestilence* (New York, 2008).
Lambert, B., *The History and Survey of London and Its Environs*, Vol. III (London, 1806).
Loach, J., *Parliament under the Tudors* (Oxford, 1991).
Loades, D., *The Tudor Navy: An Administrative, Political and Military History* (Aldershot, 1992).
Locke, A. A., *The Seymour Family: History and Romance* (1911).
Long, C. E., "Wild Darrell of Littlecote," in *Wiltshire Magazine*, Vol. IV (1858): pp. 209–225; Nos. 2 and 3, Vol. VI (1860): pp. 201–213, 390–396; "The Littlecote Legend No. 4, Vol. VII (1862): pp. 212–220.
Lysons, D., *An Historical Account of Those Parishes in the County of Middlesex Which Are Not Described in the Environs of London* (London, 1800).
McIntosh, J. L., *From Heads of Household to Heads of State: The Preaccession Households of Mary and Elizabeth Tudor, 1516–1558* (New York, 2010).

Maclean, J., *The Life of Sir Thomas Seymour, Knight, Lord High Admiral of England and Master of the Ordnance* (1869).

Merton, C. I., "The Women Who Served Queen Mary and Queen Elizabeth: Ladies, Gentlewomen and Maids of the Privy Chamber, 1553–1603," unpublished Ph.D. thesis (University of Cambridge).

Mueller, J., C. Levin, and L. Shenk, "Elizabeth Tudor: Maidenhood in Crisis," in Stump *et al.*, op. cit.: pp. 15–28.

Munk, W., The Roll of the Royal College of Physicians of London, Vol. I, *1518–1700* (London, 1878).

Nash, T., "Observations on the Time of the Death and Place of Burial of Queen Katharine Parr," in *Archaeologia*, Vol. 9.

O'Hara, D., *Courtship and Constraint: Rethinking the Making of Marriage in Tudor England* (Manchester, 2000).

Oxford Dictionary of National Biography [*ODNB*].

"Polar Ice, and a North-West Passage" in *Edinburgh Review*, No. 59 (June 1818): pp. 1–59.

Pollard, A. F., *England under Protector Somerset* (London, 1900).

Porter, L., *Katherine the Queen* (London 2010).

——, "Lady Mary Seymour: An Unfit Traveller," in *History Today*, Vol. 61, No. 7 (2011).

Rede, L. T., *Anecdotes and Biography* (London, 1799).

Rice, D. W., *The Life and Achievements of Sir John Popham, 1531–1607* (Madison, WI, 2005).

Richardson, R. E., *Mistress Blanche: Queen Elizabeth I's Confidante* (Little Logaston, Herefordshire, 2007).

——, "Lady Troy and Blanche Parry: New Evidence About Their Lives at the Tudor Court," in *Bulletin of the Society for Renaissance Studies*, Vol. 26 (2009): pp. 3–15.

Rowe, A., and T. Williamson, *Hertfordshire: A Landscape History* (Hatfield, Herts, 2013).

Seymour, W., *Ordeal by Ambition: An English Family in the Shadow of the Tudors* (London, 1972).

Shrewsbury, J. F. D., *A History of Bubonic Plague in the British Isles* (Cambridge, 1970).

Skidmore, C., *Edward VI: The Lost King of England* (London, 2008).

Somerset, A., *Ladies in Waiting: From the Tudors to the Present Day* (London, 1984).

Stansfield, C. A., *Haunted Maine: Ghosts and Strange Phenomena of the Pine Tree State* (Mechanicsburg, PA, 2007).

Starkey, D., *Elizabeth: Apprenticeship* (London, 2000).

Stump, D., L. Shenk, and C. Levin (eds.), *Elizabeth I and the "Sovereign Arts": Essays in Literature, History, and Culture* (Tempe, AZ, 2011).

Turner, E., "Sele Priory, and Some Notice of the Carmelite Friars at New Shoreham, and the Secular Canons of Steyning," in *Sussex Archaeological Collections*, Vol. 10 (1858): pp. 100–128.

Victoria County History of Hertford, Vol. III, edited by W. Page (London, 1912) [*VCH Hertford*].

Victoria County History of Middlesex, Vol. II, edited by W. Page (London, 1911) [*VCH Middlesex*].

Victoria County History of Surrey, Vol. IV, edited by H.E. Malden (London, 1912) [*VCH Surrey*].

Ward, J., "Great Bedwyn," in *Wiltshire Magazine*, Vol. VI (1860): pp. 263–316.

Warnicke, R. M., *Wicked Women of Tudor England: Queens, Aristocrats, Commoners* (Basingstoke, 2012).

Wheatley, H. B., *London Past and Present: Its History, Associations, and Traditions* (1849; reprinted, Cambridge, 2011).

Willyams, C., *The History of Sudeley Castle, Near Winchcomb, Gloucestershire* (Cheltenham, 1803).

Wilson, V., *Queen Elizabeth's Maids of Honour* (London, 1923).

INDEX

ACKNOWLEDGMENTS

There are many people to thank for their support in writing this book. My agent, Andrew Lownie, showed unwavering enthusiasm for the proposal through its many early forms. Richard Milbank at Head of Zeus and Mark Hawkins-Dady have also helped to transform and shape the book into its final form.

I cannot thank the staff at the British Library and The National Archives at Kew enough for their assistance, with the bulk of the research for this book carried out in their reading rooms. Similarly, the staff at the other local archives consulted were always unfailingly helpful and knowledgeable.

I could not have written *The Temptation of Elizabeth Tudor* without the support of my family. In particular, my husband, David, and sons, Dominic and Barnaby. My parents, Liss and Robin, have also always provided encouragement, as have my mother-in-law, Thirza, and my sister, Jo, who both very kindly provided additional childcare!

Lastly, but most importantly, I must thank my friend, Alison, who so kindly suggested the topic for the book over one of our long Tudor-related discussions.

ABOUT THE AUTHOR

Elizabeth Norton is a historian of the queens of England and the Tudor period. She is the author of biographies of Anne Boleyn, Jane Seymour, Anne of Cleves, and Catherine Parr, and of *England's Queens: The Biography.*